essentials

greg laurie

ESSENTIALS

Unless otherwise indicated, all Scripture quotations are taken from the *New King James Version*. Copyright © 1982 by Thomas Nelson, Inc. Used by permission. All rights reserved.

Scripture quotations identified (KJV) are from the *King James Version* of the Bible.

Scripture quotations marked (NIV) are taken from *The Holy Bible, New International Version*®, NIV® Copyright © 1973, 1978, 1984, 2011 by Biblica, Inc.™ Used by permission. All rights reserved worldwide.

Scripture quotations marked (NLT) are taken from the Holy Bible, New Living Translation, copyright 1996, 2004. Used by permission of Tyndale House Publishers, Inc., Wheaton, Illinois 60189. All rights reserved.

Scripture quotations identified (NASB) are from the *New American Standard Bible*®, copyright the Lockman Foundation © 1960, 1962, 1963, 1968, 1971, 1972, 1973, 1975, 1977, 1995. Used by permission. (www.Lockman.org)

Scripture quotations identified (TLB) are from *The Living Bible*, copyright © 1971. Used by permission of Tyndale House Publishers, Inc., Wheaton, Illinois 60189. All rights reserved.

Scripture quotations marked (AMP) are taken from the *Amplified*® *Bible*, copyright © 1954, 1958, 1962, 1964, 1965, 1987 by The Lockman Foundation. Used by permission. (www.Lockman.org)

Scripture quotations marked (MSG) are taken from *The Message*. Copyright © 1993, 1994, 1995, 1996, 2000, 2001, 2002. Used by permission of NavPress Publishing Group.

Scripture quotations marked (PHILLIPS) are taken from J. B. Phillips, "The New Testament in Modern English", 1962 edition, published by HarperCollins.

Copyright © 2011, 2nd edition, by Greg Laurie.
All rights reserved.

ISBN: 978-0-9828644-2-5

Published by: Kerygma Publishing
Coordination: FM Management, Ltd.
Contact: mark@fmmgt.net

Cover and interior design: Highgate Cross+Cathey
Production: Highgate Cross+Cathey

Printed in the United States of America

3 4 5 6 7 / 17 16 15 14 13

Contents

Preface 5

Part One: The Person of God

1 God Is Now Here 11

2 The God Who Cares 27

3 Jesus Christ: God with Us 43

4 The Holy Spirit and You, Part 1 .59

5 The Holy Spirit and You, Part 2 .77

Part Two: Heaven and Hell

6 Let's Talk About Heaven 95

7 What We Will Do in Heaven? 113

8 Down-to-Earth Talk About Heaven 127

9 The Reality of Hell 141

10 Angels and Demons, Part 1 157

11 Angels and Demons, Part 2 175

Part Three: Living the Life

12 The Four Ws of Evangelism 193

13 Secrets of Spiritual Growth, Part 1
The Word of God 209

14 Secrets of Spiritual Growth, Part 2
The Priority of Prayer 225

15 Secrets of Spiritual Growth, Part 3
A Pattern for Prayer 235

Part Four: Last Things

16 Signs of the Times 253

17 Israel, Magog, and the Rapture .273

18 Antichrist, America, and Armageddon. 291

19 The Second Coming of Jesus to Earth 307

20 Heaven on Earth. 323

A Final Question 339

Endnotes 341

Preface

As I get older, I seem to be forgetting things more and more. It's kind of pathetic. I wander all over the house looking for my reading glasses, only to find they've been on my head all along. Or I'll start looking for something from room to room, turning things upside down—and suddenly realize I've completely forgotten what I was looking for. (But maybe if I find it, I tell myself, I'll remember what it was.)

Then there's the matter of parking my car.

I walk into a parking structure and can't remember if I'm on level 1, 2, 3, or 4. So what do I do? I walk up the ramp from the bottom of the structure to the top, pushing the button on the little remote control thing on my car keys and hoping to hear my car honk.

The truth is, I need reminders.

The ring on my finger reminds me that I'm married. (But there's also a woman who has been living in my house for 35 years to remind me of that as well!)

In church, when we have communion, we are instructed to receive those elements that remind us of the sacrifice of Jesus, recalling His words, "This do in remembrance of Me."

Why do I need to be reminded?

Because I have such an amazing tendency to forget—even important things that I never want to forget.

In the psalms, however, David reassures our hearts with this comforting truth: "For He knows our frame; He remembers that we are dust" (Psalm 103:14). In other words, He is well aware of our failings and recognizes our weaknesses. And He's had many years of experience working with weak, failing human beings. That's why His Word is so full of reminders. In fact, in many important areas of life, the Bible tells us the same things over and over again.

Why is that? Because we so quickly forget . . . and He knows that.

In my own life, I find that I need to remind myself and refresh my memory over and over again. The apostle Peter wrote about that in his second letter.

> I plan to keep on reminding you of these things even though you already know them and are really getting along quite well! But the Lord Jesus Christ has showed me that my days here on earth are numbered, and I am soon to die. As long as I am still here I intend to keep sending these reminders to you, hoping to impress them so clearly upon you that you will remember them long after I have gone. (2 Peter 1:12-15, TLB)

In short, we need to remember, and we need to *think*.

And there is no more important area in all of life to think about than our faith. What we believe about God and what He says about Himself are the most important things we could ever focus on and think about.

We may think we know all about these things. Maybe we do, and maybe not. Either way, we need to be reminded.

Listen, please, to this next statement: *What you think about God has everything to do with how you will live your life. Your view of God will determine how you will react to what comes your way in life.*

I don't know what you are facing in your personal life right now. Perhaps as you read these words you find yourself dealing with great concerns, anxiety, worry, or fears. Maybe you feel as though you're all alone, adrift at sea, with no one to help you. Maybe you've actually found yourself wondering at times if God is even there. You feel as though He has somehow abandoned you, let you down, or just lost your file somewhere on that big desk of His.

Nothing could be further from the truth!

God is here with you. Right now. Your file is right on top, and it's open. And He wants you to fully understand that bedrock truth and begin to live in the light of its unshakable reality.

It's *essential* that you do.

And it is the first essential we will consider in these pages.

Part 1

The Person of God

God Is Now Here

I once heard the story of a hardened atheist who had led a successful life and had a nice home and family—a loving wife and a little daughter he adored. He simply had no place in his life for God. One day, unexpectedly, his health took a sudden turn for the worse, and it didn't look like he would survive. Rather than softening his heart toward God, however, he became harder and harder.

When at last he seemed to be on his deathbed, his wife called the pastor at her church to come visit her husband, hoping he could perhaps lead her atheist spouse to faith in his last days. When the stricken man saw that pastor walk into the room, however, he began to scream profanities at him. "Don't you ever let that preacher in my house again!" he yelled. "I don't want God. There is no God. In fact, I want you to take out a piece of poster board and write these words on it: 'God is nowhere.' And I want you to put it at the base of my bed so every morning when I wake up I can see that sign."

The one soft spot in this man's heart was his little daughter, who was the apple of his eye. But though he loved her, he didn't want her influenced by his wife's faith.

As the man's condition worsened and it looked like the end might be near, it was decided that this little girl should be taken out of the home for a time. The pastor and his wife kindly offered to take her in.

So the atheist's daughter lived in the pastor's home, and for the first time she saw a family praying, reading the Bible, and going to church together. Her little life was changing, and her heart eagerly responded to the truths about God and Jesus. Not only that, but the pastor's wife began to teach her how to read.

Then, again unexpectedly, the father's health began to improve. As a result, the little girl was allowed to go and spend a few moments with her dad. He was still weak, but she climbed up onto his bed, threw her arms around him, and kissed him. "I love you, Daddy," she said.

"Well, sweetheart," he replied, "I love you, too. Now, where have you been? What have you been doing?"

"I've been going to church and hearing about Jesus," she replied. "And I've even been learning how to read."

The father could hardly believe that. "But you're so little," he said. "Surely you couldn't know how to read too much at this point. You've only been gone a short time."

"No, Daddy," she insisted, "I can read now."

"Really?" he said. "Tell you what. Why don't you read that little sign there at the base of my bed? What does that say?"

The little girl looked at it for a moment and began sounding out the words. "God is . . ." she began. Thinking about it for a moment, she suddenly brightened. "Daddy, I've got it now! Your sign says, 'God is now here.'" And then she said, "And you know what, Daddy? God *is* here. And He has been with you the whole time you've been sick. And we've been praying for you."

Suddenly the father choked up, asking his wife to take their little girl from the room. In that moment, he was filled with sorrow for the way he had lived. He asked God to forgive him, and he believed in Jesus Christ.

You see, it's all in how you look at things. Some people look at life in this world and say, "God is nowhere." But others look at the same scene and see the reality that *God is now here*.

Theology Without Apology

Who is this God who is now here and has always been? This is something every believer needs to know—at a time when the church's "Bible IQ" has seemingly never been lower.

A recent Gallup poll revealed that half of Americans who describe themselves as Christians don't believe in the existence of Satan, and fully one-third think that Jesus sinned while He was on the earth. The Bible, however, clearly teaches that there is indeed a literal devil and that Jesus the Son of God never sinned.

Another 25 percent dismiss the concept that the Bible is accurate in all the principles it teaches. As a result, the pollster in the article concluded, "Growing numbers of people now serve as their own theologian-in-residence. One consequence is that Americans are embracing an unpredictable and contradictory body of beliefs."[1]

Here is what we need to do. We need to put on our thinking caps and realize that Christianity is a reasonable and logical faith. You don't have to check your brains at the door when you choose to follow Jesus Christ. In fact, in Isaiah 1:18 God says, "Come now, and let us reason together." Or in another translation, "Come. Sit down. Let's argue this out" (MSG).

In other words, the Lord says, "Let's get this right. Get this straightened out in your mind. Understand these things." We need to think and act biblically rather than emotionally.

Far too many people today simply *emote* when it comes to God. They feel, but they don't think. They will make statements like, "I don't believe in a God of love judging anyone." Or, "*My* God would never do thus and so." Or the all-time classic, "I'm not into organized religion, but I consider myself a spiritual person."

We need to think carefully about these things. We need to study God and the changeless principles and precepts in His Word. This study has a name. It's called *theology*. And whether we like that word or not, we neglect theology at our own peril. Why? Because experience is never to be the basis for theology. It's the other way around: Sound theology should be the basis for our experience.

C. S. Lewis gave this warning years ago: "If you do not listen to theology, that will not mean you have no ideas about God. It will mean you have a lot of wrong ones."[2]

That's the purpose for this book, *Essentials*. We will talk about theology without apology and break it down in an understandable way, giving you takeaway truth you can apply in your own life.

One thing is for sure: The way you think and believe will directly impact the way you live.

What the Bible Says About God

Paul writes in 1 Timothy 4:16 (NIV), "Watch your life and doctrine closely. Persevere in them, because if you do, you will save both yourself and your hearers."

Someone might say, "Oh Greg, get off it, will you? Doctrine, schmoctrine. Who cares? I just love Jesus. Can't we set these things aside and just love the Lord?"

That may be a nice sentiment, but there's a big problem with that sort of thinking.

What if you end up loving the wrong Jesus?

If you find yourself following a Jesus who sinned while He was on earth, what kind of savior is that? If the Jesus you love is not the Jesus of the Bible, then effectively you are an idolater, worshiping another god. Let's make sure we are worshiping the right God as He is presented to us in the pages of Scripture.

Imagine you're about to take off on a transatlantic flight with an airline pilot who announces over the intercom, "Fuel schmuel. Let's just see how far this bucket of bolts will go." Would that unsettle you just a bit? Or imagine you're on a gurney being wheeled into surgery, and right before you go under the anesthetic, you hear the surgeon saying, "Anybody around here got a scalpel? I'll just start cutting here and there and see what happens."

Would you like that? No, you would be alarmed and terrified. Yet there is something far more important in life than a flight across the ocean or a major surgery. Our relationship to Jesus Christ will determine our *eternal* destiny. And yet so many seem to treat that relationship casually, basically making up the rules as they go along.

Let me say it again: What you believe will enable you to get through the challenges and difficulties of life. And there is no better place to start than with God Himself. What does the Bible say about God? We must have a proper understanding of the character and nature of God.

It was A. W. Tozer who said, "Nothing twists or deforms the soul more than a low or unworthy conception of God."[3] How true. If you don't understand who God is, if your view of God is warped, it will affect the way you live.

"I Believe God"

In Acts 28, the apostle Paul was a passenger on a little sailing ship, caught in what must have seemed like a Category 5 hurricane. There was no one on board that stormy day who actually believed they could survive the pounding in those heavy seas. But then the Lord Himself came to Paul at night and personally assured him that they would have a safe arrival in Rome.

The next morning, shouting to make himself heard over the howling winds, Paul said these words:

> Last night an angel of the God to whom I belong and whom I serve stood beside me, and he said, "Don't be afraid, Paul, for you will surely stand trial before Caesar! What's more, God in his goodness has granted safety to everyone sailing with you." So take courage! *For I believe God.* It will be just as he said. (Acts 27:23-25, NLT)

We, too, live in a storm-tossed world. We can look out across our horizon and see global terrorism, rampant immorality, rogue nations threatening war and mayhem, and crippling economic recession. Sometimes as we read the paper or listen to the news, these problems seem overwhelming to us. We have no idea how these crises can be addressed or where these serious dilemmas will lead us. These are uncertain times, and we need a real certainty that will help us to get through it.

Here's what we can count on. Though times and circumstances may change, our God never changes. Everything else constantly changes all around us, but God never will. In Malachi 3:6, He says, "I am the LORD, and I do not change."

Believing in God won't necessarily alter your circumstances, though it certainly might. More often than not, however, it will change *you*. It will help you to view your circumstances properly. Paul said, "I believe God," and from that moment on, he put away his anxiety.

Our first point in this study may seem like a no-brainer. And yet it is the foundation on which everything else is built.

God Exists, and He Created the Universe and Mankind

There are no lack of militant atheists on the scene today, writing books they hope will undermine the faith of those who choose to believe the Bible. But most polls reveal that Americans by and large believe in God.

I recently heard about a group of atheists complaining because they didn't have a holiday of their own. They thought it unfair, in our pluralistic culture, that Christians had holidays like Christmas and Easter, and they didn't have any.

But wait a second. Atheists *do* have a holiday; they just haven't realized it yet. April first is their natural holiday and could be declared a national atheist day. Why April Fool's Day? Because the Bible clearly says, "The fool says in his heart, 'There is no God' " (Psalm 14:1, NIV).

It's interesting to me that the Bible never tries to prove the existence of God. Have you noticed that? Instead, it just assumes the obvious. The first words in Genesis 1:1 are, "In the beginning God …" The Bible just assumes people know this is true. (Frankly, I think it takes a great deal more faith to believe there is no God than it takes to believe there is one.)

Many people seem willing to accept the premise of a God or "higher power." But it seems today that we want a God in our own image. As Voltaire said, "God made man in His image, and man returned the favor." That's pretty much what we have today: not so much a generation that denies the existence of God, but a generation that believes in a god of their own making, a "customized" God that fits our culture, personality, desires, and inclinations.

Thanks to the ongoing technological revolution, we now have iPods, iPads, iPhones, and iTunes that we can customize to our particular whims and desires.

As a result, we may find ourselves applying that trend to God, so we end up with an iGod—programmed, personalized, and customized, He says what I want Him to say and does what I want Him to do. I edit out all the tracks I don't like and leave the ones that I do. That's what we're doing today, but that is not the way to know God. We don't mold God into our image. He wants to mold us into His.

"In the beginning God . . ."

That's where it all starts. Not in the beginning *you*; in the beginning *God*. And if I eliminate God, I have a big problem. In the beginning . . . what? Well, in the beginning a mass of gases floating in space. Oh wait, that's not the beginning. Where did the mass of gases come from? Where did space come from? Sooner or later everyone gets around to asking the question, "Where did God come from?" And that's not an easy question to answer, because the Bible doesn't tell us where God came from.

It simply tells us that He *is*.

It just says, "In the beginning God."

The truth is, God has always existed. He didn't come from something else. He was never invented or created. He has always been there. God has no beginning, nor does He have an end. It really is as simple as that.

But who is this God that has always existed? Now this is hard. Why? Because we are trying to wrap our finite minds around the infinite. It would be like trying to explain Hawaii to my baby granddaughter, Alexandra.

How can I explain Hawaii to Allie (her nickname)? "Sit down in my lap a minute, Allie, because I want to tell you about Hawaii. The sky is blue. The water is warm." She may like sitting in my lap and hearing me talk, but she has no idea what I'm talking about.

It's even more ridiculous to think you and I could grasp God or somehow make Him fit into our minds and our logic. Sometimes He does. Often He does not. This isn't a cop-out or an excuse. It's a simple acknowledgement that I will never fully be able to comprehend God this side of heaven. As it has been said, "If God were small enough for my mind, He wouldn't be big enough for my needs."

One day I will comprehend God. One day I will understand everything about God, because the Bible tells me in 1 Corinthians 13,

> We don't yet see things clearly. We're squinting in a fog, peering through a mist. But it won't be long before the weather clears and the sun shines bright! We'll see it all then, see it all as clearly as God sees us, knowing him directly just as he knows us! (verse 12, MSG)

Now, having said that we can't fully comprehend God, let me also add that we can *know* God. In fact, knowing God is the very essence of being a Christian. In His prayer in John 17, Jesus said, "Now this is eternal life: that they may know you, the only true God, and Jesus Christ, whom you have sent" (verse 3, NIV).

The apostle Paul wrote, "[For my determined purpose is] that I may know Him [that I may progressively become more deeply and intimately acquainted with Him]" (Philippians 3:10, AMP).

This is we why we are on earth: to know God. And then, as an expression of that knowledge, to honor, glorify, and magnify Him with our lives.

So what is God like? Does God literally know everything? Can God be present all around the world at the same time? Does God have limitations to His power? Are events in our universe random, or is there a plan? And does God care about someone like me?

We will find answers to those deep, searching questions in Psalm 139. At the same time, we'll discover three vital takeaway truths about God that we can begin to better understand and apply to our lives today.

God is omniscient, which means He is all-knowing.
God is omnipresent, which means He is present everywhere.
God is omnipotent, which means He has unlimited power.
Let's start with the first one.

1: God Is Omniscient

"Omniscient" simply means that God knows everything.
Here's how Psalm 139 opens:

> O LORD, you have examined my heart
> and know everything about me.
> You know when I sit down or stand up.
> You know my thoughts even when I'm far away.
> You see me when I travel
> and when I rest at home.
> You know everything I do.
> You know what I am going to say
> even before I say it, LORD.
> (verses 1-4, NLT)

Wow. How impressive is that? God knows what I'm going to say before I say it? Most of the time, *I* don't even know what I'm going to say next. And there have been times when I've said things I wish I hadn't said. But God knows what I'm going to say before I even shape the words.

From this and other verses we learn that God's knowledge is as infinite and eternal as He is. What God knows now He has always known and will always know.

You see, God doesn't learn new things, nor does He forget what He has learned, as we do. We learn new things every day, maybe every hour, but God never does. God knows all things from the beginning.

Scientists tell us that we never really forget anything. In other words, it never goes completely off our hard drive. In one magazine article I read recently, the author claims that our brains can store enough data to fill several million books. And it is estimated that in a lifetime the brain can store one million billion bits of information. Could that really be true? I will admit that certain sounds, smells, or sights have triggered vivid memories from my early childhood.

But God knows and remembers everything about everyone who has ever lived or will live. There is never the slightest lapse in His memory. He never forgets anyone or anything.

Unfortunately, that's not the case with me! Sometimes I see someone that I've known for years, and I suddenly blank out. I can't remember their name, and that can be embarrassing.

But can you imagine God having a lapse in memory? You come to Him in prayer one day, and He says, "Hello there, and you are . . . who? I'm sorry, I can't place you at the moment." Never! In contrast to that imagined scenario, God knows everything about you, down to the number of hairs on your head and the thoughts that so quickly flash through your mind.

Beyond that, of course, He knows everything there is to know about every atom of the universe—including hidden planets that no human eyes will ever see, and every star in the vastness of the heavens.

Generations ago, the astronomers of the day thought they knew the number of stars in the sky and laughed at the Bible's assertion that the stars couldn't be numbered. But then as they developed more powerful telescopes, they realized there were more stars than they had thought—and more galaxies than they had dreamed. And every year that goes by, we see more and more of these galaxies— each one like an island universe—with innumerable stars in each one of them, just as the Bible has said.

Psalm 147:4 (NIV) tells us something even more amazing. It says of God that "He determines the number of the stars *and calls them each by name*" (emphasis added).

If it were me trying to do that job, I'd run out of names in about three minutes. Astronomers estimate there are about one hundred thousand million stars in our Milky Way galaxy alone! And outside of that are millions and millions of other galaxies. Nevertheless, God knows every star, and each one has its own name. What knowledge! What creativity!

But now let's personalize it. Not only does He know all of this information about stars and galaxies and nebulas, He knows about *you*. As I mentioned, Jesus said, "The very hairs on your head are all numbered" (Matthew 10:30). Now in my case, that might not be too impressive, because there's only about eight or nine of them. For some of you, however, it would be considerably more than that.

The Bible goes on to say that God knows about every little bird that falls to the ground. Why did Jesus bring those two points—about birds and the hairs on our head—to our attention?

Because He wanted to reassure us that the Father cares about every detail of our lives. He said, "So don't be afraid; you are worth more than many sparrows" (Matthew 10:31, NIV).

This awesome God who created the universe and numbers the stars is interested in you. What bothers you? What concerns you? What makes your heart ache? What brings tears to your eyes? It is of concern to God. For the psalmist said in Psalm 56:8 (NLT), "You keep track of all my sorrows. You have collected all my tears in your bottle. You have recorded each one in your book."

So what does that mean? *It means that whatever you are facing right now, the Lord knows all about it, and He cares.* If you have made sacrifices for Him—working for His kingdom, giving financially, serving Him in some way, shape, or form—God is aware of it to the smallest detail. And you will be rewarded, for Jesus said, "Your Father who sees in secret will reward you openly" (Matthew 6:6).

Not only is God aware of what concerns you, but He is also aware of the wrongs done in our world today. We are told in Proverbs 15:3 (NIV), "The eyes of the LORD are everywhere, keeping watch on the wicked and the good."

How could it be otherwise, since He is the one who will both punish evil and reward good works? Not one single thing occurs in any place without Him being aware of it. He sees everything that happens everywhere. And He sees everything happening in our lives.

He doesn't just see you. He sees *through* you. Of course when Jesus walked this earth and was God in human form, He would read people's minds and hearts—which drove some of them crazy. He would say, "Why are you thinking [thus and so] in your heart?" How did He know that?

I'm glad I don't have that ability. I think it would be just a little bit depressing to know what people really think about me. I'm more than happy to leave that with the Lord to sort out!

God knows every thought that we think, which makes it utterly preposterous to believe that we can hide something from Him. You and I may think we are so clever sometimes, hiding this sin or that sin, covering our tracks, and fooling ourselves into thinking that no one knows.

But Someone does know. He saw it all. He isn't fooled by any of our denials, rationalizations, or spin jobs. In fact, *everything* will be made known. That which is done in secret will be shouted from the mountaintops. So if you have lived a godly life, that will be proclaimed. And if you have lived a deceptive or ungodly life, that, too, will be revealed in time.

God knows what will happen before it happens, and nothing ever catches Him by surprise. You'll never catch God off-guard or hear Him say, "Whoa! Where did that come from?" He already knows about it, and that's because God dwells in the eternal realm. Isaiah 46:10 (NIV) says, "I make known the end from the beginning, from ancient times, what is still to come. I say, 'My purpose will stand, and I will do all that I please.' "

God knows the end from the beginning. I barely know the end at the end, because I forget what happened. When God says He knows the end from the beginning, that means it's not a stretch for Him to predict what will happen in the future.

Now if I said I would "reveal" to you that the New Orleans Saints beat the Indianapolis Colts in the 2010 Super Bowl, would you think I was a great prophet? No, you would think of me as someone who watched football or maybe knew how to Google a question on my computer. God, however, can predict the future more accurately than I can describe the past. If there is to be a 2022 Super Bowl, He already knows the final scores and all the stats.

The fact is, I sometimes think I remember an event in a certain way, but later find out I had it all mixed up because my memories were fuzzy. But God not only knows what has happened, He knows what *will* happen. And because He is in the eternal realm, above and beyond time, when He says something will happen, you can be sure it will happen just as He has said.

It was A. W. Tozer who said, "In God there is no was or will be but a continuous and unbroken is."[4] In Him, history and prophecy are one and the same. You and I think in what we call the past tense or the future tense. But God thinks in the eternal tense. It's all the same to Him. Therefore the Bible is the one book that dares to predict the future—not once, not twice, but hundreds of times. How does that work? God is omniscient. God knows all things. For Him, telling the future is as effortless as describing something five minutes past. Many of the great world events described in the pages of Scripture thousands of years ago are being fulfilled today before our very eyes.

Knowing this, when we read what the Bible says about our future, we can know that it will happen just as He said.

Our God is an omniscient God. He knows everything that can be known, and nothing will ever slip His mind.

2. God Is Omnipresent

God is also omnipresent, which means He is present everywhere.

Psalm 139:7-12 says:

Where can I go from Your Spirit?
Or where can I flee from Your presence?
If I ascend into heaven, You are there;
If I make my bed in hell, behold, You are there.
If I take the wings of the morning,
And dwell in the uttermost parts of the sea,
Even there Your hand shall lead me,
And Your right hand shall hold me.
If I say, "Surely the darkness shall fall on me,"

Even the night shall be light about me;
Indeed, the darkness shall not hide from You,
But the night shines as the day;
The darkness and the light are both alike to You.

Now these words can be either comforting or frightening, depending on which side of the fence you might be on. If you are a follower of Jesus, they bring great comfort. You will never, ever be alone, not today, not tomorrow, not in a million years. Your Savior will be with you wherever you go.

What an incredible comfort! God is not bound by geographical boundaries or time zones. He is present everywhere. And no matter what you face today, no matter what you might be struggling with, He is there with you.

In Hebrews 13:5 the Lord declares, "I will never leave you nor forsake you." In the original Greek language, that statement is emphatic. It could be better translated, "I will never, no never, no never leave you or forsake you." Jesus said, "Lo, I am with you always, even to the end of the age" (Matthew 28:20).

What are you dealing with today? Whatever it is, wherever you are, you are not alone; the omnipresent God is there, walking with you through it.

In the book of Isaiah, God says it like this:

When you pass through the waters,
I will be with you;
and when you pass through the rivers,
they will not sweep over you.
When you walk through the fire,
you will not be burned;
the flames will not set you ablaze.
For I am the LORD your God,
the Holy One of Israel, your Savior.
(Isaiah 43:2-3, NIV)

Wherever you go, God is there.

C. S. Lewis said, "We may ignore, but we can nowhere evade the presence of God. The world is crowded with Him."[5]

God is with us, not just when we're in the church worshiping, but when we leave as well—wherever we go. Our God is omnipresent.

3. God Is Omnipotent

God is omnipotent, which means He is all-powerful.

We've all heard the question, "Can God do absolutely anything He wants?" We will reply, "Yes, He can do anything He wants, because God is all-powerful."

"Oh, is that so?" our questioner might reply. "Does that mean God can do anything that is ungodly? For instance, can God make a rock so heavy He can't lift it?"

Is this supposed to stump us somehow, as though it were a brainteaser? In fact, it is a foolish, lame sort of question. When we say God is all-powerful, it doesn't mean that God will do something foolish, wrong, arbitrary, or sinful. God is also righteous, good, and holy, and He won't do anything that would contradict His nature. As Scripture says, "God cannot deny Himself."[6]

We know this: God cannot lie, and God cannot die.

So what is impossible to God? Not that which is difficult to His power, but that which is contrary to His nature. It's not so much a question of whether God can't do something as much as it is an assertion that God *won't* do something.

Omnipotence means God has infinite power that can never be depleted, drained, or exhausted.

I have an iPhone that I use quite a bit, and it barely makes it through the day on a single charge. Sometime about three-quarters of the way through my day, I might notice that my battery is getting low. Then, when it hits the red zone, it's trouble. So I have to go plug it back in again and wait for it to charge.

You and I have to be aware of things like battery life in our electronic gadgets, as well as the fuel gauge in our cars, so we won't run out of gas at some inconvenient moment.

But God's resources are never exhausted. He doesn't have to

recharge at night or refuel. His power is never, ever diminished in the slightest degree. There is nothing more constant in the universe.

That's why it's so ridiculous when someone says, "Well, I've tried everything, and now all I can do is just (gulp) pray."

All right, then, let me get this straight. "All you can do now" is call out to the omniscient, omnipresent, omnipotent creator of the universe? All you can do now is cry out to the God who created all things, has named every star, and knows about every hair on your head and every bird that falls on the ground? All you can do now is call out to the unlimited God?

The simple fact is, your needs or requirements are never a drain on God's resources. You would never—in a trillion lifetimes—need more than God can supply. The Bible says that God is "able to do immeasurably more than all we ask or imagine, according to his power that is at work within us" (Ephesians 3:20, NIV).

So consider your circumstances right now. Maybe you're overwhelmed by tragedy, grief, sorrow, confusion, uncertainty, or worry. Then again, maybe you are bound by an addiction of some kind. It could be an addiction that has grown so powerful it has turned into a lifestyle, and you feel as though you will never be free from it. I want you to know that the all-knowing, all-powerful, ever-present God is here to help you.

Don't say God is nowhere. God is now here.

He is waiting for you to call out to Him and is available to meet your deepest needs.

Yes, He is infinite. But He is also knowable.

This all-powerful, everywhere-present, all-knowing God loves you. And in Jesus Christ, He welcomes you into fellowship with Himself.

chapter

2

The God Who Cares

I love the story about the little girl who grabbed a piece of paper and some crayons and started to draw with great passion. Her mom happened to notice and said, "Honey, what are drawing?"

"I'm drawing a picture of God, Mommy."

"But sweetheart, nobody knows what God looks like."

"They will when I'm done," she replied.

What is God like? That's an important question. An *essential* question. You might say that this is Theology 101.

There's that word again. *Theology.* Some people cringe or roll their eyes when they hear that term. "Oh no!" they say. "That's going to be so boring."

Really?

What is theology? It's the study of *God.* If you think that a study of God, angels, Satan, heaven, hell, the afterlife, walking in the Spirit, and the meaning of life is boring, then I don't know what to say to you. As for me, I can't imagine a more engaging, fascinating subject. And I have noticed that the older I get, the more interested I become in these things. I especially enjoy thinking and studying about heaven, since I'm getting closer to that destination with each passing day and hour.

In the last chapter we made the simple statement that God exists, and that He is the creator of the world. That's a very important place to start, and for most of us, it's pretty obvious. In today's culture, however, to say God exists and is the creator of the universe and mankind has somehow become "controversial."

G. K. Chesterton made this statement years ago:

> You are free in our culture to say that God does not exist. You are free to say that he exists and he is evil. You can even talk about God as a metaphor or a mystification. No one will protest. But if you speak of God as a fact, as a reason for changing one's conduct, then the modern world will stop you somehow if it can.

He concludes,

> We are long past talking about whether an unbeliever should be punished for being irreverent. It is now thought irreverent to be a believer.[7]

It's true, isn't it? People will say, "What? Are you crazy? You actually believe there is a God?"

But that is the direction of our culture in what I believe to be the last days before the return of Christ for His own. One minister noted that a family came in with their young teenage boy who had a question for the pastor. He wanted to know, "Who is that guy hanging up there on that plus sign?"

In other words, he knew nothing whatever of Jesus.

The study of God has never been more important, and our world has never needed it more. I find there is a great biblical illiteracy among many Christians today. They say they believe certain things, but can't tell you why they believe them. And more importantly, they can't tell you where those things are in the Bible. In this book, then, we'll take time to strengthen the foundations of our knowledge about God—or perhaps to build that foundation for the first time.

In our last chapter we noted three things about God: that He is omniscient (which means He is all-knowing), He is omnipresent (or present everywhere), and He is omnipotent (or all-powerful).

Now we come to another crucial attribute to consider and understand.

God Is Sovereign

Another way to say the same thing is to use the term "divine providence." The word *providence* comes from an interesting coupling of words: *Pro video*. We're all familiar with "video." It's something we used to watch before we had DVDs or downloadable movies. "Pro" means before. *Pro video* means that God knows or "watches" an event before it actually happens.

In the last chapter, when we said that God is omniscient, we made the point that God never learns anything, and nothing ever catches Him by surprise. But now let's expand on that and say that God not only knows everything, but God also *controls* everything.

God is able to do what He wants, when He wants, whenever He wants. Why? Because He is sovereign. God is able to do what He pleases with whomever He chooses whenever He wishes.

It's not up to a vote. God is a majority of One.

As it says in Psalm 115:3, "Our God is in heaven; He does whatever He pleases." Even the pagan king Darius acknowledged in Daniel 4:35 (NLT),

> "All the people of the earth are nothing compared to him. He does as He pleases among the angels of heaven and among the people of the earth. No one can stop him or say to him, 'What do you mean by doing these things?' "

It comes down to this. When we say that God is sovereign, it means that He is the Master, and we are the servants. He is the Potter, we are the clay. He is the Vine, we are the branches. He is the Giver, we are the recipients.

Quite frankly, God can do whatever He pleases without asking anyone's permission or explaining His reasons. Psalm 135 says, "For I know that the LORD is great, and our Lord is above all gods. Whatever the LORD pleases He does, in heaven and in earth" (verses 5-6).

Chuck Swindoll made this statement:

> To say that God is sovereign is to say that He is supreme. He is in full control of all things. All things. He is almighty. He is the possessor of power, both on earth, above earth, below earth, in all matters pertaining to all existence. Over all nature. Over all events. Over all blessings. Over all disasters and calamities. Over all of humanity. All life in the realm of the seen and the unseen. Good and evil. No one can defeat His purposes or thwart His plans. He is never surprised. He never learns. He is never frustrated. Nothing is ever an afterthought.[8]

We might protest and say, "But wait a second. Is God sovereign when I lose my job through no fault of my own? Is God sovereign when the doctor calls me with bad news? Is God sovereign when a loved one dies unexpectedly?"

The answer is yes. Yes, He is. God is sovereign.

You say, "Greg, I don't understand that."

Welcome to the club. Neither do I. This is not to say that all things that happen are necessarily done by God. By that I mean there are times that God will allow certain things that we don't understand.

Nevertheless, He is certainly aware of those things.

And if He allows them, it is for a purpose.

God has His plans and purposes, and they may become clearer to us with the passage of time. There are some happenings that will come into better focus as the years unfold and will make more sense to us. There are other things that will not come into focus and that we will never understand this side of heaven. And until that time, we simply need to remind ourselves that God is sovereign. He is God. He is Lord. And He is good.

God Is Truth

This means that He, and He alone, is the true God; His knowledge and words are true and are the final standard of truth. It's not just that He *has* truth; God *is* truth. He is the embodiment of truth, and therefore what He proclaims true is true, and what He declares false is false.

Period.

Jeremiah 10:10 says, "The LORD is the true God; He is the living God and the everlasting King." In John 17:3, Jesus declared: "This is eternal life that they may know You, the only true God, and Jesus Christ whom You have sent."

God is the final court of arbitration. This isn't up to a vote. It makes no difference at all if a bunch of us chime in and say, "Well, the majority of us don't agree with this statement by God; therefore it isn't true." No. God is the source and final standard of truth. You can't go any higher than God. You can't appeal to anyone else. It is true because God said it. You say, "But that's circular reasoning." No. It is biblical reasoning. There is no higher source to which you may go.

As Peter said, "Lord, to whom would we go? You have the words that give eternal life. We believe, and we know you are the Holy One of God" (John 6:68-69, NLT).

Remember what your parents would say to you as a child when you protested some task they had given you? They would say, "Do it anyway." You would say, "But why?" And they would reply, *"Because I said so."*

Maybe we vowed as children that we would never say that to our kids when we were parents. But we do, don't we? That fits in there with those other parental nuggets like, "If all the other kids jumped off a cliff, would you jump off, too?" And of course, "What do you think, I have a money tree in the backyard?"

Nevertheless, that's the way it is in this universe. This is reality. We know certain things are true simply because God says they are true.

God Is Holy

In the book of Isaiah, we read how the prophet had a glimpse of God's glory (and lived to tell about it). He said,

He was sitting on a lofty throne, and the train of his robe filled the Temple. Attending him were mighty seraphim, each having six wings. With two wings they covered their faces, with two they covered their feet, and with two they flew. They were calling out to each other, "Holy, holy, holy is the LORD of Heaven's Armies! The whole earth is filled with his glory!" (6:1-3, NLT)

Those seraphim could have sung, "Faithful, faithful, faithful," or, "Powerful, powerful, powerful." And they would have been right, because those things are true of God. But they said, "Holy, holy, holy is the LORD Almighty."

The mighty angels declared God's holiness, and that fact is in Scripture because it's important for us to know.

Psalm 24 says, "Who may climb the mountain of the LORD? Who may stand in his holy place? Only those whose hands and hearts are pure" (verses 3-4, NLT).

Because God is holy, He hates sin. We are told in Habakkuk 1:13 (NIV), "Your eyes are too pure to look on evil; you cannot tolerate wrongdoing." God is holy, and we need to realize that.

Have we lost sight of this? Have we traded reverence for relevance? A generation or two ago, someone might have observed that the atmosphere was just a little too uptight in Bible-believing churches. You would hear a lot of preaching on hellfire and brimstone, and you wouldn't laugh inside of a church. You would speak in hushed tones, and you always had to wear your Sunday best.

It was just a little bit rigid, to say the least.

But has the pendulum swung too far in the other direction? Now we're maybe a bit too casual and loose. And for most churches I know, it's been a long time since people have heard a "hellfire-and-brimstone" message from the pulpit.

Maybe, when you think about it, a message on hell wouldn't hurt us.

Maybe in our relaxed and casual attitude toward the things of God, we've grown just a little *too* relaxed.

How far will we go to make the message "culturally relevant"?

I am all for connection with our contemporary culture and for bringing messages week by week that are relevant to people's lives.

But do I stop being reverent?

Do I use coarse language or profanity to make my points?

Do I cuss to reach cussers or drink to reach drunks?

No, what I need to do is declare the truth of God.

I think reverence for God and His Word is the most culturally important thing we could have or show. Do you imagine that it's impressive to a nonbeliever to hear us use profanity or tell off-color jokes? Will that make us more cool in their sight? No, what they will probably think is, "What an idiot. I've done that my whole life."

How about doing something that's a little different? How about standing up for what is true? I want to be as authentic and relevant as I can be when I am preaching or teaching or writing books. But the Bible tells me that my first responsibility is to declare the truth of God.

And that is an awesome responsibility.

Listen to Paul's charge to young Timothy:

> I charge you, in the sight of God and Christ Jesus and the elect an-gels, to keep these instructions without partiality. . . . In the presence of God and of Christ Jesus, who will judge the living and the dead, and in view of his appearing and his kingdom, I give you this charge: Preach the Word. (1 Timothy 5:21; 2 Timothy 4:1-2, NIV)

This matter of representing a holy God and declaring His truth in a dark world is not a task to be taken lightly. So let's not trade rever-ence for relevance. Let's be reverent of our God and King. He is holy.

The early church showed a strong reverence for God and fear of God. In this instance, fear doesn't mean cowering in a corner because we're afraid God is going to smack us (as much as we may deserve it). Fear of God means a wholesome dread of displeasing Him. *"Oh Lord, You are so good. You are so holy. I want to live in such a way that I bring honor to Your name."*

God Is Righteous and Just

Holiness describes God's character, while righteousness and justice describe His dealings with mankind. We can be thankful we serve a righteous and a just God. We are told in Psalm 11:7 (NIV), "For the LORD is righteous, he loves justice."

In Exodus we have the account of the plague of hail, and then these words from the mouth of Pharaoh: "I have sinned this time. The LORD is righteous, and my people and I are wicked" (Exodus 9:27). Even the evil and hard-hearted Pharaoh acknowledged the justice and righteousness of God for punishing him in the way that He did.

It's important to see how these attributes of God complement one another. For instance, I pointed out that God is omnipotent, which means that He is all-powerful. But now I am bringing to your attention the fact that God is righteous. But think about it: If He were a God of perfect righteousness without the power to carry out that righteousness, we could never be sure that justice would ultimately prevail. On the other hand, if He were a God of unlimited power yet without righteousness in His character, how unthinkably horrible this universe would be.

But blessedly and happily for us, our God is all-powerful *and* He is righteous. He will not misuse His power in our lives or in the lives of any other. And besides those two important attributes, we need to know this . . .

God Is Good

Yes, it is true that God is all-knowing, all-powerful, and present everywhere at the same time. It's true that He is holy, righteous, and just.

But He is also good.

In other words, He is the final standard of goodness, and all that He is and does is worthy of approval. He determines what is good and what is bad.

The Bible tells us this over and over again. In Psalm 34:8, David urges us to "taste and see that the LORD is good." And in Psalm 106:1 we read: "Oh, give thanks to the LORD, for He is good!"

But what, you might ask, is good?

After all, I can say that God is good until something bad happens to me, and then I wonder if God truly is good. But maybe I don't know what "good" really is. Maybe my definition of good is different from God's definition. In fact, the same God who declares Himself to be good promises in Romans 8:28 that He causes all things to work together for good for those that love Him and are the called according to His purpose.

We hear that verse invoked a lot. But have we ever thought it all the way through? A better translation of that verse says, "All things *are working* together for good to those who love God and are the called according to His purpose." In other words, it's in process. All things are working together, right now, for eventual good.

What is good? That depends on whom you ask. For some people, good would be defined as blue skies, sunny days, good health, paid bills, open parking spaces, and no reruns on television. They would never regard an illness or some kind of crisis as "good." For them, good equals smooth sailing and the absence of conflict. And frankly, if most of us could have our way, that's the kind of life we would choose to live.

But a conflict-free life might actually be the *worst* thing.

In fact, God can use conflicts and hardships to produce something of immeasurable good in your life and mine. The psalmist wrote, "Before I was afflicted I went astray, but now I obey your word. . . . It was good for me to be afflicted so that I might learn your decrees" (Psalm 119:67, 71, NIV). After all he had been through, Job declared, "But He knows the way that I take; when He has tested me, I shall come forth as gold" (Job 23:10).

Think about the most important lessons you have learned in your life. Did they come when things were going well? Most of us have to admit that we have learned the most valuable and enduring life truths when we have passed through hardship and difficulty.

Little children, of course, eat only what they want to eat. They would live on candy if they were given the option. (Except, perhaps, for my little granddaughter Stella who would happily eat quesadillas for the rest of her life if she could.) In that way, we're like little children. We only want the good times, the easy times, the sweet and fun times.

Conflict, however, can bring good into our lives. Tragedy reminds us we can't do this thing called life on our own. Sometimes we get a little bit too arrogant, and we forget to acknowledge just Who it is who gives us the strength and ability to do what we are doing.

The apostle James writes:

When all kinds of trials and temptations crowd into your lives, my brothers, don't resent them as intruders, but welcome them as friends! Realize that they come to test your faith and to produce in you the quality of endurance. But let the process go on until that endurance is fully developed, and you will find you have become men of mature character with the right sort of independence. (James 1:2-4, PHILLIPS)

The trial or hardship we see as such a difficult and hurtful thing today may be regarded later as something that brought good into our lives.

God Is Love

The Bible tells us, "God is love." Not merely that He has love or even is "loving," but He Himself is love.

Bear in mind, however, that He is *not* the Hollywood version of love. What do these people in Hollywood know about love? "So-and-so is now with so-and-so. They are the beautiful couple. They are the powerful couple." Oh, and by the way, they probably won't be together for more than a few months before they drift off for other beautiful, powerful people.

God's love isn't fickle.

God's love isn't dependent on how attractive we are.

God's love doesn't hinge on our performance.

God says, "Yes, I have loved you with an everlasting love; therefore with loving kindness I have drawn you" (Jeremiah 31:3).

What's more, God doesn't just talk about love. He has demonstrated it to us, as the Scripture says: "But God demonstrates His own love toward us, in that while we were still sinners, Christ died for us" (Romans 5:8).

God is love, and God is holy. Perhaps in these two qualities we can see all the attributes of God. In His holiness He is unapproachable. In His love He approaches us.

So how should all this affect me? What is the application in my life? Here are a few things to consider.

1. Because God Is Truth, I need to be truthful

Many people seem to have missed the memo on this one. The Scripture tells us that lying lips are an abomination to the Lord. In fact, in the list of seven things that God hates, two of those things have to

deal with lying and falsehood. (See Proverbs 6:16-19.) That
is how important truth is to God.

I can think of one very practical reason why you should tell the
truth. It's just too much work to tell lies! It gets to be hard to remember
which lie you told to whom and how you told it. The way it usually
works is you have to lie to cover up something you did wrong, and then
tell another lie to back up that lie—and tell a real whopper to cover
for the first two. After a while a person gets confused and has difficulty
sorting out or remembering what was truth and what was lie.

Just be truthful. Speak the truth in love. Walk in truth.

2. Because God Is holy, I should seek to be holy

We are told in 1 Peter 1:15-17 (NIV),

> But just as he who called you is holy, so be holy in all you do; for it
> is written: 'Be holy, because I am holy.' Since you call on a Father
> who judges each man's work impartially, live out your time as
> foreigners here in reverent fear.

When we use the word "holy," most of us tend to regard it in a negative light. Think about it. When was the last time you heard or even used
the word *holy?* It's usually said in a sarcastic tone of voice, as in, "Are you
telling me how to live? Don't give me that holier-than-thou stuff."

Do you know what? It's okay to be holy. The Bible commands you
to be holy.

Now when I say holy, I don't mean that you are arrogant or conde-
scending or that you go around with a false piety. Some people might
call that "holy," but it's really nothing more than pride. Or being a jerk.
In reality, the most holy people are the most humble people.

Going back to that famous passage in Isaiah, the prophet had
a vision and "saw the Lord sitting on a throne, high and lifted up,
and the train of His robe filled the temple" (6:1). What was his
reaction? He cried out, "Woe is me, for I am undone! Because I
am a man of unclean lips, and I dwell in the midst of a people of
unclean lips" (6:5).

As he saw God in all of His holiness, he became painfully aware of his unholiness. In the same way, when you are seeking to live a holy life, you will usually be very aware of how far you have to go. The person who says he or she has got it all together and has reached some spiritual plateau above all others is in reality someone who has barely left the starting blocks in the Christian life. The person who is truly seeking to live a holy life will usually say, "I'm a work in progress. I have so much to learn. I have a long way to go, but I want to be like Jesus."

Even the apostle Paul, after years of walking with God, said,

> Friends, don't get me wrong: By no means do I count myself an expert in all of this, but I've got my eye on the goal, where God is beckoning us onward—to Jesus. I'm off and running, and I'm not turning back. (Philippians 3:13-14, MSG)

All of this goes for me, too, as an author and pastor. I too am a work in progress and have a long, long way to go. As we all do.

It might help us to take another look at this word *holy* and try spelling it another way. Instead of spelling it H-O-L-Y, let's spell it W-H-O-L-L-Y.

Wholly.

When we think of "holy," we might find that term distant or unapproachable. The word *wholly*, however, simply means fully committed to something. We talk to people all the time who are fully committed to this or that. Some people are wholly committed to their career. Others are wholly committed to surfing, fantasy football, or video games. We all know people who are wholly committed to making money. Or wholly absorbed with their physical appearance.

If, however, you are *wholly* committed to God, you will find that you are *holy* as a result.

In the Old Testament, it was said of Caleb, "He wholly followed the Lord His God."[9] Even though his whole generation had turned away from God, there was old Caleb at age eighty-five, raising up his bony arm and saying, "Give me this mountain." He's the guy who took the portion of land that was given to him and conquered it. He not only started well in his life, but he also finished with a sprint. Why? Because he wholly followed the Lord his God.

• • •

Let's close out this chapter now with six important things God wants us to know about Himself.

In the book of Numbers, God gave the priests a blessing to pronounce over the people of Israel on a regular basis. It was as though God was saying, "I want this ingrained in the brains of My people. I want them to hear this over and over and over again. I want them to know that I am the God who cares."

Here is how Scripture records that blessing:

> "The LORD bless you and keep you;
> The LORD make His face shine upon you, and be gracious to you;
> The LORD lift up His countenance upon you, and give you peace."
> (Numbers 6:24-26)

1. "The Lord bless you"

I love that word . . . blessing. It really is a believer's word. Yes, I know the world has hijacked it and used it for all sorts of silly, empty things. But the reality of the word is powerful, because it speaks of God's favor on a man or a woman. Jesus both began and ended His ministry by blessing people. He took the little children into His arms, the Scripture says, and He blessed them. Prior to His ascension into heaven, He blessed His disciples.

It's no different today. He wants to bless you and me, too.

2. "The Lord keep you"

We sometimes worry about safety and security—not only for ourselves, but also for our loved ones. But God will never forget or "lose" those whom He loves.

Not long ago, we took our granddaughter Stella to Disneyland. I couldn't help noticing that a lot of parents have their little ones on leashes nowadays. While I understand a parent's concern for a child's security, I would never do that. I choose to carry my granddaughter instead. I carry her in my arms and never take my eyes off of her. The fact is, you don't lose someone you love.

In the same way, God protects His investment. He keeps you moment by moment, and He will keep you until the very end.

We all pray for His protection on life. But you might ask the question, "What about when some accident or tragedy happens to the child of God? Where was the keeping power of God then?"

I will answer that question with another question. Are we assuming that we have a right to live a long, relatively easy life and one day die peacefully in our sleep at an advanced age? The Bible makes no such promise. Our very life—every breath that we draw into our lungs—is a gift to us from God. Even in an accident, illness, or death, God will keep us. When the day of our passing from this earth arrives, He will take us safely into His presence, where every wound will be healed and every sorrow will fall away.

God's commitment to keep you doesn't just stop with this life alone but continues right on until He has taken you into His presence in glory.

This is something I have struggled with. As a dad, I'm always fixing things and protecting my loved ones. So when my son Christopher died in a car crash in 2008, I suddenly ran into something I couldn't fix and felt like I had somehow failed to protect him.

Fathers fix things. Fathers make things right. Fathers protect. That's just what we do. But then I realized that Christopher is now in the presence of my heavenly Father—and He *has* fixed things in a way much better than I can even imagine.

I don't need to fix this.

I need God to fix me.

And I need to trust my Father, who holds my son safely in His arms. He will keep us.

3. "The Lord smile on you"

"The Lord bless you and keep you; the Lord make His face shine upon you. . . ."[10]

That part about the face of God could be literally translated, "May God smile on you." Do you think of God as smiling? It probably depends on what kind of father you had. Did you have one of those grumpy dads? ("Don't talk to Dad yet. He hasn't had his coffee, and he's grouchy.") Aren't you glad we don't serve a grumpy God?

("Don't bother praying today. God's in a really bad mood.")

Praise the Lord, He is never grumpy. How does God react when you come walking into the room? Probably in the same way I react when one of my little granddaughters comes into the room. I smile. My face lights up. I'm just a crazy grandfather who's head-over-heels in love with his granddaughters. Even when they're doing something wrong, I still think it's cute.

No, don't misunderstand me here. I'm not suggesting that God looks approvingly on bad behavior. I'm simply trying to make the point that when God the Father sees you, He smiles.

What about all your failures? Do you think they're somehow a surprise to God? No, but He wants to continually change you and transform you to become just like His Son. In the meantime, imagine yourself walking into His presence, and imagine that He smiles when He sees you. His face lights up with joy.

4. "The Lord be gracious unto you"

Grace is God's unmerited favor. It's not something we earn. Sometimes we find ourselves thinking, "I really worked hard this week. Maybe I will find God's favor."

No. The Lord is *gracious* unto you. He pours His favor upon you because He is good and gracious. The Bible says, "For by grace you have been saved through faith, and that not of yourselves; it is the gift of God, not of works, lest anyone should boast" (Ephesians 2:8-9).

Thank God for that grace! *Justice* is getting what you deserve. *Mercy* is not getting what you deserve. *Grace* is getting what you don't deserve. Don't ask for justice. "Oh God, give me justice today." No, you don't want what you deserve. You want the love and unmerited favor and kindness and provision that you don't deserve and never will deserve.

The Lord looks on you with a smile. He looks on you with grace. And here is another wonder: the God of the universe is *attentive* to you.

5. "The Lord lift up His countenance upon you"

Another way to say the same thing is to "look at someone with interest." When you do that, when you turn to look at someone with interest in your eyes and in your face, they know they have your full attention. God is saying, "I watch out for you each and every day. You have my full attention. I care."

Have you ever been in a conversation with someone who wasn't really paying attention? Maybe they were looking over your shoulder instead of looking into your eyes, or maybe their gaze was glazed over and you could tell they were not really tracking with you. It's never that way with God. "Busy" as He might be, He is never distracted from you for a moment. You never, ever lose His full attention.

In Psalm 139, David marveled over this fact, writing,

> How precious it is, Lord, to realize that you are thinking about me constantly! I can't even count how many times a day your thoughts turn towards me. And when I waken in the morning, you are still thinking of me! (verses 17-18, TLB)

6. "The Lord give His peace to you"

There is no peace anywhere like the peace of God. Jesus told His disciples, "Peace I leave with you, My peace I give to you; not as the world gives do I give to you. Let not your heart be troubled, neither let it be afraid" (John 14:27).

This is the peace that comes as a result of knowing all these things about God's character and His attitude toward me—and that I am safe in Him. It's really hard to relax or sleep when your heart is in turmoil. But when you are at rest and you feel safe, you can close your eyes.

If you know Jesus as your Savior and Lord, you are safe in the arms of God. And you can trust Him. You know that He will see you through, come what may, until He finally takes you home to be with Himself.

• • •

The omniscient, omnipotent, omnipresent, righteous, true, holy, good, and sovereign God of the universe is watching over you. He will bless, smile on, and keep you, and give you His full attention and peace.

He is the God who cares.

3

Jesus Christ: God with Us

What is God like? We've been exploring that question together in the opening pages of this book.

Where should we go to get an answer to that question? Who has an "expert opinion"? A theologian? A pastor? Not necessarily.

How about a child? Sometimes children will get it right before the adults do. Even our Lord said, "Truly I tell you, unless you change and become like little children, you will never enter the kingdom of heaven" (Matthew 18:3, NIV).

I read about a group of children who were asked the question, "What is God like?" Ashley, age ten, said, "God is like a never-ending story that you want to read again and again. When I hear about Him I want to know more. Although I can't see Him, I feel Him. He is perfect and pure. I know He has felt pain and has suffered greatly to take away my sins."

Well said!

is Jesus."

Caleb nailed it. If you want to know what God is like, take a long look at Jesus Christ, because Jesus is God in human form. If you want to see all of the wonderful attributes of God embodied and put on display, look at Jesus. When Jesus walked this earth, He wasn't a mere representative of God; He was God Himself walking among us. Jesus Messiah. God with us. He wasn't a glorified man, but God in human form, "God with skin on."

He embodied all the attributes of God that we've already talked about in the first two chapters, yet He was also a man who walked our planet, breathed our air, and felt our pain.

He was so wise that He could predict the future events of the world.

He was so humble that He could get on His knees and wash His friends' dirty feet.

He was so powerful that He could calm the wind and waves with a word.

And He was so approachable that children climbed into His arms.

As someone has said, Jesus was God spelling Himself out in language we could all understand.

Jesus Christ. There has never been a man who strode across the human stage quite like Him. He stands apart from all others. We literally, and rightfully so, divide human time from the date of His birth. His very name ripples with power.

If you don't believe me, just say it sometime. Let's say you're in a crowded room—one voice among many. You can say the names of various religious leaders, gurus, or prophets and get no reaction at all. People won't even notice.

But if you simply and clearly say the name "Jesus," you'll get a reaction.

It's almost like a hush will fall over the room. People will start looking around. "Who said that? Did that person actually just say *Jesus Christ*?" Even an atheist who says there is no God at all will use His name to punctuate a point or even use it in a profane way. Why? Because even the nonbeliever knows, deep down, there is power in the name of Jesus.

In Philippians 2:9-11 we read these powerful words:

> God also has highly exalted Him and given Him the name which
> is above every name, that at the name of Jesus every knee should
> bow, of those in heaven, and of those on earth, and of those under
> the earth, and that every tongue should confess that Jesus Christ is
> Lord, to the glory of God the Father.

There is no other name like *that* in all the universe.

Who Is Jesus?

Jesus Christ is the most controversial figure who has ever lived. He is
loved, adored, and worshiped and followed by some . . . hated, despised,
and rejected by others . . . and is disregarded and ignored by most.

Who is Jesus? Two thousand years ago our Lord Himself posed
this question to the Pharisees when He said, "What do you think of
Christ? Whose Son is He?" Interestingly, that question perplexed the
people in His day just as it does the people in ours. The general public was confused about Jesus. Some thought He was Jeremiah the
prophet. Others thought He was Elijah. Herod thought He was John
the Baptist, returned from the dead.

People in that day were confused about the identity of Jesus. They
still are.

Many opine on Him and speak about Him. Some have it right, and
others have it as wrong as can be. Pontius Pilate, who personally exam-
ined Christ and then sent Him to be crucified (though he knew He was
innocent of any crime), said of Jesus, "I find no fault in this man."[11]

Napoleon, the great French general, said, "I know men, and Jesus
was no mere man." Strauss, the German rationalist, described Jesus
as the highest model of religion. John Stuart Mill called Jesus "the
guide of humanity." The French atheist Renan said that Jesus
Christ was "the greatest among the sons of men." Theodore Parker
said Jesus was "a youth with God in his heart."[12]

More contemporary figures have given their opinions as well.
Mahatma Gandhi said of Jesus, "A man who was completely

innocent, offered Himself as a sacrifice for the good of others, including his enemies, and became the ransom of the world. It was a perfect act."[13] Larry King said that if he could interview anyone throughout human history, he would choose Jesus. And then he said, "I would ask Him if He was indeed virgin born, because the answer to that question would define history."[14]

Rock star Bono of U2 gave this opinion of Jesus:

> The secular response to the Christ story always goes like this: He was a great prophet, obviously a very interesting guy, had a lot to say along the lines of other great prophets. But actually Christ doesn't allow you to do that. He doesn't let you off the hook. Christ says: "I'm not saying I'm a teacher, don't call me teacher. I'm not saying I'm a prophet. I'm saying: 'I'm the Messiah.' I'm saying: 'I am God incarnate.'"[15]

Everybody has an opinion about Jesus. But the fact is, He did indeed claim to be God incarnate, and in John 14:6 He said very clearly that He is the only way to God the Father.

Speaking of Jesus, C. S. Lewis summed up the matter as only he could:

> You must make your choice. Either this man was, and is, the Son of God; or else a madman or something worse. You can shut Him up for a fool; you can spit at Him and call Him a demon; or you can fall at His feet and call Him Lord. But let us not come with any patronizing nonsense about Him being a great human teacher. He has not left that open to us. He did not intend to.[16]

What Did the Disciples Say?

If I wanted to know about you, one of the best ways I could find out about you—get the inside story, so to speak—would be to spend time with people who know you best.

In the case of Jesus, those people would be the apostles. For three concentrated years, they walked, talked, ate, and stayed with Jesus.

They saw Him in every circumstance imaginable. And of those apostles, there were three who were singled out for special privileges and attention: Peter, James, and John. These three were present at the transfiguration of Jesus, up on the mountain, when His face and clothing were changed, and He shone brighter than the sun. They were there when Jesus raised a child from the dead. They were there in the Garden of Gethsemane when His anguished sweat fell like great drops of blood.

John was probably the most perceptive of the lot and seemed to pick up on things that others often missed. It was John who would often lean his head up close to the chest of Jesus, so as to not miss a word.

In John's own book, then, the Gospel called by his name, we would expect to find an intimate, insightful portrait of Christ . . . and we do.

Jesus Was—and Is—God

In the opening words of John 1 we read:

> In the beginning was the Word, and the Word was with God, and the Word was God. He was in the beginning with God. All things were made through Him, and without Him nothing was made that was made. In Him was life, and the life was the light of men. And the light shines in the darkness, and the darkness did not comprehend it. (verses 1-5)

A study of these words in the original language reveals something interesting: There is no definite article—no "the"—before the word *beginning*. What that means is that no one can pinpoint this beginning in a moment of time. Why? Because Jesus predates Creation. He predates everything. He existed in eternity past, just as He will live forever into the future. Our limited, finite minds can't even conceive or imagine that concept, but it's true.

It's just another way of saying, as John says repeatedly in his Gospel, that Jesus is God. Before there was a world, before there were planets, before there was light or darkness, before there was any matter at all, before there was anything but the godhead, there was Jesus. He is a member of the Trinity, and coequal, coeternal, and coexistent with the Father and the Holy Spirit. He was with God, He was God, and He came to this earth as a Man.

Verse 14 of John 1 tells us, "And the Word became flesh and dwelt among us." That word, *dwelt*, also means He *tabernacled* among us. In *The Message* we read, "The Word became flesh and blood, and moved into the neighborhood. We saw the glory with our own eyes."

Hard as it may be to grasp or understand, the almighty God became an embryo. He was deity in diapers, and He grew into a Man. He walked in our shoes, lived our life, and then He died our death.

But note this distinction: While Jesus *identified* with us, He did not become *identical* with us. That's important. No one was ever more identified with humanity than Jesus. It was total identification without any loss of identity, for He became one of us without ceasing to be Himself. He became human without ceasing to be God. Jesus did not exchange deity for humanity; He was deity *in* humanity.

Scripture also makes clear that Jesus Himself was the creator of the universe. In John 1:10 we are told that "He was in the world, and the world was made through Him." In Colossians, Paul writes,

> For by Him all things were created that are in heaven and that are on earth, visible and invisible, whether thrones or dominions or principalities or powers. All things were created through Him and for Him. And He is before all things, and in Him all things consist. (1:16-17)

Jesus was—and is—God.

Jesus, Who Was God, Became a Man

When we think about that first Christmas, now over 2,000 years ago, we celebrate the birth of our Lord in the manger in Bethlehem.

When you think about it, however, it wasn't only the story of an arrival on earth, it was also the story of a departure from heaven.

The prophet Isaiah looked hundreds of years into the future and wrote about that event:

For unto us a Child is born, Unto us a Son is given;
And the government will be upon His shoulder.
And His name will be called Wonderful, Counselor,
Mighty God, Everlasting Father, Prince of Peace.
Of the increase of His government and peace
There will be no end. (Isaiah 9:6-7)

From earth's perspective we say, "Unto us a Child was born."
But from heaven's perspective, it was, "Unto us a Son is given." To
further remind us of the deity of this Baby, the Bible tells us that
His name will be "Wonderful, Counselor, Mighty God, Everlasting
Father, Prince of Peace."

Clearly, Isaiah was speaking here of God in human form. Your
eyes have to be closed (or veiled) to miss that. In the first chapter of
Matthew, we are reminded of the prophet's words: " 'Behold, the virgin shall be with child, and bear a Son, and they shall call His name
Immanuel,' which is translated, 'God with us' " (verse 23).

We also know the Lord chose that the Messiah would be born
of a virgin, as the prophesies declared. He would be supernaturally
conceived in the womb of a woman who had never known a man.

People through the years, of course, have struggled with this
defining miracle. Some will say, "I believe in Jesus, but I don't know if
I believe in that Virgin Birth stuff." The fact is, however, I don't think
you can be a true Christian without believing in the Virgin Birth. If
He wasn't supernaturally conceived in the womb of the virgin, then,
friend, He wasn't God. And if He wasn't God, then His death on the
cross wasn't of any great significance.

There were many men who died on Roman crosses 2,000 years
ago, and one of them happened to be named Jesus. But there was
only one Man who died on a cross *who was God in human form, atoning
for the sin of the world, and then bodily raised again from the dead.*

The Lord's Virgin Birth was a claim to His deity. And going back
to the point I made in the first chapter, if you believe God exists and
is the Creator of all things, the rest of the Bible will be relatively easy
for you to believe. If you can accept Genesis 1:1, "In the beginning
God created the heavens and the earth," then you can believe in all

the miracles that we find in the pages of Scripture.

When you stop to consider it, the Virgin Birth makes total sense. How else could God have accomplished sending His Messiah to earth? How could Jesus have been born as a complete yet sinless human being without a human parent?

What if God had suddenly sent a fully-grown Jesus in a blinding flash of light from heaven? He suddenly appears, and says, "I am the Messiah!" It certainly would have impressed people, but how could we have related to Him in all our human troubles and trials? If He talked about walking in our shoes and facing the challenges we face, we might reply, "Well, Lord, I'm not sure you understand what I'm going through. After all, You came down from heaven in a shaft of light, and You can't really understand what I'm facing right now."

What, then, if God had sent Jesus into the world through two human parents? It would be difficult for us to accept His divinity. We might say, "You say that He is divine, but He has human parents like the rest of us. What's the difference?"

So you see, the Virgin Birth makes total sense. Yes, He was supernaturally conceived in the womb of a human mother, but He did not inherit her sinful nature because His Father was God.

Christ was God, but not because He was virgin-born. Rather, He was virgin-born because He was God.

Dietrich Bonhoeffer said, "If Jesus Christ is not true God, how could He help us? If not true man, how could He help us?"[17]

There was never a moment when Jesus became God. He was always God. He was God before He was born, and He remained God after He became man. His deity was prehuman, preearthly, pre-Bethlehem, pre-Mary. He was always God—even as a tiny fetus in His mother's womb.

How much, then, did Jesus know about His mission when He was a baby or a little child? Did that baby know all things?

Babies, of course, are amazing. Particularly my granddaughters, Stella, Lucy, and Allie (short for Alexandra). As I write these words, Allie is still a little baby, but she is learning something new every day.

With each passing hour and day, she is becoming more alert and more aware. But she isn't talking yet, like her cousins Stella and Lucy. She doesn't call me Papa yet. She looks and smiles and doesn't say anything intelligible, because she's at a different mental state than her older sister, Rylie.

How much did Jesus know in the womb? How much did He grasp as a newborn infant, lying in that hay-filled manger? Did He look around Him that first Christmas night and say, "Hello, Mother. Hello, Joseph. I am Jesus. How are you? I'm the creator of all things. I would really appreciate it if someone could get Me out of this manger, because I have a ministry to get started."

That's not the picture we get in Scripture.

The Bible indicates that Jesus went through a learning process like every other human child. In Luke 2, we're told, "And Jesus matured, growing up in both body and spirit, blessed by both God and people" (verse 52, MSG).

"But wait a second!" you say. "If you are omniscient, which means you know all things, how can you learn anything?" That's a valid question. And here's my view: Jesus possessed these divine attributes without using them. When He became a man, he "emptied Himself, taking the form of a bond-servant, and being made in the likeness of men" (Philippians 2:7, NASB).

Self-emptying is not self-extinction. He humbled Himself. When Scripture says He emptied Himself, it doesn't mean that He laid aside His deity; it means He laid aside the privileges of deity.

So yes, He went through a learning process. When Luke 2:52 says He "increased in wisdom and stature," it literally means "He kept on advancing."

Because Jesus was truly man, enduring heat and cold, pain and grief, weariness and strength, laughter and tears like any one of us, the Bible tells us that He is able to sympathize with us in our weaknesses. We can never say to Him, "Jesus, You just don't understand."

> But Jesus the Son of God is our great High Priest who has gone to heaven itself to help us; therefore let us never stop trusting him.
> This High Priest of ours understands our weaknesses, since he had

the same temptations we do, though he never once gave way to them and sinned. So let us come boldly to the very throne of God and stay there to receive his mercy and to find grace to help us in our times of need. (Hebrews 4:14-16, TLB)

Jesus Veiled, but Never Violated, His Deity

God among us!

Imagine what that would have been like. Imagine if you had been one of the apostles, and you could lay your actual eyes on Jesus, the eternal Son of God. John, who wrote the Gospel of John, also wrote the letter we know as 1 John. In the opening words of that letter, he wrote,

We proclaim to you the one who existed from the beginning, whom we have heard and seen. We saw him with our own eyes and touched him with our own hands. He is Jesus Christ, the Word of life. This one who is life itself was revealed to us, and we have seen him. (1 John 1:1-2, NLT)

The phrase that John used here for "saw with our own eyes" could be translated "to view, to contemplate, to gaze upon as a spectacle."

It amazes me to think about this. As one of those original twelve disciples, you could look at Jesus as He was teaching or walking ahead of you or sleeping, and think to yourself, "What I am seeing right now is God in human form. That's *God* standing there. That's *God* speaking to us. I can reach out my hand right now and touch *God!*"

All of this brings us to the natural question, "What did Jesus look like?" Was He strikingly handsome, as He is usually depicted in the movies or in paintings? Maybe, and maybe not. My understanding is that if we saw Him, we might describe His appearance as "ordinary." Isaiah 53:2 says: "He had no beauty or majesty to attract us to him, nothing in his appearance that we should desire him" (NIV).

Many times He could walk right through a crowd unnoticed. When Judas was planning to betray Him, he said, "It's the man that I kiss. He's the one." If Jesus appeared as He did in some religious art, Judas would have only had to say, "He's the guy who looks like a movie star. Wavy hair, blue eyes . . . you can't miss Him."

Since Jesus was Jewish, it's very doubtful He had blond hair or blue eyes. His skin, hair, and eyes would have been dark. I don't imagine that He looked anything at all like modern artists or actors portray Him.

I remember an incident many years ago in a mental hospital. (I was there as a visitor, not a patient.) I was visiting with my friend and fellow pastor, Mike MacIntosh. At that time, in the sixties, I had shoulder-length hair, parted down the middle, and a full beard. (I told you it was a long time ago.) And some people said I resembled Jesus a little bit.

Mike and I were talking to a patient in the mental hospital, and Mike said to him, "Has anyone ever introduced you to Jesus Christ?" Without missing a beat, the patient turned to me, grabbed my hand, shook it, and said, "Jesus, it's good to meet You."

"Oh," I said. "I'm . . . uh . . . not Jesus. I'm Greg."

The truth is, Jesus looked like your average "man on the street." He didn't have a halo, and He didn't glow in the dark.

Isn't it interesting that in all four of the Gospels, we don't have a single physical description of Jesus? I've sometimes wondered, *Couldn't one of those guys have spared maybe two verses to describe what Jesus looked like?*

But no, we can safely conclude that wasn't God's will. Perhaps, with our propensity for idol worship, God knew that a physical picture of Jesus might lead us astray. We might become more caught up in what He looked like than in what He said. And it is the words of Jesus that are life to us. Jesus Himself said, "The Spirit gives life; the flesh counts for nothing. The words I have spoken to you—they are full of the Spirit and life" (John 6:63, NIV).

Remember the time when the disciples were crossing the Sea of Galilee and encountered a great storm? It must have been an incredibly violent storm, because these seasoned sailors began to despair of life. They thought, *This is it. We're all going to drown.*

Meanwhile Jesus was sleeping in the boat's stern. It had been a difficult day, and He was exhausted. They woke Him up, yelling over the howling wind and crashing waves, "Lord, don't You care that we are perishing?" Christ stood up, faced the storm, and said, "Peace, be still." A more literal translation would be, "Peace, be *muzzled*," as though He were talking to a wild animal. And then He rebuked them for not having faith.

That's a perfect example of deity and humanity on display. What could be more human than being exhausted after a day's work and falling asleep? And what could be more divine than rebuking the elements? His authority that day caused His own disciples to say, "Who can this be, that even the wind and sea obey Him?" (See Mark 4:35-41).

Who can this be? He who was both God and man.

A Man Like Us

When Jesus needed to get from point A to point B, He walked, like everybody else in His day.

Now if I had been Jesus, I wouldn't have done this. I would have said to the guys, "I'll meet you in Jerusalem."

"Aren't You walking with us, Jesus?"

"Um, no, not this time." And then as they started down that long, dusty road, I would have just floated through the air and landed in Jerusalem. No fuss. No muss.

But Jesus didn't do that. He walked. He put mile after mile on those sandals of His. He walked until He was tired, perhaps even exhausted. He fell asleep from exhaustion like anyone else would do in those circumstances.

Jesus experienced physical hunger. The account of His temptation in the wilderness tells us that after He had fasted forty days and forty nights, He was hungry. When Satan tempted Him to turn a rock into a piece of bread, He refused to do that—and it's worth noting that Jesus never performed a miracle for His own benefit.

He also experienced physical thirst. When He hung on the cross, He said, "I thirst." He could have created water to refresh Himself. But instead, He humbled Himself, set aside all the privileges of deity, and suffered for our sakes.

He experienced physical weakness. I think you could safely say that Jesus was a man's man. He wasn't weak and scrawny, as often depicted in religious art. We can assume that because He had been raised by Joseph and worked as a carpenter. In John 4:6, we read that when Jesus and His disciples arrived in Samaria, He sat down by a well, "being wearied from His journey." When He was forced to carry His own cross—which must have had a considerable weight—He did that until He finally stumbled. This was after having His back lacerated with thirty-nine lashes from a Roman cat-o'-nine-tails, resulting in a severe loss of blood.

He bled real blood, experienced real human agony, and finally, died like a man, in that His body ceased to function.

Jesus also knew anger. No, He never "flew off the handle" or "lost His temper" as you and I have been known to do. (Isn't it great to know that God doesn't have temper tantrums? Can you imagine the stars and planets flying around?) No, God's wrath is always a measured and righteous wrath, and anger in Jesus was always righteous indignation. We see it on display in the Gospels, when the Temple money changers were preying on the people rather than praying for the people. Jesus upset their tables and drove them out with a whip. He was angry with the religious leaders who continually and stubbornly misrepresented God to the people.

At the same time, however, He was tender and approachable. So much so that little children would run to sit in His lap and play at His feet.

Jesus felt sorrow, too. Deep, soul-wrenching sorrow. At the tomb of His personal friend Lazarus, brother to Mary and Martha, the Bible tells us that "Jesus wept." Why did He weep? Because His friend was dead? I don't think so. He knew very well that Lazarus was in paradise in that moment, perfectly safe and happy. I think He wept because He saw how death brought such devastation to Mary and Martha and the people who loved Lazarus and mourned for him. I think He shed tears because He knew that death had never been part of God's plan. He wept for a world where sin had entered in, allowing things like illness, pain, sorrow, and death to become part of human experience.

He also understands your sorrow. He knows and feels whatever you may be going through as you read these words.

In Isaiah 53, the Bible says of Him:

> We despised him and rejected him—a man of sorrows, acquainted with bitterest grief. We turned our backs on him and looked the other way when he went by. He was despised and we didn't care.

> Yet it was *our* grief he bore, *our* sorrows that weighed him down. And we thought his troubles were a punishment from God, for his *own* sins! But he was wounded and bruised for *our* sins. He was beaten that we might have peace; he was lashed—and we were healed! *We*—every one of us—have strayed away like sheep! *We*, who left God's paths to follow our own. Yet God laid on *him* the guilt and sins of every one of us! (verses 3-6, TLB, emphasis in original)

It wasn't just your sins that weighed Him down, it was your *sorrows*. A contemporary politician might say, "I feel your pain." But that's just an expression, because he or she doesn't know or feel your pain at all. But Jesus, God's Son, truly does feel your pain and understand your sorrow. In the book of Hebrews, we're told that He is a "merciful and faithful High Priest" who sympathizes with our weaknesses (Hebrews 2:17; 4:15). Someone else might say to you in your grief or sorrow, "Get over it. Grow up. Don't cry. Wipe your tears." Jesus would say, "I understand. I know why you feel that way. I know why you hurt like that. I have been there, and I know what it's like. And I am here for you."

That's why Jesus is so wonderful! When we talk to Jesus, we know that we're talking to a God who has walked in our shoes, breathed our air, lived our life, died our death, and is now preparing a place for us in His Father's house.

The essential message of Christmas, the birth of our Lord, is that Immanuel came. God is with us and walked among us. And now we never, never have to be alone in this world. One of the most remarkable teachings in the Bible is that Jesus Christ is not only with us, but that He actually comes and makes His home in the human heart that welcomes Him. Jesus said in John 14:23, "If anyone loves Me, he will keep My word; and My Father will love him, and We will come to him and make Our home with him."

God wants to make His home with you. He doesn't want to just stop by as a house guest or pay you a visit or have a nice little chat. He wants to move in. He wants to indwell you and transform you from the inside out.

He wants you to know that no matter what happens on these sometimes-dark roads that we walk on this side of heaven, we are never alone.

God is with us!

Maybe your marriage fell apart this past year, and you feel all alone. *God is with you.* Perhaps your children have forgotten about you, and you never hear from them. *God is with you.* Maybe a loved one who was with you last year is not here today. You need to know something. *Immanuel. God is with you.* If your loved one was a believer, he or she is with the Lord now, and you will join him or her one day in a great reunion. Maybe you feel isolated in a hospital, a prison, a convalescent home, or on military duty in some alien and faraway place. If you have faith in Christ Immanuel, *God is with you.*

God with skin on.

God spelling Himself out in language we can all understand.

We have access to the very presence of God through Jesus Christ. C. S. Lewis summed it up beautifully when he said, "The Son of God became a man that men might become sons of God."[18]

The Holy Spirit and You, Part 1

We talk about God as a Father, and we talk about God as a Son. To some degree, we can grasp images like these, because we've all had fathers, and we may have had sons or be a son.

But God as Spirit?

A spirit, almost by definition, is hard to grasp. A spirit can't be seen with human eyes. And then if you use the old King James verbiage it gets even a little harder to grasp. God the Holy Ghost? Uh-oh.

And maybe all of the old cartoon images of ghosts float into our minds, and we think, *How do we understand something like this? How can God be a Father, Son, and Holy Ghost?*

The fact is the Bible teaches that God is a triune being. A Trinity.

Now some would protest, asserting that you can't find the word *trinity* anywhere in the Bible. That is true. But you find the *teaching* of the Trinity from Genesis to Revelation.

But doesn't it say in Deuteronomy 6:4 that "the LORD our God, the LORD is one"? Yes. And so He is. The Lord our God *is* one God. We worship and serve one God, not multiple gods. We aren't polytheistic; we are monotheistic. And yet the Bible clearly teaches that God is a Trinity.

We're not talking here about modes or manifestations of the same Persons, but rather three Persons who are all simultaneously active. In other words, the Father is not the same Person as the Son. And the Son is not the same Person as the Holy Spirit. There is one God, and this true God exists in three distinct, co-equal, co-eternal Persons. Not three Gods, but one. One substance, in perfect harmony.

Analogies Don't Cut It

How could God be three in one? Many try to offer word pictures or analogies to help explain this difficult concept, but all such comparisons break down quickly. Some teachers point to the example of water, noting that we experience water in three different forms—liquid, steam, and ice. The forms are different, but the substance is the same. Others might mention an egg, with a shell, a yolk, and a white. They're all part of the same egg.

But those simple analogies really don't begin to do justice to the biblical reality of one God in three Persons.

The fact is, no one can really explain the Trinity, and all our best attempts fall short. Jonathan Edwards said of the Trinity that it was "the highest and deepest of all divine mysteries."[19] If you and I could fully explain God, then we could fully explain the Trinity. But we can't fully explain either one.

It has been well said, "Try to explain this, and you will lose your mind. Try to explain it away, and you will lose your soul." You must believe in the Trinity to be a believer.

The Trinity in Scripture

Perhaps you say, "Where do we find the Trinity in the Bible?" You could start with the very first page, where you would see the Trinity at work in the creation of the world.

Who created the heavens and the earth?

Genesis 1:1 says, "In the beginning *God* created the heavens and the earth." So there was the Father at work in creation.

But Jesus was there as well. As a member of the Trinity, Christ was hands-on at the creation of everything. John 1:3 says, "All things were made through Him, and without Him nothing was made that was made." And also we read in Colossians 1:16, speaking of Christ, "By Him all things were created that are in heaven and that are on earth, visible and invisible, whether thrones or dominions or principalities or powers. All things were created through Him and for Him."

The Bible says that God the Father created the heavens and the earth, and it also says that God the Son created all things. And then of course, we read in Genesis 1:2 and 3, "The earth was without form and void; and darkness was on the face of the deep. And the spirit of God was hovering over the face of the waters. Then God said, 'Let there be light' and there was light."

So God the Father, God the Son, and God the Holy Spirit all played a part in Creation. In the book of Genesis, one of the names that is used for God is *Elohim*, which means "more than one." Again, we're not talking about "more than one God" here. *Elohim* is a unique word describing God's essential nature.

For instance, in Genesis 3:22 we read of God saying, "Man has become like one of *Us*." Then we read in Genesis 11:7, God speaking, "Let *Us* go down." That's the Trinity having a conversation.

Perhaps one of the clearest examples of the Trinity in action—all simultaneously participating—is at the baptism of Jesus. Here we have Jesus, who is God in human form, going into the Jordan River to be baptized. God the Father speaks from heaven and says, "This is my beloved Son in whom I am well pleased." And God the Holy Spirit comes upon Jesus in the form of a dove.[20]

Finally, when we baptize people we are to baptize them in the name of the Father, the Son, and the Holy Spirit.

So let's talk a little bit about the Holy Spirit in particular.

Called Alongside to Help

When Jesus walked this earth as God in human form, He was on scene and available to be seen, heard, and touched.

Years after Jesus left the earth, the apostle John reflected on that unique and precious opportunity. He wrote,

> Christ was alive when the world began, yet I myself have seen him with my own eyes and listened to him speak. I have touched him with my own hands. He is God's message of life. This one who is life from God has been shown to us and we guarantee that we have seen him; I am speaking of Christ, who is eternal Life. He was with the Father and then was shown to us. Again I say, we are telling you about what we ourselves have actually seen and heard, so that you may share the fellowship and the joys we have with the Father and with Jesus Christ his son. (1 John 1:1-3, TLB)

The disciples could hear the timbre of His voice, look at His unique features, and even reach out and grab Him by the arm. But then Jesus made it clear that He was going to leave them and ascend to His Father. Before He departed, however, He promised them another Helper, who would come in His place. That incomparable Helper is God the Holy Spirit.

One of the words that Jesus used for the Holy Spirit is *parakletos*, "One called alongside to help." Jesus said in John 14:16-18,

> I will pray the Father, and He will give you another Helper, that He may abide with you forever—the Spirit of truth, whom the world cannot receive, because it neither sees Him nor knows Him; but you know him, for He dwells with you and will be in you. I will not leave you orphans; I will come to you.

In these verses, Jesus promised His disciples that the Holy Spirit would be *with* them and would be *in* them. In the same way, that same Holy Spirit is with and in every believer in Christ today, as we will note in the following chapter.

In John 16:7, Jesus tells his disciples, "'Nevertheless I tell you the truth. It is to your advantage that I go away; for if I do not go away, the Helper will not come to you; but if I depart, I will send Him to you."

Now, take note of what He says next:

> And when He has come, He will convict the world of sin, and of righteousness, and of judgment: of sin, because they do not believe in Me; of righteousness, because I go to My Father and you see Me no more; of judgment, because the ruler of this world is judged. (verses 8-11)

Notice that Jesus says, "When *He* has come, *He* will convict." The Spirit is a "Him," not an "It." Now I know that's difficult for us to grasp, because we read in Scripture about the Spirit being like a mighty rushing wind or divided flames of fire on the Day of Pentecost, and then we read about His appearing as a dove. So how can the Spirit be a *Him*?

These are word pictures. In the same way, we read about Jesus being called "the Bread of Life" and "the Door." And the Father is described as a consuming fire and a refuge. We're told that He hides us under the shadow of His wings. Does that mean that Jesus is a loaf of bread or a door? Or that the Father is a giant bird in heaven? Of course not. These are metaphors that are employed to help us to understand God better.

So yes, the Spirit is compared to a dove or a mighty rushing wind. But at the heart of it all, He is a *person*. He has intelligence, emotion, a will, and all the other aspects of personality. And He has a specific work He wants to do in this world.

An inanimate object or "force" does not express love or have emotion. But the Spirit is not an object. He is not an It. He is a He. And He has come for a purpose. What, then, is this purpose and work He wants to do in the world?

The Purpose and Work of the Holy Spirit

1. The Holy Spirit has come to convict us of our sin

Another way to put it is He has come to *convince* us of our sin. In John 16 we read, "And when He [the Spirit] has come, He will convict the world of sin, and of righteousness, and of judgment" (verse 8).

In other words, He has come to show us that we are sinners. The Holy Spirit takes the message of the death and resurrection of Jesus, shows us it is true, and convinces us that we need to turn to God. Without the convicting power of the Spirit, you would never have come to Jesus. The Spirit shows you that you need God, that you need the salvation of Jesus Christ. There is nothing that I or any preacher, teacher, or author in the world could say to convince you of those things. It takes the power of the Spirit Himself.

When I find myself praying for a nonbeliever, then, I will say, "Lord, convict this person by your Holy Spirit." I can certainly tell someone Jesus has made my life richer and better, and that I have great joy and peace in knowing God and having my sins forgiven. And that individual might think, *Well that's fine for you.* But what that person needs to realize is that he or she is a sinner, in desperate need of a Savior.

I can't convince them of that.

But guess what?

The Holy Spirit is able to do that. That is His work, and His specialty. As you read these words, you may remember the day or even the moment when it dawned on you, *I am a sinner. I am separated from God. I am in deep trouble.* That was no preacher or book or even your own thought process that convinced you of those facts. It was the supernatural work of God's Holy Spirit.

Why does the Spirit convict us of our sin? To drive us to despair? No. He does it to send us into the open arms of Jesus. In the book of Acts, we read about how Simon Peter got up to preach on the Day of Pentecost, speaking to the very people who were culpable in the crucifixion of Jesus. As they listened to Peter's words, something amazing happened. We read, "Now when they heard this, they were cut to the heart, and said to Peter and the rest of the apostles, 'Men and brethren, what shall we do?' "[21] *"Cut to the heart."* That's an interesting phrase that appears only here in the New Testament. It means to pierce or stab, and it describes something that is sudden and unexpected. Stabbed in the heart! And who is wielding this knife? It is the Holy Spirit Himself. And we all know what it's like to come under that kind of sudden conviction.

Consider this: If you stab someone in the heart, you have to face them! It doesn't say the Holy Spirit stabbed them in the back. We have all been stabbed in the back at one point or another. Someone is sweet and nice to our face and as soon as we walk away, they say, "Let me tell you about this guy." Stabbed in the back!

The Holy Spirit never stabs you in the back; He stabs you in the heart.

Yes, I know it's a graphic and unsettling phrase that I use here. But let's change our verbiage a little bit, and instead of thinking about a dagger in the hands of an assassin, think about a scalpel in the hands of a surgeon. If I have a cancerous tumor growing in my body and find an expert surgeon who knows how to remove that deadly growth, what do I want him to do? I want him to pierce my body with that razor-sharp scalpel of his and remove that thing that will eventually kill me. Or to use another example, a heart surgeon might even open up my chest, remove my diseased heart, and put in a new heart in its place.

So the idea here is, yes, the Holy Spirit will "stab" you, but it is not to destroy you. It is to show you your need for Jesus.

2. The Holy Spirit has come to bring us to Christ

John 16:8 tells us that when the Holy Spirit comes He will convict the world of sin, and verse 9 tells us why: "because they do not believe in Me."

One of the Holy Spirit's tasks is to show the world their sin in rejecting and refusing to believe in Jesus Christ.

3. The Holy Spirit has come to show us our need for righteousness

In John 16:10 Jesus speaks of the Spirit convincing the world "of righteousness, because I go to My Father and you see Me no more."

Earlier in His ministry, Jesus said, "For I say to you, that unless your righteousness exceeds the righteousness of the scribes and Pharisees, you will by no means enter the kingdom of heaven" (Matthew 5:20).

I remember the first time I read that as a young Christian. And I thought to myself, *Now wait a second. Weren't these scribes and Pharisees very devout men? How could my righteousness possibly exceed theirs?*

Here is how. Theirs was a false righteousness and a self-righteousness. The Holy Spirit has come to all of us to say, "Friend, you are not righteous enough on your own. You need the righteousness of Christ credited to your account because you are a sinner. But if you will trust in Jesus, this righteousness will be given to you." That is why the Holy Spirit has come.

Sins Against the Holy Spirit

The Holy Spirit also has emotion, and because He has emotion, He can be offended. Did you know there are six specific sins identified in the Bible that could be committed against the Holy Spirit? When I hear something like that, I want to know immediately what they are. And I want to make as sure as I can that I am not committing any of them!

Sins believers can commit against the Spirit

In Acts 5, we note the first three of these six sins that can be committed against the Holy Spirit. These are sins that believers can commit against the Spirit.

1. Lying to the Holy Spirit

> But a certain man named Ananias, with Sapphira his wife, sold a possession. And he kept back part of the proceeds, his wife also being aware of it, and brought a certain part and laid it at the apostles' feet. But Peter said, "Ananias, why has Satan filled your heart to lie to the Holy Spirit and keep back part of the price of the land for yourself? While it remained, was it not your own? And after it was sold, was it not in your own control? Why have you conceived this thing in your heart? You have not lied to men but to God." (Acts 5:1-4)

This is a page of history from the first-century church, and it's one of those supernatural acts that, quite frankly, God is not doing today. This was the miracle of two people being struck down dead for being hypocrites and lying to the Holy Spirit.

Two things jump out to me from those verses. First, we can see yet another declaration that the Holy Spirit is God. Peter said that Ananias and Sapphira had lied to the Holy Spirit, and then later said, "You lied to God."

The second thing I notice is that the Holy Spirit can be specifically sinned against. And in this instance, they lied to Him.

Now what does that mean? It means they pretended to be something they were not. The worst kind of sin is the kind committed by a person who doesn't think he or she is really a sinner.

Let's just think for a moment about a "garden-variety sinner." They use profanity. They drink. They smoke. They cheat when they can get away with it. They're mean and ornery. We all know people like that. Most of us used to *be* people like that. And then let's think of someone who goes to church every Sunday morning. What we have trouble realizing is that the person in the pew of the church could be in worse shape than the garden-variety sinner I just described! If that person who is a nonbeliever knows he is a nonbeliever, and knows he is separated from God, there is hope for him that one day he will come under the conviction of the Holy Spirit, turn from that sinful lifestyle, and believe in Jesus. But if that person who goes to church every Sunday has no intention of responding to what he is hearing, he is actually a hypocrite.

Better to just be what you are.

It's better to say, "I am not into this Christianity stuff . . . I don't believe in this . . . I don't care anything about this . . ." than to pretend to be spiritual when you aren't at all. God really hates hypocrisy.

Now that doesn't mean we won't be inconsistent at times or fall short of the mark now and then. We've all had our moments of hypocrisy, and that's not what I mean. I'm talking about people who consistently wear a mask in order to deceive people into believing they're a different man or woman than they actually are.

As a kid, I remember how we would wear rubber masks on Halloween. (I can still remember the way they smelled.) Your face would be sweating under that mask, and you couldn't really see very well through the eyeholes. As you went door to door with your trick-or-treat bag, you were pretending to be someone you were not. In other words, you were portraying a character.

There are people who actually do that at church. They slip on their little Christian mask and put on a beautiful show. And people look at them and say, "Now there is a committed Christian." But the truth is, that individual may have little or no interest in God at all. Outside of church, they're doing things that openly contradict the clear teaching of God's Word. Yet they show up every Sunday with a Bible in hand and a big smile on their face.

That's hypocrisy. And that was the sin of Ananias and Sapphira. They were lying to God.

It was Cicero who said, "Of all villainy there is none more base than that of the hypocrite who at the moment he is most false makes it his business to appear virtuous."

The hypocrite extraordinaire, if you will, was Judas Iscariot. He seemed like a stand-up guy—and especially when that woman brought her sacrificial gift of perfume with which she anointed Jesus. Judas, you'll remember, stood up and indignantly said, "That perfume was worth a year's wages. It should have been sold and the money given to the poor" (John 12:5, NLT).

The other disciples might have thought, *Wow. He is so holy.* But then the gospel writer adds this note: "Not that he cared for the poor—he was a thief, and since he was in charge of the disciples' money, he often stole some for himself" (verse 6, NLT).

Things aren't always as they appear! And then to add insult to injury, when Judas betrayed Jesus in Gethsemane, He did it with a kiss. He could have just pointed and said, "There is Jesus. Arrest Him. My job is done." Or he could have touched Him on the shoulder. But no, Judas kissed Him—repeatedly. At the moment he appeared to be the most virtuous, he was the most sinful. That is lying to God.

2. Grieving the Holy Spirit

Another sin you can commit against the Holy Spirit is grieving Him.

Ephesians 4:29-32 says this:

"Don't use foul or abusive language. Let everything you say be good and helpful, so that your words will be an encouragement to those who hear them. And do not bring sorrow to God's Holy Spirit by the way you live. . . . Get rid of all bitterness, rage, anger, harsh words, and slander, as well as all types of malicious behavior. Instead, be kind to each other, tenderhearted, forgiving one another, just as God through Christ has forgiven you." (NLT)

The word *grieve* means to make sad or sorrowful—to bring sadness to the Holy Spirit. What makes the Holy Spirit sad and sorrowful?

FOUL AND ABUSIVE LANGUAGE

Verse 29 says, "Don't use foul or abusive language." In the original language, the phrase that is used here means something rotten—something that has gone bad. And rotten speech includes profanity, dirty stories, vulgarity, and double entendre—where everything has a sexual connotation.

We're all aware that some people speak that way all the time. But if God has cleaned up your heart, it should also affect the words that come out of your mouth.

For out of the abundance of the heart his mouth speaks. (Luke 6:45)

Blessing and cursing come pouring out of the same mouth. Surely, my brothers and sisters, this is not right! Does a spring of water bubble out with both fresh water and bitter water? Does a fig tree produce olives, or a grapevine produce figs? No, and you can't draw fresh water from a salty spring. (James 3:10-12, NLT)

Sweet water and bitter water shouldn't be gushing out of the same spring, and rotten talk shouldn't be coming out of the same mouth as praises to God. He wants us to clean up our vocabulary. God wants to change this area of our life. Why? Because it brings sorrow to the heart of the Holy Spirit.

BITTERNESS

Bitterness means an embittered and resentful spirit that refuses to be reconciled. Did you know that some people like to be mad? They live for conflict, arguments, and fighting. In a perverse sort of way, they actually enjoy it.

Other people will walk around the block to avoid a conflict, and I am one of those people. I don't like conflict, unless I'm forced to it. And even then I dread it. I know that it's necessary at certain times, but it's not something that I look forward to or relish.

On the other hand, some people are just looking for a fight. And you can see them moving from fight to fight in their lives, no matter who they're with or where they go. These folks are always mad at someone. They always have their nemesis—a person who is supposedly the source of all their misery. These same people are often very critical and nitpicky as they try to uncover sources of contention, dissatisfaction, and conflict in the lives of others.

I have found that the person who has covered up sin in his or her life is often the one who keeps trying to uncover sin in other people's lives. It never surprises me when I find that the most critical people are guilty of something far worse themselves.

Don't live this way! It makes the Spirit sad. Why? Because if you let bitterness go unchecked, it naturally leads you to the next thing that grieves His heart.

FITS OF RAGE AND UNCONTROLLED ANGER

In the book of Ephesians, Paul writes, "Get rid of all bitterness, rage and anger, brawling and slander, along with every form of malice" (4:31, NIV).

Rage speaks of a person who is easily angered and prone to shout or scream in their anger or frustration. We say people like this "have a short fuse," and we find ourselves having to "walk on eggshells" around them. The least little thing seems to set them off. That sort of behavior grieves the Spirit of God.

SLANDER AND MALICE

Slander speaks of saying evil things about others behind their backs. *Malice* speaks of ill will—even to the point of plotting evil against someone.

The truth is, we've all been hurt by certain people in our lives.

Every one of us has been wounded by someone who took advantage of us or did us wrong. Now what are you going to do? Are you going to be like Shylock in Shakespeare's *Merchant of Venice*, and demand your "pound of flesh" and be obsessed with destroying the person who hurt you? Or are you going to instead live according to the truth of Ephesians 4:32, which is to be tenderhearted and forgive them?

"Well," you say, "they don't deserve forgiveness."

Yes. But if the truth were known, you don't deserve it, either.

You are to forgive as God in Christ has forgiven you. And if you don't do that, you are grieving the Holy Spirit. The Lord says, "Vengeance is Mine, I will repay" (Romans 12:19). Commit it to God.

It is said that St. Augustine had a sign that hung on his wall that said, "He who speaks evil of an absent man or woman is not welcome at this table." Wow. That would end a lot of conversations, wouldn't it?

Maybe you ought to apply the acronym THINK the next time you wonder whether or not you should say a certain thing. It goes like this:

"T" is for truthful. Is what I'm about to say actually true? Do I know it for a fact, or is it just something I've heard second- or third hand? We are so quick to spread gossip. And we all know that just because someone *says* something doesn't make it true. Don't repeat anything if you don't have the facts.

"H" is for helpful. Is what you're about to say going to help anyone? Or will it just tear someone down?

"I" is for inspiring. Is it inspiring?

"N" is for necessary. Does it really have to be said?

"K" is for kind. Is what you're saying characterized by kindness?

You say, "Greg, if I apply that acronym, I may never say anything again!" Amen. So be it. Maybe you can start using your mouth for what it was created for: to glorify God, honor Him, build up your brothers and sisters, and preach the Good News to those who don't know Jesus.

3. Quenching the Holy Spirit

Another sin believers can commit is quenching the Spirit. First Thessalonians 5:19 says, "Do not quench the Spirit." Now the idea of quenching is related to putting a fire out. Let's say that you went out to the woods or down to the beach, and you built a fire in one of those designated fire rings. When you leave, you completely extinguish that fire, pouring water or sand on it. You're careful to make sure that the fire is out. You've quenched it!

In the same way, we can quench the Spirit of God in our lives. For instance, the Holy Spirit may be prompting you to do a certain thing. Maybe He's saying, "I want you to share the gospel with that individual."

Has that ever happened to you? You find yourself in the company of a stranger, someone you don't know from Adam's house cat, and you hear the Spirit whisper in your heart, "I want you to talk to that person about Jesus."

What? you say. *I can't do that! I don't even know that person. He'll think I'm crazy if I walk up to him and just started chatting. I won't do it.*

But if the Holy Spirit asks you to do something, and you continually refuse to listen to His voice or obey Him, it has the effect of quenching Him in your life. Maybe the Spirit has been saying, "You need to repent over this thing in your life and stop rationalizing it." But you reply, "No. I'm not willing to give it up. I'm going to keep doing it."

That is quenching the Holy Spirit. It's a refusal to respond to His leading, urging, and nudging in the deepest part of your life. As a result, you lose the ability to hear Him . . . and that causes Him grief.

Sins nonbelievers can commit against the Spirit

When we talk about quenching and grieving the Spirit, we're talking about sins that believers can commit. But there are also sins that nonbelievers can commit. In fact, there are three in particular that happen to go together.

4. Resisting the Spirit

When Stephen stood before the unbelieving Sanhedrin in Acts 7:51 (NLT), he declared, "You stubborn people! You are heathen at heart and deaf to the truth. Must you forever resist the Holy Spirit? But your ancestors did, and so do you!"

These words remind us that the Spirit wants to speak to an

unbeliever and lead him or her to God.

The Holy Spirit is patient and persistent. But listen: It is possible to resist all of His pleadings. God says in Genesis, "My Spirit shall not strive with man forever" (6:3). Apparently the spiritual leaders of Israel whom Stephen addressed with such passion that day had rejected the truth—again and again. In other words, the implication here is that they believed what He was saying was true, but simply refused to accept it. For that reason, they were resisting the Spirit of God.

This is a different issue from simply not believing. It's as though a person is saying, "Yes, I acknowledge that what you're saying is true, but I'm simply not going to admit it or respond to it." That is resisting the Spirit, and it's a dangerous thing to do.

5. Insulting the Holy Spirit
In Hebrews 10:29 we read,

> Think how much worse the punishment will be for those who have trampled on the Son of God, and have treated the blood of the covenant, which made us holy, as if it were common and unholy, and have insulted and disdained the Holy Spirit who brings God's mercy to us. (NLT)

Now what does this mean? Let's say someone took the time to explain to me that Jesus gave His life and shed His blood for me on the cross, dying in my place to save me and gift me with eternal life. In response to that, let's imagine that I just totally blew it off and said, "Who cares? You know I don't believe in that. I don't believe the blood of Jesus means anything. I don't believe the death of Jesus means anything."

If I were to do such a thing, I would be insulting the Holy Spirit. And anyone who does this had better be careful, because they will find themselves on very thin ice.

What is the worst sin a person can commit? Adultery? Murder? Rape? There are many terrible things we might think of, but the most devastating sin a person can commit, with the most far-reaching conse-quences, is not believing in Jesus. Those other sins I mentioned—and any others beyond those—can be forgiven if a person will repent of that sin and put his or her faith in Christ. But if you reject Jesus Christ as Savior and Lord, you are insulting the Holy Spirit, and you are resisting Him. And this can lead to the sixth sin on our list.

6. Blaspheming the Holy Spirit

Jesus said,

> Every sin or blasphemy can be forgiven—except blasphemy against the Holy Spirit, which will never be forgiven. Anyone who speaks against the Son of Man can be forgiven, but anyone who speaks against the Holy Spirit will never be forgiven, either in this world or in the world to come. (Matthew 12:31-32, NLT)

Sobering words!

But what does it mean to blaspheme the Holy Spirit? As a pastor, I am probably asked this question more than any other. Why do we ask this? Because deep down, we wonder if we've ever done it. Maybe in our nonbelieving days, in a drunken stupor, we started cursing everything in sight, and we may have just cursed the Holy Spirit. Does that mean that we have committed the unforgivable sin?

No.

To blaspheme the Holy Spirit doesn't mean that you said a bad thing about Him. *To blaspheme the Holy Spirit is to reject His mission.* What is the mission of the Spirit? It is to show us our sin—to open our eyes to the fact that we don't have enough righteousness to get to heaven. And it is to bring us to Jesus. To blaspheme the Spirit means to reject the work the Spirit has come to do, which is to bring us to Christ. And the Bible asks the question, "How can we escape if we neglect so great a salvation?"

Quite frankly, almost everyone I can imagine reading this book shouldn't be worrying about this. I think the person in the greatest danger of committing this sin is the one who could care less about what I've written here and doesn't think about these things at all. These are the people who simply live their lives the way they want to live, allowing their hearts to become harder and harder as the days, weeks, and years slip by.

Is there a point of no return?

Yes, I believe there is.

You can go so far that it's too far. Where or when that might be, I can't say. And I would never, never say that a man or woman has reached that point. As a matter of fact, I've seen some pretty crazy people get saved. You write them off in the back of your mind and say to yourself, *There's no way that person could respond to the gospel.*

And then, miraculously, they do.

Look at the thief on the cross beside Jesus. If you had been standing there at the base of those crosses that day, you might have easily written him off. In fact, just a few minutes before his heart turned, he had been heaping abuse on the dying Jesus. (See Mark 15:32; Luke 23:39-43.)

As I have said before (half jokingly), there will be three big surprises when we get to heaven. Surprise number one: Some of the people we thought would be there won't be there. Surprise number two: Some of the people we never thought would be there will be there. And surprise number three: *We* will be there.

As we walk through this brief life on our way to heaven, we need to focus on making sure that we are yielding to the Spirit, obeying the Spirit, and being filled with the Spirit. That is our objective as followers of Jesus.

5

The Holy Spirit and You, Part 2

The Holy Spirit is probably the most misunderstood and misrepresented member of the Trinity. Why? Because it seems whenever something weird or far-out is done in Christian circles, it gets blamed on the Holy Spirit.

If you don't believe me, watch Christian television sometimes and check out some of the people who talk about "coming under the power of the Holy Spirit."

I remember watching a program once where people were shrieking, screaming, running around in circles, rolling on the ground, and making animal noises. And it was all attributed to the Holy Spirit.

Frankly, none of that interests me. Not in the least.

I'm happy to take a pass on those things. Yes, I very much want God's Spirit active in my life, and I want to be filled with Him and walk with Him daily—even moment by moment. But I don't want to have anything to do with these bizarre, unbiblical misrepresentations of the Holy Spirit.

The Bible certainly instructs us to be filled with the Spirit. Ephesians 5:18-19 gives us practical specifics: "Be filled with the Spirit, speaking to one another in psalms and hymns and spiritual songs, singing and making melody in your heart to the Lord."

Is the filling of God's Spirit an emotional experience?

It can be. But then again, you can be filled with the Holy Spirit and feel absolutely nothing. What does it really mean to be filled with the Spirit?

The Greek word translated "filled" in Ephesians 5 speaks of wind filling a sail. So there you are in your little sailboat out on a lake, and a gust of wind comes, filling your sails and moving you forward toward the desired destination.

I love that imagery. There is power and beauty and practicality in the picture of a wind-filled sail thrusting a boat forward through the waves. In the same way, God's Spirit wants to empower us, move us, guide us, and direct us.

But that Greek term translated "filled" could also mean "to permeate." It's the idea of salt permeating meat. Back in the days the New Testament was written, the way they preserved meat was by rubbing salt deep into its fibers. This tells us that the Holy Spirit wants to permeate our lives—touching everything we think, do, and say, entering every fiber of our being.

Being filled with God's Spirit does *not* mean losing control of your faculties. No matter what people tell you, this does not have to happen. The book of 1 Corinthians clearly tells us that "the spirits of prophets are subject to the control of prophets. For God is not a God of disorder but of peace" (14:32-33, NIV).

Another translation says it like this: "Remember that a person who has a message from God has the power to stop himself or wait his turn. God is not one who likes things to be disorderly and upset. He likes harmony" (TLB).

In other words, when God's Holy Spirit is working through you, you still have control of what you say. You have control of your volume. You are not an automaton, and you are not "taken over" by some freaky force. The Holy Spirit wants to fill you, permeate you, and influence you. This is a joyous, incredibly helpful, practical power that God wants to work through our lives.

The Holy Spirit has a specific work He wants to do in the world. You remember that Jesus said, "When He has come, He will convict the world of sin, and of righteousness, and of judgment" (John 16:8). In other words, the work of the Spirit in the lives of non-believers is to convince them of the fact that they are sinners. And then it is to bring them into the open arms of Jesus and show that their own righteousness is not enough to get them to heaven. They need the very righteousness of Christ Himself deposited into their account.

For the next few pages let's focus on the work of the Spirit in the life of the believer, pointing out some practical things the Spirit has done in you and wants to do for you.

The Work of the Holy Spirit in Our Lives

1. The Holy Spirit converts us

> It is the Spirit who gives life; the flesh profits nothing. The words that I speak to you are spirit, and they are life. (John 6:63)

> Most assuredly, I say to you, unless one is born of water and the Spirit, he cannot enter the kingdom of God. (John 3:5)

When you became a Christian you did not do so by an act of your own will. In other words, yes, you believed—but it is the Holy Spirit who showed you and convinced you of your need for Jesus.

It is the Holy Spirit who ultimately brings about the work of conversion; it is not a work I do for myself. I couldn't have saved myself any more than a drowning person with cramps out in the middle of the sea could save themselves. They have to call out for help or they will go under, and we have to do the same, calling out to the Lord.

Once we do put our faith in Jesus Christ, it is the Holy Spirit who personally gives us the assurance that Christ has come into our lives. Romans 8:16 (NLT) says, "For his Spirit joins with our spirit to affirm that we are God's children."

This deep-down inner witness of the Spirit is wonderful beyond words. He speaks from the center of your being, and you just "know that you know." Difficult as it may be to explain sometimes, it's as real as the breath you're drawing into your lungs at this very moment.

It is the Holy Spirit who gives us that matchless inner assurance that we are sons and daughters of God.

2. The Holy Spirit indwells us

When you become a Christian, the Spirit comes to live in you. First Corinthians 3:16 (NLT) says, "Don't you realize that all of you together are the temple of God and that the Spirit of God lives in you?" In John 14:17 (NIV), Jesus said of the Holy Spirit that "you know him, for he lives with you and will be in you."

3. The Holy Spirit seals us

In Him you also trusted, after you heard the word of truth, the gospel of your salvation; in whom also, having believed, you were sealed with the Holy Spirit of promise, who is the guarantee of our inheritance until the redemption of the purchased possession, to the praise of His glory. (Ephesians 1:13-14)

What does this mean, to be sealed by the Spirit?

Back in the first century, when goods were shipped from one place to another, they would be stamped with a waxed seal and imprinted with a signet ring bearing a unique mark of ownership. It was the same with important documents—from a king, for instance. The dispatch or document would be sealed with wax and imprinted with the royal seal. As a result, no one would dare tamper with or break that seal until it was delivered to the person to whom it had been addressed.

When the Bible, then, says, "You were sealed with the Spirit," it means that God has put His imprint on your life.

Let's try to make that illustration a little more contemporary by saying that God has put His ID tag on you—just as you would put a tag on your personal luggage.

Let's say you're a thief in an airport, you want to steal something, and you happen to see a very expensive briefcase on the luggage conveyer belt. Looking around, you can't see anyone who seems to be claiming it. What a prize that briefcase would be! It has gold-plated hinges on it, and the handle is studded in diamonds. You say to yourself, *Wow, that case alone is valuable. Imagine what's in it!*

As you walk over to it, intending to quickly steal it and walk away, you notice an ID tag attached to it, and it has the word "Tyson" on it.

You think, *Tyson? As in Tyson chicken?*

And then you see a very large, muscular man walking toward you, and you realize, it's *Mike* Tyson, the professional fighter, who owns that briefcase. As a result, you decide to walk away and leave the briefcase alone. Why? Because you enjoy life. And you fear the owner.

In the same way, the devil—the one who has come "to steal, and to kill, and to destroy"—approaches you. In his hatred and malice, he says, "I will wreak havoc in this life. I will ruin this person. I will—oh, wait. Is that an ID tag? What does it say? Property of the Lord Jesus Christ? Uh-oh." And he backs off.

Satan does not have free reign to attack and destroy a son or daughter of God, because we have been sealed with the Holy Spirit of promise.

But as they say in those commercials on cable TV, "Wait . . . there's more!"

This really gets interesting now. That passage in Ephesians 3 says: "You were sealed with the Holy Spirit of promise, who is the guarantee of our inheritance until the redemption of the purchased possession."

Another translation speaks of the Spirit as the One "who is a deposit guaranteeing our inheritance." Another way to put that would be "a down payment."

Let's say you want to purchase a car. You locate a particular make and model you want to buy, and say to the car dealer, "I want to come back tomorrow and purchase that car."

The car dealer (who of course would never deceive or mislead you) tells you that someone else is already interested in that car, and they may swoop down and buy it before you have the chance. He suggests that you put down a large, nonrefundable deposit until you can come the next day with the full purchase price.

In the same way, Jesus says to us, "One day you will go to heaven when you die."

"Well, that's great," you reply. "I believe You, but it's a difficult concept to grasp and hold on to sometimes."

So God replies, "Okay. I want you to know I am serious about this, so I'm going to prove it to you. I'm going to give you the Holy Spirit, who will be a down payment guaranteeing your future inheritance."

It's called proof. We all want proof that God is at work in our lives. It's all very nice that someone else says they have proof, but I want personal proof in my life to know that God is working in me.

Some people look for proof or a sign of God's presence in the strangest of places, claiming to see the image of Jesus on a garage door or even on a toasted cheese sandwich or a tortilla.

My wife and I saw an article in the paper about a mother and daughter here in Southern California who claim to have seen the face of Jesus on their plum-colored armchair in the living room. Apparently, this has become a big deal to a number of people. Some claim they have even seen and photographed the sandaled footprints of Jesus leading up to the chair. One of the people handing out photographs of the footprints was quoted, saying, "Everyone has a purpose in life, and we believe this has been the purpose of our lives."

Did this really happen? Did Jesus tiptoe into that home wearing sandals and imprint His face on a chair?

Sometimes we might even feel a little intimidated when people talk about God's saying this and that to them and doing extraordinary things in their lives. And maybe you find yourself thinking, *Why doesn't God work in my life like that? Why doesn't He show me some proof that He is there and that He is working in me?*

In fact, there is more proof than you realize.

You have the Holy Spirit, God Himself, actually in residence in your life. Has your life changed for the better since you put your trust in Jesus? Do you sense His presence in you, giving you strength you never had before? These are proofs that God's Holy Spirit is at work in your life. As time goes by and you daily seek to be filled and empowered by the Spirit, He will make known to you (in countless ways) that He is working in you and through you. You don't have to look for the image of Christ in clouds, tortillas, or in sandaled footprints following you around. You have God's Word and the inner witness of His Spirit to daily convince You that He is there and that He is at work in your life.

4. The Holy Spirit helps us bring forth spiritual fruit

> But the fruit of the Spirit is love, joy, peace, longsuffering, kindness, goodness, faithfulness, gentleness, self-control. (Galatians 5:22-23)

How do I know that I am a Christian? It probably boils down to this: You look for results in my life. You can't see my heart, and you can't really see my faith. However, you can look for the outcomes or results of my faith. Jesus said, "Therefore by their fruits you will know them" (Matthew 7:20).

So the way you can determine whether or not I am a follower of Jesus won't be because I simply say so. You will know I belong to Jesus because of the evidence you see in my life. And that evidence is sometimes called spiritual fruit.

Fruit, of course, doesn't grow overnight; it takes time. You don't see apple blossoms on a branch one day and ripe apples the next. There's a waiting period involved. In the same way, we can become discouraged about our growth in Christ, because we don't seem to see the kind of change we had hoped to see. You can become worried and introspective and ask yourself every night, "Have I become more like Jesus in the last twenty-four hours?"

It would be like trying to watch your kids grow physically. You might say to yourself, "Well, they don't seem to be growing to me. I've watched for a week or two, and I don't see any change." Why? Because growth is often slow and subtle. But then maybe some friend or relative you haven't seen for months comes to visit your family, and they will exclaim, "Oh my goodness, your children have sure grown!"

But you didn't see it.

In the same way, we don't necessarily see the changes the Spirit of God may be working in our own lives. That's why it's so incredibly encouraging when someone comes along and says to us, "You have really changed. I see you are becoming more like Jesus. You're a lot more thoughtful and kind than you used to be."

Don't you love to hear comments like that? (Maybe that should prompt us to say those kinds of things when we notice God's Spirit working in someone else's life, too.)

This is a big deal to Jesus. Over in John 15:16, He said, "You did not choose Me, but I chose you and appointed you that you should go and bear fruit, and that your fruit should remain."

He was saying, "I want there to be fruit in your life."

But what is this fruit? We have the answer in Galatians 5:22. The passage begins, "But the fruit of the Spirit is love. . . ." Sometimes people talk about the *fruits* (plural) of the Spirit. But if you want to get a little technical here, you should say the *fruit* (singular) of the Spirit.

What is the fruit of the Spirit?

The fruit of the Spirit is love.

Love for what? Love for whom? Love for God and love for others. Jesus said, "By this all will know that you are My disciples, if you have love for one another." But He also said, "If you love Me, keep My commandments" (John 13:35; 14:15).

So if you really are a Christian, you will love God—and you'll show this by doing what He says. And if you really are a Christian, you will also love others. Even unlovable people. But we'll need His strength for that, won't we? We can't do it on our own.

If, then, the *fruit* of the Spirit is love, then that love is defined by characteristics such as joy, peace, patience, kindness, and goodness. Another translation of Galatians 5:22 puts it like this:

> But what happens when we live God's way? He brings gifts into our lives, much the same way that fruit appears in an orchard—things like affection for others, exuberance about life, serenity. We develop a willingness to stick with things, a sense of compassion in the heart, and a conviction that a basic holiness permeates things

and people. We find ourselves involved in loyal commitments, not needing to force our way in life, able to marshal and direct our energies wisely. (MSG)

In certain Christian circles, we will hear people say (with exuberance), "I have Holy Spirit power!"

When you ask them what they mean, they will say, "The Holy Spirit manifests Himself through me in signs and wonders."

Maybe He does, and maybe He doesn't; it isn't for me to say. But what really impresses me more than flashy signs and wonders is spiritual fruit.

• *A man or woman who will honor their marriage vows for life.*

• *A young couple committed to maintaining sexual purity until their wedding day.*

• *A person who is willing to forgive someone who has deeply wronged them.*

• *A dad or mom who remains patient, kind, and firm while raising a houseful of kids.*

Those are the lives that really impress me.

Am I denigrating the more spectacular spiritual gifts or "signs and wonders"? Not at all. But I think what we really need to see in these days is some of that beautiful spiritual fruit described in Galatians 5. These are the qualities that will make our lives stand out from the crowd and cause people to say, "That person right there is a follower of Jesus Christ."

How do you bring forth this fruit? Jesus said in John 15:7-8, "If you abide in Me, and My words abide in you, you will ask what you desire, and it shall be done for you. By this My Father is glorified, that you bear much fruit; so you will be My disciples."

How do you bear fruit?

Jesus says, "Abide in Me."

What does it mean to abide? It's just like planting a tree that sinks its roots deeply into the soil. The way to bring forth fruit is to walk in daily conversation and communion with Jesus. To stay close to Him. To consciously depend on Him in a thousand situations throughout your day. Fruit will come as a result of this relationship with the Lord who loves you.

5. The Holy Spirit helps us to pray

There are times when you and I don't know what or how to pray.
You may be discouraged or grieving. You might find yourself
gripped with fear, deeply depressed, or overwhelmed by some worry.

It is then—right in that very moment—when the Holy Spirit
will help you. Jesus referred to the Holy Spirit as a Comforter. He
said in John 14:16-17, "I will pray the Father, and He will give you
another Helper, that He may abide with you forever—the Spirit of
truth."

Comforter?

We don't even know what this word means anymore. Isn't that a blanket you have on the foot of your bed that you pull up when you get cold?

As we noted earlier, the word *Comforter* that Jesus used comes from
the Greek word *parakletos*, which means "called alongside to help."
It could also be translated a helper, an aide, or an assistant. Some
versions translate the word *parakletos* to the word *advocate*, which is
applied to Jesus in 1 John 2:1, "If anyone sins, we have an Advocate
[a *parakletos*] with the Father. Jesus Christ the righteous."

The Holy Spirit has come to help you, to aid you, to assist you in
your prayer, and to be an advocate who intercedes and pleads your
cause before the Father. Why? Because we don't always know how to
put words to our prayers.

Here's the good news. *Sometimes just a sigh or a groan will do.*

Maybe you're praying with some people and someone will say,
"Okay, we're all going to pray. We'll start with Joe, there, and just
pray around the circle." The problem is, if there are a lot of people
in the group, everything gets prayed for before they get to you. All the
good stuff is taken. So by the time it's your turn, you're not sure what
to pray, and all you can do is mumble a few words. You think to yourself, "Oh man, everyone will think I don't even know how to pray!"

Here is what people sometimes miss. Prayer isn't so much about the
petitions or specific words you bring before God, though it can include
that. Prayer is what's in your heart, your spirit. Sometimes the most
profound prayer you could ever make is a sigh or a groan, because
you're overwhelmed and don't know what to say. Trust me, I've done

this quite a bit over the last few years. When I think about the reality of my son Christopher being gone, it's really difficult for me.

I want to pray during these times of grieving, but I don't always know what to pray. So sometimes I'll just say, "Oh, Lord." And maybe I will groan, sigh, or cry. But do you know what? I think that's good enough, because I'm crying out to God for help.

Here is what we're told in Romans 8:26-27 (NLT), one of the most encouraging passages in the New Testament that I can think of.

> And the Holy Spirit helps us in our weakness. For example, we don't know what God wants us to pray for. But the Holy Spirit prays for us with groanings that cannot be expressed in words. And the Father who knows all hearts knows what the Spirit is saying, for the Spirit pleads for us believers in harmony with God's own will.

6. The Holy Spirit helps us in our study of and memorization of Scripture

In John 14:26 Jesus says, "But the Helper [*parakletos* again], the Holy Spirit, whom the Father will send in My name, He will teach you all things, and bring to your remembrance all things that I said to you."

Have you ever had the experience of being down or discouraged or unsure what to do when suddenly a verse of Scripture seems to jump into your mind? And here is the interesting thing: Sometimes you don't really remember memorizing that particular Bible verse. It might have been a passage you heard quoted in a sermon a month ago—or ten years ago—and there it is, vividly displayed on the screen of your mind.

Where did that come from?

It came from the Holy Spirit. It was He who brought that word to your remembrance, just when you needed it.

That's the reason I always pray before I open God's Word to study, that the Holy Spirit will illuminate, or shine a light on, the passage I'm looking at. Here's what it says in 1 Corinthians:

No eye has seen, no ear has heard, and no mind has imagined what God has prepared for those who love him.

But it was to us that God revealed these things by his Spirit. For his Spirit searches out everything and shows us God's deep secrets. (2:9-10, NLT)

So as I open the Bible, I breathe a prayer like this: "Lord, speak to me from Your Word. Reveal these things to me. Show me what You want me to see and know. Show me how to apply what You want me to apply to my life."

Here's another great thing about the Holy Spirit and our memory. Sometimes someone will ask you a question about spiritual things, and you don't have an answer. Your mind just goes blank for a second, and you don't know what to say next. And then . . . all of a sudden . . . four little thoughts jump into your mind, all in order, and you begin sharing with that person. Sometimes what you're saying is so good and makes so much sense that you want to take notes on yourself!

In the back of your mind you're thinking, *This is good stuff. Where did this come from?* And you know very well it didn't come from your own mind; it came from the Holy Spirit. He is bringing things to your remembrance as you seek to speak a word for Jesus.

Let me quickly add here that this does *not* excuse you from the discipline of Bible study. You don't put your Bible under your pillow and pray that all that knowledge and insight will seep into your brain while you're asleep. No, Bible study takes diligence and dedication, and there aren't any shortcuts to simple time spent in the Word. You still have to discipline yourself to read it, to study it, and to memorize it. But having done those things, the Bible promises that the Holy Spirit will bring important truths into your memory as you need them.

7. The Holy Spirit wants to come upon you

But you shall receive power when the Holy Spirit has come upon you; and you shall be witnesses to Me in Jerusalem, and in all Judea and Samaria, and to the end of the earth. (Acts 1:8)

You will receive power . . . to be a witness for Jesus Christ.

You will receive power . . . to boldly share your faith.

You will receive power . . . to speak up and be counted.

You will receive power . . . to turn your world upside down.

This power was poured out on the church at the Day of Pentecost. But don't think of this as merely a historical event. The same power that came upon and filled those first century believers is available to us today.

On that same day of Pentecost, Peter spoke of this Holy Spirit power and said these highly significant words:

> *"Repent and be baptized, every one of you, in the name of Jesus Christ for the forgiveness of your sins. And you will receive the gift of the Holy Spirit.* The promise is for you and your children and for all who are far off—for all whom the Lord our God will call." (Acts 2:38-39, NIV, emphasis mine)

In other words, the promise of the indwelling Holy Spirit is for us just as much as it was for them.

But here's a question. Didn't those believers gathered on the Day of Pentecost *already* have the Holy Spirit living in them?

Yes, they did. Back in the Upper Room, while Jesus was still on the earth, we read that "He breathed on them, and said to them, 'Receive the Holy Spirit' " (John 20:22).

At that time the Spirit came into them just as the Holy Spirit has come into us. They were indwelt by the Spirit, as every believer is. As we have already seen, the Holy Spirit indwells us and takes up residence in our lives when we put our faith in Jesus. The Spirit seals us to mark us as God's own and bears witness with our spirit that we are children of God.

But this is something different.

This is talking about the Spirit coming *upon* you.

Jesus said, "You shall receive power," which is translated from the Greek word *dunamis*.

We've all heard of the Nobel Peace Prize named for Alfred Nobel. The fact is, however, that in his day Nobel was known for something quite different. He had discovered a power stronger than anything the world had known up to that time, an explosive element he had created in the laboratory. Following his discovery, he went to see a friend of his who was a Greek scholar and asked him what the Greek word was for "explosive power."

The man said, "It is *dunamis*."

From that term, Nobel named his new invention, calling it "dynamite." And Jesus said that *dunamis*—explosive power—would be given to the disciples when the Holy Spirit came upon them.

Just think how that power transformed these first believers. Look at Simon Peter. Prior to Pentecost, he couldn't even stand up for his faith before strangers who had asked him point-blank if he was a follower of Jesus. Yet after the power of the Spirit was poured out on Pentecost, that same Peter stood up and boldly preached the gospel, resulting in 3,000 people being saved in one day.

Saul of Tarsus is another example. After he was converted on the Damascus Road and became a believer, the Lord led a man named Ananias to go to Saul and pray for him. At that moment Saul, a former enemy and persecutor of Christians, became Paul, a bold and fearless preacher and apostle who proclaimed Jesus Christ throughout the known world.

My point is simply this: the power of the Holy Spirit is for a purpose. It isn't power to be crazy or do weird things; it is power to be a witness. It's power to speak to someone you don't even know and tell them about Jesus Christ. It's power to confront someone about their sin. It's power to initiate conversations and tell people about what Jesus has done for you.

Do you have this power in your life right now? Has your prayer life become dry and one-dimensional? Do you feel like there is something lacking in your spiritual walk? Are you stricken with fear at the very idea of sharing your faith? Then you, my friend, are a candidate for the empowering of the Holy Spirit.

You may reply, "But I have already received this power."

Well and good. But check this out: *God gives refills*. When your car runs out of gas, what are you supposed to do? You're supposed to fill it up again!

This comes as a revelation to my wife. It seems like every time I get in her car, the low fuel light on the dash comes on. The other day it was on the bottom of the bottom. I said, "Cathe, we have to go straight to the gas station."

Frankly, that's how many believers operate in their lives. They're driving around on a nearly empty tank, running on fumes, and that warning light keeps blinking, *"Low Fuel! Low Fuel!"*

It's time to refuel and refill. And God will do that for us.

When I go into a restaurant and order a big iced tea, they usually come around and keep filling and refilling my glass. Refills are generally free.

God's refills are free too. In the book of Acts we read about the believers who were commanded by the authorities to "cease and desist" preaching the gospel and proclaiming the name of Jesus. So what did they do? They prayed for more boldness to preach the gospel.

Here's an account of what happened next:

> While they were praying, the place where they were meeting trembled and shook. They were all filled with the Holy Spirit and continued to speak God's Word with fearless confidence. (Acts 4:31, MSG)

I like that! God gave them a mighty refill of the Holy Spirit.

Final Notes

In Ephesians 5:18, when the text says, "be filled with the Spirit," the Greek term translated *be filled* is in the imperative mode. In other words, it is a command. It's not a suggestion. God is saying, "I am commanding you. You need to be refilled every day. You need to get your life recharged by My Holy Spirit."

But here's something else about that command, "Be filled." In the Greek, the word denotes a *continuous action*. In other words, it is saying, "Be constantly filled with the Spirit. Keep on being filled with the Holy Spirit. Do it over and over again."

We can't rely on a past filling or live merely in the expectation of future filling. Let's get a present filling for present challenges and opportunities.

You say, "All right. What do I need to do?"

The answer is so simple, it will amaze you.

In Luke 11:13, Jesus said, "If you then, being evil, know how to give good gifts to your children, how much more will your heavenly Father give the Holy Spirit to those who ask Him!"

Just ask Him.

You don't have to plead. You don't have to beg. Just ask.

My granddaughter and I like to go to toy stores together. And if she sees something on a shelf and says, "Papa, will you get this for me?" you can pretty much count on the fact that it's going to happen. What can I say? I love her and I'm a soft touch. She just has to ask. Sometimes I will get it for her without her asking. It is my joy.

In the same way, the Father will give the Holy Spirit to those who ask Him.

So ask. Be filled and refilled. Be fueled and refueled. Walk in the joy of His presence and power.

Part 2

Heaven and Hell

Let's Talk About Heaven

E ver since I was a little boy, I have always been a fan of Disney.

When I was growing up, of course, Walt Disney himself was still the creative genius behind the whole Disney empire. Like so many in my generation, I was raised watching *The Mickey Mouse Club* on our black-and-white TV. (With rabbit ears. Remember those? That was before cable or satellite.)

And then, around the time when color television was introduced, there was *The Wonderful World of Disney* on Sunday nights (right before *Bonanza*). Even prior to that time, I remember when Walt Disney came out before the cameras, unrolled some architectural plans on his desk, and said, "I want to tell you about something we are building now. We call it Disneyland."

Disneyland. As a little kid watching this, it was more like the Promised Land. I could hardly wait to get to this place. To me, it seemed like the ultimate escape from the crazy, alcoholic home I was raised in and all the different men living with my mother and coming and going through my life.

Most of all, it was a promise of something better.

Living in Southern California as we did, I made my mom take me to Disneyland for my birthday. To this day, I can remember making a vow as we approached the park, and I looked at the Matterhorn in the distance. I said to myself: "Someday, when I become an adult, I'm going to go to Disneyland every single day."

I haven't quite lived up to that vow, though I'm sure I've had more than my share of days at the Magic Kingdom. But why did Disneyland draw me so strongly when I was a child? Because, as I said, it held so much promise.

Disney was a dreamer. He called the people who worked with him "imagineers," as the whole Disney team spent time imagining what could be. He was raised in the Midwest and didn't have much money. But he always dreamed of a better world—or possibly even creating a better world. You might even say he was trying to create a heaven on earth.

In his Disney biography, author Pat Williams wrote,

> I know that Walt Disney felt a longing for heaven. He had that longing when he was a boy in Kansas City peering through the fence at Electric Park, wanting what he couldn't have because he didn't have a dime in his pocket. I believe it was that longing for heaven that drove Walt to build a perfect place where children could ride merry-go-rounds and always catch the brass ring. A place where yesterday and tomorrow were always within walking distance. A place where anyone can be perfectly happy, if only for a day. In Walt's mind, heaven is a beautiful park all shining and clean filled with wonderful things to see and do, with a castle rising over it all and a train that goes around it.[23]

Walt Disney isn't really so much different from you and me. We, too, have been pre-wired to want something more in life. The Bible says that we have been born with eternity in our hearts (see Ecclesiastes 3:11). That is something that is unique to mankind, to men and women made in the image of God.

It's not true of the animal kingdom. I don't think animals sit around and wonder about the meaning of life. Dogs don't. I can't imagine one of my dogs lying in the backyard thinking, *What is the meaning of my life? Why am I here? I've tried everything this world has to offer. Road kill. Chasing cats. Still, there is an emptiness . . .*

No, dogs don't think things like that.

But people do.

All kinds of people, religious and nonreligious, Christians and atheists, have pondered the meaning of our brief lives "under the sun," as Solomon put it. We wonder, *Why am I here? What will it take to fill the emptiness? Maybe if I just reached this goal, climbed that mountain, formed this relationship, or had this degree, life would take on new meaning.*

In a sense, unless we've simply given up on life altogether, we're always moving forward; we're always on a quest. Why?

Because I think, deep down, we know that we were meant for another, better world. When we become Christians, we realize that our citizenship is in heaven and our life on earth just comes and goes, whether you live to be nine or ninety.

David said of life on earth, "We are here for only a moment, visitors and strangers in the land as our ancestors were before us. Our days on earth are like a passing shadow, gone so soon without a trace" (1 Chronicles 29:15, NLT).

The truth is, as Christians we are already citizens of heaven. We long for something more. Paul wrote,

> But we are citizens of heaven, where the Lord Jesus Christ lives. And we are eagerly waiting for him to return as our Savior. He will take our weak mortal bodies and change them into glorious bodies like his own, using the same power with which he will bring everything under his control. (Philippians 3:20-21, NLT)

It was Augustine who said of God, "You formed us for Yourself, and our hearts are restless until they find their rest in You." Because of this, we want to know more about what is in our future and more about our heavenly home as we begin to see this world for what it is.

Just for a moment, let me distinguish what I mean when I say "the world," as opposed to speaking of "earth." We live on the earth. God Himself created it. He both filled it and surrounded it with His handiwork. You can see His fingerprints everywhere. His signature is written across our planet and all of the marvelous things He has made.

The Bible says, "The earth is the LORD'S, and everything in it." Paul reminds us that we are not "to trust in uncertain riches but in the living God, who gives us richly all things to enjoy" (Psalm 24:1, NLT; 1 Timothy 6:17).

I believe that Christians, more than anyone else, have the capacity to appreciate a beautiful sunset, a rainbow, or a night sky filled with radiant stars, because we know the One who created it all, and we have an intimate relationship with Him.

That's "the earth."

But sometimes we speak about "the world."

When Christians refer to the world, they're often speaking of a godless world system that is under control of Satan, "the god of this world," and "the prince of the power of the air."[25] And the closer we get to God, the better we begin to see the world for what it truly is and has become.

In his first letter to the church, the apostle John wrote:

> Do not love this world nor the things it offers you, for when you love the world, you do not have the love of the Father in you. For the world offers only a craving for physical pleasure, a craving for everything we see, and pride in our achievements and possessions. These are not from the Father, but are from this world. And this world is fading away, along with everything that people crave. But anyone who does what pleases God will live forever. (1 John 2:15-17, NLT)

Deep down inside, we long for a place we have never been to before. C. S. Lewis wrote,

> There have been times when I think we do not desire heaven, but more often I find myself wondering in our heart of hearts if we have ever desired anything else. It is the secret signature of each soul. The incommunicable and unappeasable want.[26]

I'm reminded of the story of a little boy who was flying his kite. Apparently he had plenty of string, because as the kite went up higher and higher, he eventually lost sight of it altogether. About that time a man came along and saw the boy holding on to the string.

"What are you doing?" he asked.

"I'm flying my kite," the boy replied.

The man looked up and said, "I can't see your kite anywhere. How do you know it's even there?"

"I *know* it's there," the boy replied, "because I can feel its tug."

In the same way, you and I know there is a heaven because we can feel its tug. It goes back to the earliest days of our childhood. And I will tell you this: When you know someone who is already there, heaven becomes much more important—and much more real.

But thoughts of heaven aren't only for people who have recently lost loved ones or who are getting on in years and adjusting to a new reality. Actually, all of us should be thinking aggressively about heaven. And here's why. In the book of Colossians, Paul writes, "Since, then, you have been raised with Christ, set your hearts on things above, where Christ is, seated at the right hand of God. Set your minds on things above, not on earthly things" (Colossians 3:1-2, NIV).

To "set your mind" speaks of a diligent, active, single-minded investigation—as if you had lost something and were searching for it.

That is how we should be looking forward to heaven.

Another way to translate this verse is simply, *"Think heaven."* The verb used in this verse is in the present tense, which could be translated, "Keep seeking heaven."

What is Paul saying? He's saying that we who belong to Jesus Christ should constantly keep seeking and thinking about heaven. Our feet must be on earth, but our minds must be in heaven.

Even so, many of us will go through a day—or even a week—without a single thought of heaven. E. M. Bounds made this statement:

Heaven ought to draw and engage us. Heaven ought to so fill our thoughts, our hands, our conversations, our character, and our features that all would see that we are foreigners and strangers to this world. The very atmosphere of this world should be chilling to us and noxious. Its suns eclipsed and its companionship dull and insipid. Heaven is our native land and it is home to us. Death to us is not the dying hour but the birth hour. [27]

What a great quote.

And it was Warren Wiersbe who said, "Heaven is more than a destination; it is a motivation." [28]

But *how* are you and I to be thinking about heaven, a place where we have never been? What's our point of reference? One of our problems is that we may have a caricatured version of heaven in our brain. Even though we may know better, we kind of imagine going to heaven, having wings sprout on our backs, and floating around through the clouds and the mist with a golden harp.

First of all, people don't become angels. Only angels are angels. And we will certainly not sit around on fluffy clouds, spending eternity in endless boredom. That's about as far from the mark as you could possibly get. We need to understand what the Bible actually has to say about our future, eternal home.

Periodically, people will write books about their alleged experiences of dying, going to heaven, and returning to earth. I was looking at one just recently, and I found it fascinating.

Are they true? Any of them?

Who knows? The only way I would say outright that some account of a heavenly visit wasn't true would be if it contradicted Scripture. But even if it didn't contradict Scripture, I would read it with interest and say, "Well, maybe that's true, and maybe it isn't. Maybe they're making it up, and maybe they're not."

What I need—what we all need—is a more authoritative source. And of course that takes me to the pages of Scripture, so I can know how to think when I think about heaven.

What Is Heaven?

Heaven is the dwelling place of God Himself.

In a broad sense, of course, God is everywhere. We use the word *omnipresent*, which basically means that wherever you go, God is already there.

The psalmist said it like this:

> I can never escape from your Spirit! I can never get away from your presence! If I go up to heaven, you are there; if I go down to the grave, you are there. If I ride the wings of the morning, if I dwell by the farthest oceans, even there your hand will guide me, and your strength will support me. (Psalm 139:7-10, NLT)

So yes, on one hand, God is everywhere. On the other hand, God has chosen to dwell in heaven in all of His glory. I believe that when we find ourselves longing for heaven, we're really longing for God Himself.

In the psalms, David cried out, "O God, you are my God; I earnestly search for you. My soul thirsts for you; my whole body longs for you in this parched and weary land where there is no water" (Psalm 63:1, NLT).

Sounds like he's homesick to me. Homesick for heaven, and homesick for the God of heaven.

In his wonderful book *Heaven*, the author (and my friend), Randy Alcorn, makes this statement:

> We may imagine we want a thousand different things, but God is the only One we really long for. His presence brings satisfaction; His absence brings thirst and longing. Our longing for heaven is a longing for God. . . . Being with God is the heart and soul of heaven. Every other heavenly pleasure will derive from and be secondary to His presence. God's greatest gift to us is and always will be Himself."[29]

We long to be with God. We long to see God. And yet if God were to show Himself to us today, we wouldn't be able to handle it. We would melt like a Popsicle on a hot sidewalk—or simply disintegrate on the spot. Why? Because God is perfect and flawless and holy . . . and I am imperfect and flawed and unholy.

One day Moses, the man of God, said to the Lord, "Show me your glory." God replied, in so many words, "No. I can't do that for you. But I will let you see Me as I pass by. You can sort of catch the afterglow."[30] Why? Because God knew that no one could see Him and live.

But there is a day coming when we *will* see God. Jesus said so. In

His Sermon on the Mount He said, "Blessed are the pure in heart, for they shall see God." (Matthew 5:8). In a burst of faith, right in the midst of his grief and suffering, Job cried out,

> But as for me, I know that my Redeemer lives, and he will stand upon the earth at last. And after my body has decayed, yet in my body I will see God! I will see him for myself. Yes, I will see him with my own eyes. I am overwhelmed at the thought! (Job 19:25-27, NLT)

When will you see God? When you get to heaven. As Asaph says, "Whom have I in heaven but you? And earth has nothing I desire besides you" (Psalm 73:25, NIV).

Seeing God will be like seeing everything we have ever seen for the first time. Why? Because not only will we see God, but He will be the lens through which we will see everything else: people, ourselves, and all the varied events and ups and downs of this earthly life. When I see God, I will see everything. I will get it, and I will say, "Now I understand."

What Do We Know About Heaven?

Heaven is an actual place.

It isn't an idea, a metaphor, an ideal, a philosophy, a happy thought, or a state of mind.

No, it's an *address*.

I can't relate to some spacey, weird, mystical dimension. I live in the real world. I am a real person. Tell me about real things. And heaven is a real place. More real than anything you and I have ever seen.

As He was preparing to depart this earth, Jesus told His grieving disciples, "I go to prepare a place for you" (John 14:2).

Most of us have heard the verse quoted from the King James Version that says, "In my Father's house are many mansions." The word *mansion* could be translated *dwelling place*. As to whether or not that is speaking of an actual residence that we will live in or of the new body God will give us when we arrive, I don't know for sure.

But one thing is certain. Heaven is a place. A real place.

The late science fiction writer Isaac Asimov once wrote,

I don't believe in an afterlife, so I don't want to spend my whole life fearing hell or fearing heaven even more. For whatever the tortures of hell, I think the boredom of heaven would be even worse.[31]

What an unbelievably foolish statement.

For all his intelligence and success, Asimov had obviously done no research at all on the subject of heaven.

It will most certainly *not* be a boring place. It will be wonderful, exciting, and joyful beyond words. Remember Paul's words?

Eye has not seen, nor ear heard, Nor have entered into the heart of man The things which God has prepared for those who love Him. (1 Corinthians 2:9)

Randy Alcorn writes,

Think of friends or family members who loved Jesus and are with Him now. Picture them with you, walking together in this place. All of you have powerful bodies, stronger than those of an Olympic athlete. You are laughing, playing, talking, and reminiscing. You reach up to a tree to pick an apple or orange. You take a bite. It is so sweet that it's startling. You have never tasted anything so good. Now you see someone coming towards you. It is Jesus, with a big smile on His face. You fall to your knees in worship. He pulls you up and embraces you.[32]

Now, I understand that Randy is taking a little liberty there in painting that picture. But at the same time, everything that he said is based on Scripture. Heaven is a real place for real people who belong to God through faith in Jesus Christ, and the Bible uses a number of words to help describe it us.

1. Heaven is a paradise

What do you think of when you think of paradise?

As I cited earlier, the thief on the cross, dying beside Jesus, finally came to his senses and said, "Lord, remember me when You come into your kingdom." And Jesus immediately responded, "Truly, truly I say unto you, today you will be with Me in Paradise."[33]

But what is this paradise Jesus was speaking of?

Translated literally, that word in the first century would have been used to describe the garden of a king. It's almost impossible for us to imagine how luxurious and splendid a king's garden would appear to an average person in this era. If you were a relatively impoverished person and were unexpectedly given the privilege of stepping inside the walled and well-tended garden of a king, you would be overwhelmed by that experience. The fragrance and beauty of it all would blow your circuit breakers.

So "paradise" was a reference point for people—the best human language could do.

Imagine if you had the privilege of dying and going to heaven, and then at some point came back to earth to try to describe the experience. That's precisely what happened to the apostle Paul.

Try to imagine a group of people sitting around discussing the beautiful places they had visited. One guy says, "I've been to Hawaii, and I've never seen anything like it. The water is so blue, the sky is even bluer, and the air is balmy and warm. And oh—those soft trade winds that come in the evening. So wonderful."

The next guy says, "Yes, but have you ever been to Tahiti? Oh, man, the water in Tahiti makes the water in Hawaii pale in comparison. It's an even deeper blue, and even warmer."

Then a third guy says, "Well, I have been to the Seychelles Islands, and it's better than either Hawaii or Tahiti—the sky, the ocean, the flowers, the birds. It's the most beautiful place I've ever seen."

And then the apostle Paul could say, "Well, guys, I have been to heaven. And it is *way* better than all of those places you're talking about."

Paul actually went to heaven and spoke about it—even if he didn't say as much about it as we might wish.

I know a man who, fourteen years ago, was seized by Christ and swept in ecstasy to the heights of heaven. I really don't know if this took place in the body or out of it; only God knows. I also know that this man was hijacked into paradise—again, whether in or out of the body, I don't know; God knows. There he heard the unspeakable spoken, but was forbidden to tell what he heard. (2 Corinthians 12:2-4, MSG)

I love that. Paul is saying, "I'm not really even sure what happened! I don't know if I was in the body or out of the body. All I can tell you is I can't even describe it."

But he does use one word. *Paradise.* (See 2 Corinthians 12:4.)

2. Heaven is a place

Some would say, "We really can't know what heaven will be like, because it will simply be beyond our wildest dreams, so we have to leave it at that."

That is true, to a degree. But it's not totally true.

The apostle John, for instance, described heaven in great detail. Just listen to some of His words. In Revelation 21 he says,

The city wall was broad and high, with twelve gates guarded by twelve angels. And the names of the twelve tribes of Israel were written on the gates. There were three gates on each side—east, north, south, and west. The wall of the city had twelve foundation stones, and on them were written the names of the twelve apostles of the Lamb. (Revelation 21:12-14, NLT)

It's obvious, isn't it? John is talking about a real place. Not just some weird, foggy land of nothingness. He goes on:

The angel who talked to me held in his hand a gold measuring stick to measure the city, its gates, and its wall. When he measured it, he found it was a square, as wide as it was long. In fact, its length and width and height were each 1,400 miles. Then he measured the walls and found them to be 216 feet thick (according to the human standard used by the angel).

The wall was made of jasper, and the city was pure gold, as clear as glass. The wall of the city was built on foundation stones inlaid with twelve precious stones: the first was jasper, the second sapphire, the third agate, the fourth emerald, the fifth onyx, the sixth carnelian, the seventh chrysolite, the eighth beryl, the ninth topaz, the tenth chrysoprase, the eleventh jacinth, the twelfth amethyst. The twelve gates were made of pearls—each gate from a single pearl! And the main street was pure gold, as clear as glass.

I saw no temple in the city, for the Lord God Almighty and the Lamb are its temple. And the city has no need of sun or moon, for the glory of God illuminates the city, and the Lamb is its light. The nations will walk in its light, and the kings of the world will enter the city in all their glory. Its gates will never be closed at the end of day because there is no night there. And all the nations will bring their glory and honor into the city. Nothing evil will be allowed to enter, nor anyone who practices shameful idolatry and dishonesty—but only those whose names are written in the Lamb's Book of Life. (Revelation 21:15-27, NLT)

A real place. You'd better believe it.
In Revelation 22, John writes,

Then the angel showed me a river with the water of life, clear as crystal, flowing from the throne of God and of the Lamb. It flowed down the center of the main street. On each side of the river grew a tree of life, bearing twelve crops of fruit, with a fresh crop each month. The leaves were used for medicine to heal the nations. (verses 1-2, NLT)

The reference to the tree of life goes all the way back to the Garden of Eden. After Adam and Eve ate of the Tree of the Knowledge of Good and Evil, and sin entered the human race, they were forbidden to eat of the Tree of Life. Why? Because if they ate of it they would live forever in that fallen state. So the angels were sent to protect the Tree of Life from Adam and Eve—and Adam and Eve from the Tree of Life. In heaven, however, that tree will be available to everyone.

3. Heaven is a city

Our eternal home is also described in Scripture as a city. In Hebrews 11:10 (NIV), the writer says that heaven is a "city with foundations, whose architect and builder is God." And then in Hebrews 13:14

(NIV) he adds: "For here we do not have an enduring city, but we are looking for the city that is to come."

Heaven . . . a city?

That's a bit hard for us to grasp, because we tend to think of cities as noisy, crowded places, with urban decay, graffiti, trash, and violent crime. But I want you to think of cities in a different way for a moment, if you would. Think of a perfect city where there is no crime, where everyone loves everyone, where the very streets and walls and sidewalks and buildings are translucent and glow with an inner radiance.

Cities have culture. Cities have art, music, goods, services, events, and restaurants. Restaurants in heaven? Why not? We know there will be feasting there.

Even earthly cities, for all their problems, have a certain unique quality to them. I think about Jerusalem at sunset, bathed in a golden light. Or Paris in springtime. Or Rome in the morning.

These are all places and cities right here on our home planet. And heaven is a city too. It is real, and we already have a placed reserved within its borders.

4. Heaven is a country

Speaking of those who were persecuted or martyred for their faith, the author of Hebrews said, "But as it is, they desire a better country, that is, a heavenly one. Therefore God is not ashamed to be called their God; for he has prepared a city for them" (Hebrews 11:16, NASB).

A heavenly country. A land of indescribable beauty and infinite dimensions. Perhaps this is the ultimate fulfillment of the psalmist's desire: "He brought me out into a spacious place; he rescued me because he delighted in me" (Psalm 18:19, NIV).

You and I tend to think of earth as the "real thing" and heaven as the surreal thing. But it's the other way around. In reality, heaven is the real thing. When we're trying to get a handle on what heaven might be like, we tend to start with earth and reason up to heaven, when we ought to start with heaven and reason down toward earth.

Earth is the imitation, the "shadowlands," as C. S. Lewis called them. The temporary dwelling place. He said, "The hills and valleys of heaven will be to those we now experience not as a copy but as an original. Nor as the substitute is to the genuine article, but as the flower to the root or the diamond to the coal."[34]

There is an interesting statement in Hebrews 8:5 (NIV). The writer speaks of the priests of that day at the temple in Jerusalem and notes that, "They serve at a sanctuary that is a copy and shadow of what is in heaven."

A copy. A shadow. Could you say that about all of earth, as well as an earthly temple slated for imminent destruction?

The fact is, heaven will be infinitely better than anything we imagine, and Scripture only gives us tantalizing hints about what it will be like.

Minds on Heaven, Feet on Earth

So how should these thoughts about heaven affect us here on earth? Paul instructed us to "aim at and seek the [rich, eternal treasures] that are above, where Christ is, seated at the right hand of God" (Colossians 3:1, AMP). In other words, our minds must be in heaven, but our feet must be on earth. How do we do that?

Let's go back to Colossians 3, where Paul continues:

Therefore put to death your members which are on the earth: fornication, uncleanness, passion, evil desire, and covetousness, which is idolatry. Because of these things the wrath of God is coming upon the sons of disobedience, in which you yourselves once walked when you lived in them.

But now you yourselves are to put off all these: anger, wrath, malice, blasphemy, filthy language out of your mouth. Do not lie to one another, since you have put off the old man with his deeds, and have put on the new man who is renewed in knowledge according to the image of Him who created him. (Colossians 3:5-10)

"*Therefore . . .*"

As I often say, whenever you see the word *therefore*, find out what it is there for. After telling us to seek heaven, think about heaven, and investigate heaven, Paul says, in effect, "Now . . . in light of all of this, here's how you ought to live."

It has been said of some people that they're "so heavenly minded they are no earthly good." I think there are some people who are so earthly minded, they are no heavenly good. If you are heavenly minded, in the best sense of that expression, you will be of the *greatest* earthly good.

If you are heavenly minded, it will affect the way you live on earth. And if heaven doesn't affect the way you live your daily life, just how heavenly minded could you really be?

As he develops that thought, Paul deals with three categories of sins that you might say keep us "earthbound," grounded, and miserable.

Sins That Keep Us Earthbound

1. Sexual sin keeps us earthbound

In verse 5, Paul used the word *fornication*, which is from the Greek word *pornea*. We get our word *pornography* from that term, and it speaks of sexual immorality in general—including illicit sex, whether it is extramarital, homosexual, or premarital. In other words, all sex out of God's order.

And what is God's order? It's very, very important, but it isn't rocket science.

One man. One woman. Marriage.

That's it. That's His order for life. And it applies not only to our actions but to our *thoughts* as well.

Jesus said, in so many words, "You have heard that it has been said, 'Do not commit adultery,' but I say to you if you look on a woman with lust in your heart it is the same thing." Oh, the Pharisees didn't like that. They prided themselves on the fact that they didn't commit the actual deed.

But Jesus essentially said, "If you are thinking about it and fantasizing about it, it's the same thing."[35]

It shouldn't surprise us, because the battle against sin—especially sexual sin—always begins in the mind. And let me warn you: *If you don't win the battle there, you won't win it in the way that you live.* Show me any person who has fallen into any kind of immorality, and I will show you a person who toyed with those things in his or her imagination—perhaps feeding those thoughts with pornography or trashy media or inappropriate conversations.

These are sins that will steal our joy and put the lights out on our testimony of life in Christ. And that's not how a citizen of heaven ought to live.

2. Idolatry keeps us earthbound

In verse 5, Paul calls covetousness idolatry. Isn't it interesting that the number one program in America (at this writing) is *American Idol*? I'm told that more people vote for their favorite idol candidate than vote for the president of the United States of America.

In the interest of full disclosure, it's a program I watch, too, on occasion . . . even though the title makes me uncomfortable.

What is an idol? *An idol is anyone or anything that takes the place of God in your life.* Everybody is a worshiper, whether they claim to believe in God or not. Everyone worships someone or something. An idol is simply something that we allow to divert us from worshiping, walking with, obeying, and serving the true and living God.

In other words, we can make a good thing into a bad thing by moving it from its proper and rightful place in our lives. A car can be an idol. A house can be an idol. Your career can be your idol. A college degree could be an idol. A boyfriend or a girlfriend could be an idol. Your child could be an idol. There are any number of things we might put in the place that belongs to God alone.

If you are dedicated to something, passionate about it, and can't stop thinking about it so that it becomes the primary interest or love in your life, that thing in effect becomes your god.

What, then, does Paul mean when he says that covetousness is idolatry? What does it mean to covet? Actually, *covet* is an interesting word. It comes from two root terms, which are *to have* and *more*. To have more. (And more and more and more.) It's the sin of never being satisfied or content, but always wanting more.

It starts with kids. Child A has a toy that Child B wants to play with. Child B bonks Child A on the head and then claims the toy. After a few minutes, Child B abandons the toy and moves on. (It was more the thrill of the hunt, I think, than the actual toy.)

Then we grow up, and we become adults. And one day you say, "You know what? I'm tired of my husband. I like *her* husband. I want him." So you go get him. And then you hear yourself saying, "You know what? My other husband was better than this guy. What am I doing here with this loser?" In the process, of course, lives and marriages and homes and families are destroyed—perhaps for generations.

Coveting is a serious life issue . . . and quickly becomes idolatry. This is not how a heavenly minded person ought to live.

3. Anger, meanness, and slander keep us earthbound

In verse 8, the apostle goes on with other things that can keep us from living like citizens of heaven: "But now you yourselves are to put off all these: anger, wrath, malice, blasphemy, filthy language out of your mouth."

Anger in this context speaks of a settled and habitual anger, mixed in with thoughts of revenge. This isn't a person who just gets a little ticked off and then gets over it. This is a person who says, "I don't get mad, I get even." You need to stop that. That is inappropriate behavior for a citizen of heaven.

Wrath speaks of a boiling agitation of the feelings. Sudden, violent anger. In context, the word *blasphemy* here is not speaking so much of blaspheming God as much as it is talking about slandering others.

We are a culture that is obsessed with gossip. The very word *gossip* makes a hissing sound, doesn't it? *Gosssssssip*. Just like a serpent. We all fall into this trap from time to time; we can find it kind of enjoyable to be spreading negative information about someone else. But it isn't so much fun when you find out that someone has been gossiping or telling lies about you. Don't let this be part of your lifestyle as a child of God . . . and as a citizen of heaven.

Let me offer a fresh way to look at these all-too-human struggles. You don't need to *turn away* from one thing as much as you need to *turn* to another. What do you do when you want a child to let go of something? You put something better and more interesting in front of him—and he will let go in a hurry to reach for that new something.

You and I need something that is more important to us than the earthly attractions that keep tripping us up. As one old preacher put it, we need "the expulsive power of a new affection." I like that phrase. This new affection causes that old thing to be seen for what it is, and I don't want it any more.

What is the new affection?

Heaven.

I want to be a heavenly-minded person. That simply means I desire to be a person who thinks about God and wants what God wants more than anything else. Yes, I'm still a real person living a real life on the earth. But at the same time, I'm not letting the worries and cares and preoccupations of life on earth become the most important things in my life.

I have higher priorities.

I want that expulsive power of a new affection, where I am loving God, and therefore I don't want to be tied up with the love of this world.

If you have asked Christ to come into your life, you are now His child, and you are a citizen of heaven. It's time to start living like one, because this life is fading like a puff of vapor in the wind. Sooner than any of us imagine, we'll be stepping into eternity.

Don't waste the precious life God has given to you. Make every year, every month, every week, every day, indeed every hour count for Him.

C. S. Lewis said it best: "Aim at heaven and you will get earth thrown in. Aim at earth and you will get neither."[36]

Makes sense, doesn't it?

7

What Will We Do in Heaven?

E ven with my GPS device in my car, I seem to be navigationally challenged.

Maybe my trouble is that I try to out-guess it.

The GPS will try to guide me to such-and-such a freeway, but I'm thinking to myself, *I know a better way than that.* But then it keeps telling me I've made a mistake and need to get off or go back . . . or maybe get a life.

I actually read about a motorist in the Midwest who followed her GPS directions onto a snowmo-bile trail, got stuck in the snow, and had to dial 911. The officer who responded said, "People shouldn't believe everything these gadgets tell you."

We think we're pretty smart as a culture, because we've invented this global positioning technology. But the truth is, what we've invented isn't half as amazing as the sophisticated homing instincts God has built into certain animals and birds.

I read about one species of bird known as the Manx Shearwater that make their nests somewhere off the coast of Wales. Scientists took a number of these birds, tagged them, and released them at different points around the globe to see whether they could find their way back home to the Coast of Wales.

And they did. All of them. Within twelve days, they were back.

One bird in particular made it all the way from Boston, traveling 250 miles a day from a place it had never been before to get back home. Now that's what you call a homing instinct!

Another bird, the Golden Plover, is native to the Hawaiian Islands but migrates every summer to the Aleutian Islands off of Alaska, some 1,200 miles away. I guess the Plover thinks Hawaii gets a little too hot in the summer—or maybe it's fed up with all the tourists and says, "Let's go to the Aleutians for a while."

When they arrive after their long trip, they mate, lay their eggs, and their little fledglings are born. And then the parent birds say, "See ya. Come visit." And they fly back to Hawaii, leaving the little fledglings to fend for themselves. Then, when a certain time of year rolls around, the young birds somehow know how to make a 1,200-mile journey to Hawaii, a place they have never been before.

Without question, these birds have a God-given GPS—a homing instinct from the Lord.

Guess what? God has placed a homing instinct in you and me as well. But it's not a homing instinct for the Hawaiian or Aleutian Islands.

Ours is a homing instinct for eternity.

Or to put it another way, it's a homesickness for heaven. We are pre-wired to long for a place we have never been before. Again, as we are told in the book of Ecclesiastes, God "has put eternity in [our] hearts."[37]

Made for Another World

Heaven is the real deal, the eternal dwelling place of every follower of Jesus Christ. C. S. Lewis wrote,

> All the things that have ever deeply possessed your soul have
> been hints of heaven—tantalizing glimpses, promises never quite

fulfilled, echoes that died away just as they caught your ear. If I find in myself a desire which no experience in this world can satisfy, the most probable explanation is I was made for another world. Earthly pleasures were never meant to satisfy, but to arouse, to suggest, the real thing.[38]

Yes, heaven is the real thing that we long for.

But questions often arise, and we wonder about heaven. Let's consider a few of these questions.

What Will Our New Bodies Be Like?

God is going to give you a brand-new body, but it won't be unrelated to your existing body. The blueprint for your eternal, glorified body is in the body you now possess. It's already there. There will be a connection between the Greg Laurie of earth and the Greg of heaven. And the same is true for all of us.

Job said, "And after my skin has been destroyed, yet in my flesh I will see God; I myself will see him with my own eyes—I, and not another" (Job 19:26-27, NIV).

The Bible promises that these bodies of ours will be resurrected, and there will be that unmistakable connection and correlation between the old and the new. Heaven is the earthly life of the believer, glorified and perfected.

For all its similarities, however, there will be wonderful differences.

When we get to the other side, our minds and our memories will be clearer than they have ever been before. Paul tells us in 1 Corinthians 15, that our bodies now disappoint us.

Amen to that! But here's the whole reference:

Our bodies are buried in brokenness, but they will be raised in glory. They are buried in weakness, but they will be raised in strength. They are buried as natural human bodies, but they will be raised as spiritual bodies. (1 Corinthians 15:43-44, NLT)

That means our new bodies will in some ways be the same as our old bodies, but at the same time they will be different. Without question they will be radically improved. No more physical disabilities. No signs of age. No sinful tendencies.

Joni Eareckson Tada, who has had to endure a paralyzed body for over forty years, says this about our new bodies:

> No more bulging middles or balding tops. No varicose veins or crow's feet. No more cellulite or support hose. Forget the thunder thighs and the highway hips. Just a quick leapfrog over the tombstone and it is a body you have always dreamed of. Fit and trim. Smooth and sleek. [39]

In fact, our new, resurrection bodies will resemble the resurrection body of Jesus Christ. As we know, Christ was crucified and rose again from the dead three days later. And we know that after His resurrection He walked around in a real physical body. You could touch Him. He ate fish in front of everyone, the Bible says. And yet He could appear in a room without using the door. And of course, He ascended to glory.

Will we be able to do the same things? I don't know. But the Bible does say in 1 John 3:2, "Beloved, now we are the children of God; and it has not yet been revealed what we shall be, but we know that when He is revealed, we shall be like Him, for we shall see Him as He is."

Do you long for that day? Do you look forward to that moment when you will see the Lord face-to-face?

Life goes by so quickly. Billy Graham was asked awhile back what the greatest surprise of his life had been. He answered: "The brevity of life."

When you're young, it seems like life goes on forever. When I was in elementary school, it seemed like each school day lasted months. I still have one of my old report cards from those days. The teacher wrote on it, "Greg spends too much time looking out the window and daydreaming and drawing cartoons. He will never amount to anything."

At least part of that was true: I did a lot of daydreaming and looking out the window . . . watching the clock and wondering why it wasn't working.

But then when you get out of elementary school, junior high goes a little bit faster. Then high school flies by. And then adult life. And then pretty soon you start remembering decades instead of years. Then one day you look in the mirror and you hardly recognize the old person looking back at you. *When did that happen? When did I get old?*

I started getting AARP magazines delivered to my house recently. I didn't ask for that, and I really don't want it. But then someone told me that because of my age, which is 58, I now qualify for a discount at the movie theater as a senior citizen. And guess what? I am taking advantage of it. Why not?

But there are those telltale signs that you are getting old. You know you are getting old when you get winded playing chess. You know you are getting old when you try to straighten the wrinkles in your socks, and then you realize you're not wearing any. You know you are getting old when your pacemaker accidentally opens the garage door. You know you are getting old when you bend over to tie your shoes and then wonder what else you can do while you're down there. You know you are getting old when you actually look forward to a dull evening at home. You know you are getting old when your mind makes commitments that your body can't keep. You know you are getting old when someone calls you at 9:00 in the evening and asks, "Did I wake you?" You know you are getting old when your ears are hairier than your head!

So often we think of ourselves as a body that happens to have a soul. But the reality is, you are a soul wrapped in a body. Yes, your body is "the real you." But there is more than your body! The thing that gives you spark and personality is your soul, the part of you that lives forever in the presence of God.

Will We Recognize One Another in Heaven?

Yes. Of course. Absolutely.

Why would you think that you would know less in heaven than you know on earth? In heaven, we will be perfected. Glorified. In fact, in 1 Corinthians 13:12 we are told that we will "know just as [we] also [are] known." There will be no more mysteries. No more questions. Everything will be resolved. You will *know*. Will you still love your family and friends? Of course you will! In fact, it will be a stronger, purer, and sweeter love.

Death breaks ties on earth, but it renews them in heaven. And we will be the same people in heaven that we were on earth. We won't become different people. You will still be you, and I will still be me, but the *perfected* version of me, without all the flaws, shortcomings, and sinful tendencies.

Do you remember the story in Matthew 17, where Jesus appeared on the Mount of Transfiguration with Moses and Elijah? Did you ever wonder how it was that everyone *knew* it was Moses and Elijah, without their saying so? Do you think Moses was standing there with the stone tablets under his arm or that maybe Elijah was calling down fire from heaven? Or do you imagine they had one of those newcomer badges people wear that said, "Hi, I'm Moses"?

No. I don't think so. Somehow, they were simply recognizable, and the men on the mountain with Jesus that day knew instantly who they were. I believe it will be the same for us in heaven. Somehow, I don't think there will need to be lengthy introductions, "icebreakers," or get-acquainted sessions when we first arrive.

I love the way Jesus stated it after He rose from the dead and met with His followers. He said, "It is I myself! Touch me and see" (Luke 24:39, NIV).

It's Me, guys. It wasn't a different Jesus. It was (and is) the same Jesus in a glorified body.

But What Will We Do in Heaven?

Why do we even ask this question? Because we think about the word *forever*, and we fear that we'll soon be bored. Someone will say, "Am I just going to sit around on a cloud, strum a harp now and then, and sleep?"

That might sound nice to some, but not to me! So it's good news to know there will actually be activities in heaven. One of the things you will be doing in heaven is worshiping God. And by the way, that is why you were created in the first place—to bring honor and glory to your Creator. In a sense, we will be reclaiming our original purpose, one that was so distorted and damaged by the fall.

I feel pretty certain that in our perfected, eternal bodies, we will all have perfect voices. No one will be going sharp or flat. We will harmonize perfectly as we sing the praises of God. Here's what we read in Revelation 15:

> I saw before me what seemed to be a glass sea mixed with fire. And on it stood all the people who had been victorious over the beast and his statue and the number representing his name. They were all holding harps that God had given them. And they were singing the song of Moses, the servant of God, and the song of the Lamb:
>
> "Great and marvelous are your works, O Lord God, the Almighty. Just and true are your ways, O King of the nations. Who will not fear you, Lord, and glorify your name? For you alone are holy. All nations will come and worship before you, for your righteous deeds have been revealed." (verses 2-4, NLT)

Maybe one of the reasons we will be able to sing out without hesitation in heaven will be because our problems, sorrows, conflicts, and worries will be gone. All of our questions will be answered and resolved.

One of the reasons we have a hard time worshiping on earth is because we don't always "feel like it."

We say, "I'm not in the mood to worship right now. I think I have a cold." Or, "I have this situation in my life that's weighing on me right now, so I don't really feel like singing praises to God." Or we may even allow ourselves to be critics of the worship service, even while it's underway. "I didn't really like that worship set as much as last week's—it was a little too loud." Or, "I've never liked that instrument. I don't know why they keep using it."

Yes, we all have our preferences and prejudices. But worship isn't something we should critique; it is something we should *do*, and we should do it whether we feel like it or not, or whether we are in the ideal circumstances or not.

That is why the Bible talks about the "sacrifice of praise" (Hebrews 13:15), because there are times when praise is a sacrifice. I don't *want* to offer it, my flesh resists offering it, but I offer it anyway because I know that God is in control. I know that He loves me and that He is worthy of my praise. So I offer it up.

Let me be straightforward here: *Worship is not about you, it's about Him.* If we keep that in mind when we sing our praises to God, it can make all the difference in the world.

Yes, we will worship the Lord when we are in heaven, but we won't worship all the time. Sometimes people have this idea that we'll just be laying on our stomachs worshiping for aeons. Yes, we will certainly worship. But we will also be busy, traveling across the new heavens and the new earth (at the speed of thought) doing our Father's business.

The Bible tells us in Revelation 7:15 (NLT) that the Lord's saints "stand in front of God's throne and serve him day and night in his Temple. And he who sits on the throne will give them shelter."

Serving Him . . . how?

Who knows. But you can bet that it will be the most exciting, fulfilling, joyous experience you have ever known.

Yes, heaven is a place of rest, but I can only rest for so long. It will also be a place of productivity. One wonders what the Lord has in store for us when we get there. We wonder if we will be able to perhaps finish some of the tasks that remain uncompleted on earth. Maybe you had dreams that were shattered here that will in some sense be fulfilled there. Who is to say that God would not allow us to complete what He inspired us to start on the other side?

Remember that verse in Philippians? "He who began a good work in you will carry it on to completion until the day of Christ Jesus." (Philippians 1:6, NIV). God is all about finishing what He begins.

We don't determine when we are born, nor do we determine when we die. But we have everything to do with that little dash in the middle, the thin line on our memorial stone that marks the years between our birth and our passing. I would simply remind us that life does not end after life on earth. It continues on in heaven.

And the best is yet to come.

Earth it is like a stopover. When I'm flying, I don't like stopovers at all.

Whenever I book a flight, I try to get a direct flight, because sometimes during stopovers, bad things happen. Inclement weather rolls in and you get stuck, or the scheduled flight crew doesn't show up, or whatever. So I like to get from A to B as quickly as possible.

Nevertheless, life on earth is a stopover. An airport lounge. A bus terminal. A train station. We're not at our destination yet, but we're on our way. And the last stage of that journey won't be long at all. It will come much sooner than we may realize.

What else will we do in heaven?

We're going to eat!

Revelation 19:9 (NIV) says, "Blessed are those who are invited to the wedding supper of the Lamb!"

I like the fact that the word *supper* is used. Here in California, where I live, we usually refer to the evening meal as "dinner." In the South, however, it's "supper." They will say, *"Wash up for supper!"*

I heard this a lot growing up, because for a good part of my childhood I was raised by my grandparents Stella and Charles, who were from Arkansas.

I called my grandmother Mama Stella and my grandfather Daddy Charles. My grandmother, I'm happy to say, was from the old school of home cooking. Mama Stella never saw a TV dinner, never reheated anything, and didn't care much for processed foods period. She made everything from scratch. I can still close my eyes and taste that fresh fried chicken. And of course, all of those fresh vegetables—string beans, black-eyed peas, okra, collard greens, and real mashed potatoes.

Mama Stella's crowning achievement was her biscuits. I have never had one as good since she went to heaven. And it strikes me as perfectly logical that the Lord would employ her abilities in heaven at the supper of the Lamb.

But we will also be able to sit down with the great saints of old. Matthew 8:11 (NIV) says, "I say to you that many will come from the east and the west, and will take their places at the feast with Abraham, Isaac and Jacob in the kingdom of heaven."

Can you even imagine this? Sitting at a table and saying, "Moses, excuse me, would you please pass the manna?" Or maybe, "Elijah, my meat is a little undercooked. Would you get a little extra fire on it?"

Imagine being able to pick the brain of some great man or woman of faith and find out all about him or her. Talk to Mary about having the Son of God conceived in her womb. Talk to Moses about seeing the Red Sea parted. Talk to Noah about the ark. Talk to Shadrach, Meshach, and Abednego about the fiery furnace. ("Did you guys use sunscreen?") Talk to Daniel about the lion's den. The list goes on, and how amazing it will be.

The thing biggest in my heart right now, however, will be the opportunity to reunite with loved ones. I think especially of my son Christopher, who, as I mentioned earlier, went to be with the Lord in 2008 at the age of thirty-three. Needless to say, I miss him very much and look forward to seeing him with all my heart.

When Christopher was just a boy and I would carry him around, he was always a curious little guy, and he would point to things and ask me what they were. And because he was very little he didn't say, "What's that?" He just said *"S'at."*

He would point to a truck. *"S'at—?"*

"That's a truck."

"S'at—?"

"That's a tree."

"S'at—?"

"That's another tree."

"S'at—?"

"That's a house."

He said it over and over, *S'at . . . S'at . . . S'at,* until it really began to wear me out.

So now, Topher (his nickname) has gone on to heaven ahead of me. And after I arrive and we're walking around together, I will say, *"S'at—?"*

"That's the sea of glass, Dad."

"S'at—?"

"That's an angel, Dad."

"When do we eat dinner?"

"Anytime, Dad."

But the main event of heaven will be Jesus. Yes, we long for heaven, but what we are really longing for is God Himself. Jesus said, "When everything is ready, I will come and get you, so that you will always be with me where I am" (John 14:3, NLT).

Paul said,

> As long as I'm alive in this body, there is good work for me to do. If I had to choose right now, I hardly know which I'd choose. Hard choice! The desire to break camp here and be with Christ is powerful. Some days I can think of nothing better. (Philippians 1:22-23, MSG)

D. L. Moody wrote, "It is not the jeweled walls and pearly gates that are going to make heaven attractive. It is being with God."[41]

God will be there. You can ask Him anything, tell Him anything, and hear everything He has to say to you. You will have all the time in the world when you get to heaven. It is our future home, the place we desire and long for with a homing instinct we can't explain any other way.

When I travel, I start missing home almost as soon as I leave the ground. If you are overseas very long, you long for your country, you long for your house, you long for your bed, and you certainly long for your family.

And in the same way, we all long for our home in heaven.

Years ago Audio Adrenaline recorded a song called "Big House," about heaven. They sang it at one of our crusades years ago. Speaking of heaven they sang:

> It's a big, big house with lots and lots of room,
> A big, big table with lots and lots of food,
> A big, big yard where we can play football,
> A big, big house. It's my Father's house.

Steven Curtis Chapman, a contemporary Christian recording artist, lost his little adopted daughter Maria in an accident in 2008, the same year we lost Christopher.

Maria was adopted from China, and he was able to speed up the adoption process because Maria had been born with a hole in her heart. And Steven and his wife Mary Beth loved her with all their hearts. She was a beloved part of the family.

In a recent radio broadcast, Steven spoke with Dr. Dobson about that event. Within the interview, he mentioned a postcard I had written to him that I never knew he had received. It surprised me when I heard him mention it. And in my card I had told him that his little girl was going to be much more a part of his future than his past. He told Dr. Dobson that the thought encouraged him very much.

He also related a story about when little Maria came to his wife Mary Beth and asked her about this place she had heard about in Sunday school. She had heard about a big, big house, with lots and lots of food, and a big, big yard, and so forth. Immediately, Mary Beth recognized that little Maria was talking about that Audio Adrenaline song. So she said, "Oh, you mean where we will play football?"

"Yeah, Mommy. That is the place."

"Well, that is a song about heaven."

Little Maria said, "I want to go to there."

And of course Mommy said, "Well, one day. Later. Not anytime soon."

But the Lord had prepared this little girl, and that is where she is now. In heaven. In that big, big house, sitting at that big, big table. I don't know about the football part. But then again . . . why not?

A Prepared Place for Prepared People

If I plan on taking a plane trip, I have to first book a ticket. I don't just walk into the airport and walk onto a plane. In the same way, if you want to be sure you're going to heaven, you need the ticket.

You say, "How much will it cost?"

You couldn't afford it. Not in a million years.

But the good news is that Jesus Christ came to this earth and died on a cross for your sin and rose again from the dead, and in effect purchased your ticket for heaven and eternal life. Here is how you receive it. You just say, "Lord, I accept the gift that You have offered to me. I turn from my sin and I put my faith in You."

If you have done that, then you have a reserved place and a future home that no one can ever take away from you. As Peter said,

> Now we live with great expectation, and we have a priceless in-heritance—an inheritance that is kept in heaven for you, pure and undefiled, beyond the reach of change and decay. (1 Peter 1:3-4, NLT)

It's a big, big house.

And more than anywhere else in the universe, it is where you belong.

8

Down-to-Earth Talk About Heaven

S ometimes it's difficult for us to wrap our minds around this eternal destination called heaven.

What will it be like for us? Will it seem strange? Will it really feel like home? The mental pictures we conjure up seem so surreal, so mystical, so misty and foggy at times.

But there is nothing misty or foggy about heaven. The Bible presents heaven as a future destination, identifying it as a real place, and a home that will be inexpressibly better than anything we are experiencing now. The Bible promises that in heaven we will be given new bodies that will be strong and healthy, and that we will never have to deal with pain or sorrow or fear again.

As I talk to people about our life in the presence of God, however, several questions invariably surface. You might call them down-to-earth questions about a beyond-the-earth reality.

Let's consider two of them.

Question 1: Will we still be married in heaven?

Some people would be very happy to think that there will be marriage in heaven. Others would not be so happy. So what's the answer?

It's really yes and no.

You will still have many of the relationships in heaven that you had on earth. Yes, you will be receiving a new body, made to last forever, and you will be relocating to heaven and ultimately to the new earth that God will establish. But that won't erase history. No, it will *culminate* history.

But what about the marriage relationship? Actually, Jesus was asked that very question by a group of religious leaders known as the Sadducees. Now this group of leaders, in contrast to the Pharisees, didn't believe in the resurrection of the dead or life after death.

Maybe that's where they got their name, because they were so sad . . . you see. It's a pretty bleak outlook to have no hope of life beyond the grave. This group of Jewish leaders thought they would trap Jesus with a hypothetical situation they'd dreamed up. Here's how it went:

> But that same day some of the Sadducees, who say there is no resurrection after death, came to him and asked, "Sir, Moses said that if a man died without children, his brother should marry the widow and their children would get all the dead man's property. Well, we had among us a family of seven brothers. The first of these men married and then died, without children, so his widow became the second brother's wife. This brother also died without children, and the wife was passed to the next brother, and so on until she had been the wife of each of them. And then she also died. So whose wife will she be in the resurrection? For she was the wife of all seven of them!" (Matthew 22:23-28, TLB)

With that question, these guys smugly supposed they had the Lord trapped, and that He wouldn't be able to answer. Jesus quickly put that idea to rest, however, with His response: "Your error is caused by your ignorance of the Scriptures and of God's power! For in the resurrection there is no marriage; everyone is as the angels in heaven" (verses 29-30, TLB).

So . . . isn't that saying that we won't be married in heaven? Not necessarily. You won't be married to your spouse in heaven, but you will be married to the Lord, because the Bible clearly describes us as the bride of Christ. When we go to heaven, then, we will join our Groom, and in that sense there will be marriage on the other side.

But what about our relationship with our spouse? If you have been married to someone for 25, 35, 45, or 55 years, the idea of not having any connection with that husband or wife in eternity is troubling at the very least. But here's what you need to know. Your relationship with your spouse will not end. In heaven, Cathe and I will know each other. We won't be husband and wife in the same sense that we were on earth, but we will certainly still be in relationship.

Author Randy Alcorn puts it like this: "Earthly marriage is a shadow, a copy, an echo of the true and ultimate marriage. . . . *'The purpose of marriage is not to replace Heaven, but to prepare us for it.'*"[42]

The human institution of marriage culminates in heaven, and we will no longer be married in a technical sense. But that doesn't mean our relationship will end. God's plan for our lives doesn't stop in heaven, it continues. God doesn't abandon His purposes in heaven, He fulfills them. Therefore, friendships and relationships that have begun on earth will continue in heaven, richer than ever.

Question 2: Do people in heaven know about events on earth?

Some people think those who have gone on before us know nothing of what is happening on earth. Others think they are watching everything. Sometimes people will even say, "I sense the presence of my loved one with me. I think he or she was guiding me during that difficult time."

Let me be a little blunt here, because we can't allow our emotions alone to guide us to sound conclusions. The fact is, when loved ones die and go to heaven, you can no longer communicate with them, and they can no longer communicate with you. That doesn't mean there is no connection. It simply means there can be no real communication. People who are desperate to make contact with departed loved ones will reach out to psychics or mediums, wanting so much to have one last conversation or obtain one last word of advice.

The Bible says to have nothing to do with such things.

Here is what we need to know.

First, people in heaven may indeed be very aware of what is happening on earth.

In Luke 16, which we will consider in more detail later on, we encounter the story of Lazarus and the rich man. Both men died, one going to a place of comfort in "Abraham's bosom," and the other to a place of torment on the other side. The rich man, suffering in Hades, was both fully conscious and aware of those he had left behind. In Luke 16:28, he expresses concern for his five brothers, not wanting them to end up where he is. If someone in hell was aware of relatives on earth, couldn't we conclude that it would be even more likely for someone in heaven?

Second, when people believe in Jesus on earth, it is public knowledge in heaven.

In Luke 15, He gives us three vignettes about three things that are lost and found: a lost sheep, a lost coin, and finally a lost son. The woman who found her lost coin and the shepherd who found his lost sheep rejoiced greatly over what had been restored to them. And Jesus adds these words: "I say to you that likewise there will be more joy in heaven over one sinner who repents than over ninety-nine just persons who need no repentance." And again, "Likewise, I say to you, there is joy in the presence of the angels of God over one sinner who repents" (verses 7, 10).

Then finally it culminates with the parable of the prodigal son. You remember the story—the youngest son takes his share of the inheritance, leaves home, and blows it on riotous living. Then, reaching the bottom, he resolves to return home, and his father welcomes him with open arms.

I want you to notice something in this passage. Jesus doesn't say there will be joy *among* the angels over a sinner who repents; it says joy *in the presence of the angels*.

Could that be referring to those who have gone on before us as well as the angels? In heaven, we will know *more* than we know on earth, not less. Isn't it possible we could be aware of the fact that someone had placed faith in Christ because of our testimony? If there was a party breaking out in heaven, don't you think you would know about it?

Years ago we were in San Jose for one of our crusades, and I was staying in a hotel. I'm usually a light sleeper, so if there is noise in a room nearby, it's hard for me to fall asleep. We'd had an event that night, and the next night we were having another one, so I really wanted to get my rest.

In the room next to me, however, I heard music . . . which became louder and louder and louder. Pretty soon (and I'm not exaggerating) the bass speakers next door were moving the wall. *Thump. Thump. Thump.*

I thought, "This is crazy." So I finally called hotel security, and they called the police. It turns out there was a bachelor party going on next door with at least a hundred people in the room. It was complete with a DJ, sound system, and strobe lights. I watched through the little peephole in my door as the people began carting their equipment out of the room. They basically threw them out of the hotel.

Did I know there was a party going on? Was I aware of it?

You'd better believe it!

Now don't you think that if there was a celebration in heaven with angels singing and dancing or doing whatever they do to celebrate, that you would be aware of it? Of course you would. Maybe you would even understand how your simple testimony had a part in that person's finally coming to Jesus Christ.

Third, people in heaven may know about the time and place of certain events on earth.

In Revelation 6 we read:

When He opened the fifth seal, I saw under the altar the souls of those who had been slain for the word of God and for the testimony which they held. And they cried with a loud voice, saying, "How long, O

Lord, holy and true, until You judge and avenge our blood on those who dwell on the earth?" Then a white robe was given to each of them; and it was said to them that they should rest a little while longer, until both the number of their fellow servants and their brethren, who would be killed as they were, was completed. (verses 9-11)

I find it interesting how much these men and women seem to be aware of. These people are aware they were put to death on earth for their faith. They also seem to be conscious of the passing of time on earth. Why else would they say, *"How long, O Lord, holy and true, until You judge and avenge our blood . . . ?"* And they are given the answer that "they should rest a little while longer."

Notice also that there is some connection between the believers in heaven and those on earth. In Revelation 6:11, those in heaven are conversing about "their fellow servants and their brethren" still on earth.

Fourth, those who have gone on before us may be cheering us on in our walk with Christ.

Listen to the writer of Hebrews:

Since we have such a huge crowd of men of faith watching us from the grandstands, let us strip off anything that slows us down or holds us back, and especially those sins that wrap themselves so tightly around our feet and trip us up; and let us run with patience the particular race that God has set before us. (Hebrews 12:1-2, TLB)

The King James version speaks of our being "compassed about with so great a cloud of witnesses." Who are these witnesses? Are they the loved ones who have gone on before us, cheering us on from the grandstands of heaven?

Hebrews 12, of course, follows Hebrews 11, which many have described as "the hall of faith." It's something of a "who's who" of God's people, including names like Abraham, Moses, Joseph, Gideon, Samson, David, Rahab, and Daniel. In the first verse of Hebrews 12, the writer speaks of our being surrounded by a great cloud of witnesses. He seems to be saying, "In light of the fact that these men and women of God served the Lord so faithfully, you'd better run a good race, too."

The writer could be saying, "They have set a good pace. Follow it!" But he might also be saying, "These believers who have gone on before you are watching your progress." I don't think we can say for sure if they are or if they aren't. But we know for sure that our Lord Himself is watching our progress!

One Foot in Heaven?

There are things that can happen to us in this life that make us more aware of heaven and our future destination.

I was speaking with a lady the other day who has a severely handicapped son, and caring for this boy has been extremely difficult for her. Referring to her son, she told me, "His life has placed one of my feet in heaven and one on earth."

I understood what she was saying and felt compassion for her. But when you think about it, that's not such a bad place to be.

The presence of pain and suffering can bring this about, as can the unexpected death of a loved one. You long to see that person, and you feel connected to heaven by stronger ties than you had ever experienced before.

C. S. Lewis once said, "A continual looking forward to the eternal world is not a form of escapism or wishful thinking, but one of the things a Christian is meant to do."[43]

For the believer, death is not only the great separator; in Jesus Christ, death is the great uniter. When we get to heaven we will not only be reunited with those who have gone before us, but we will be united with those we may have helped bring us to faith.

In 1 Thessalonians 2:19-20 (NIV), the apostle writes: "For what is our hope, our joy, or the crown in which we will glory in the presence of our Lord Jesus when he comes? Is it not you? Indeed, you are our glory and joy."

I love that! Paul is saying that these spiritual children of his will be his crown of rejoicing in the Lord's presence when He comes. This passage seems to be implying that when we get to heaven, we will in some sense have grouped around us those we helped to believe in Jesus.

Maybe that thought discourages you a little, instead of encouraging you. Maybe you would say, "I don't know that I have really helped that many people believe in Jesus."

The fact is, you really don't know how many people you have helped along in their journey of faith. You haven't seen the big plan, and you don't know how touching one person's life ended up touching another person's life . . . and on and on it goes. On this side of heaven, you and I don't really know how it will all play out.

The important thing is to simply be faithful with the opportunities that God sets before you. The truth is, you may have reached more people than you realize. Ultimately it is God who converts people, not you or me. The Bible says that one sows, another waters, but it is God who gives the increase (see 1 Corinthians 3:6-8). God is the one who brings men and women into the kingdom of God.

When you pray for the work of evangelism you become invested in it. When you give financially to support the work of evangelism you become invested in it. When you are kind to someone and help or bless someone in the name of Jesus, you become invested in evangelizing that life.

In fact, Jesus said, "Truly I tell you, anyone who gives you a cup of water in my name because you belong to the Messiah will certainly not lose their reward" (Mark 9:41, NIV).

The Judgment Seat of Christ

In the book of Revelation, John speaks of the terror of the final judgment known as the Great White Throne. That will be the dreadful moment when those who have rejected Jesus Christ and His forgiveness and salvation will have to stand before God and give an accounting of their lives.

How terrible will that be?

John wrote, "And I saw a Great White Throne and the one who sat upon it, from whose face the earth and sky fled away, but they found no place to hide" (Revelation 20:11, TLB).

We'll talk more about that event later, but the fact is, we who believe in Jesus Christ won't appear before that Great White Throne. We will already be in heaven, secure for all eternity. But the Bible does teach that each one of us will stand before the judgment seat
of Christ, where He will dispense His rewards.

Maybe it would help to think of it more as an awards ceremony—like the Grammys or the Oscars.

Sometimes when you're watching the Academy Awards you find yourself pulling for a certain movie or a particular actor that you liked. And when that movie gets completely bypassed, you feel some disappointment.

In the same way, we may feel disappointed at times that our efforts or sacrifice or the investment of our time and skill goes unnoticed and unacknowledged. Granted, we do what we do for the Lord, and for His approval, not the approval of people. But even so, we're human, and it hurts sometimes to have our work or our best efforts get totally ignored.

At the judgment seat of Christ, our Lord takes care of that. Because God doesn't miss anything—not a single detail—of what we do for Him or for others on His behalf. Jesus said, "Your Father who sees what is done in secret will reward you" (Matthew 6:6, NASB).

In 2 Corinthians 5:10, Paul says: "For we must all appear before the judgment seat of Christ, that each one may receive the things done in the body, according to what he has done, whether good or bad."

Somehow, this judgment will take place individual by individual. We will all have our appointment before the Lord, where He will review our lives. Don't imagine that God will at this time drag up all your old sins. He won't, because those sins are gone and forgotten! They have all been washed away and forgiven by the blood of Christ. And we should not choose to remember what God has chosen to forget.

That's not what this occasion will be about. It will be a time when the Lord will say to us, "What did you do with your life? What did you do with your resources? What did you do with your time and your opportunities?"

We all have one life, and the Lord will ask us how we invested what He gave us. It's possible for a believer to simply waste his or her opportunities on earth instead of taking advantage of them. You can have a saved soul and a lost life.

The Bible tells us the story of the wicked King Belshazzar, who was confronted by the prophet Daniel. Daniel looked the king in the eye and said, "You have been weighed in the balances, and found wanting." (See Daniel 5:18-30.)

Now, normally when we get on a scale we want to weigh less. But when you get on God's scales, you want to weigh more. You want to have substance and depth and purpose and weight to your life. Effectively Daniel was saying, "Belshazzar, you are a spiritual lightweight. You have done nothing with your life and all your wonderful privileges and opportunities."

Speaking of this judgment seat of Christ, Paul wrote:

> For no one can lay any foundation other than the one we already have—Jesus Christ. Anyone who builds on that foundation may use a variety of materials—gold, silver, jewels, wood, hay, or straw. But on the judgment day, fire will reveal what kind of work each builder has done. The fire will show if a person's work has any value. If the work survives, that builder will receive a reward. But if the work is burned up, the builder will suffer great loss. The builder will be saved, but like someone barely escaping through a wall of flames. (1 Corinthians 3:11-15, NLT)

So the topic before Christ's throne at that time won't be so much about the bad things you've done; it's more about *what did you do with your life?* Did you accomplish anything? Did you impact anyone? Did you seek to glorify Him with your time and opportunities? Or did you spend it on empty pursuits and worthless activities?

I think most of us envision this day as being monopolized by the great heroes of the faith. As we ponder this awards ceremony, we think about people like Corrie ten Boom or Jim Elliot or Billy Graham. We imagine that these great men and women of God will get all the rewards, and there won't be anything left for us.

But I suggest to you there might be some surprises in heaven. I think we will also see the Lord reward some people you have probably never heard of before.

People like Pearle Goode.

Who is Pearle Goode? She was an older woman who heard of the ministry of Billy Graham and committed herself to pray fervently for every crusade that he did. Word reached Billy Graham of the faithful prayers of this woman, and he was so moved by her ministry that they started flying her out to the crusades, so that she could pray on site. And that is what she faithfully did, until she passed away at the age of ninety. At her funeral service, Billy's wife Ruth paid tribute to Pearl. She said, "Here lie the mortal remains of much of the secret of Bill's ministry."

Pearle wasn't a preacher, missionary, or author. But while Billy did his part, Pearle did hers. While Billy was out preaching, Pearle was praying.

In the same way, you have your own part. So don't worry about what God has called someone else to do. Just focus on what God has called you to do, because the key in that final day is not how much you did but why you did it. God is far more interested in significance than He is in success. God is far more interested in faithfulness than He is in success.

In that final day, He won't say, "Well done, good and successful servant." No, He will say, "Well done, good and *faithful* servant." It's all about faithfulness. It's all about doing what God has set before you, doing it well, and doing it with all of your might. That is what we will be judged for in that final day.

At that time, crowns will be given out as rewards for faithful service.

As the grandfather of young granddaughters, I am learning how little girls like to dress up like princesses. Having raised two boys, this is all new territory for me. Little girls love being Cinderella or Sleeping Beauty, with the full gown, the crown, the scepter, and the whole nine yards.

The crowns the Lord gives out on that day, however, won't be plastic or paper or aluminum. They will be eternal and beautiful beyond description.

There will be a crown of rejoicing

Paul wrote to the Thessalonians, "For what is our hope, or joy, or crown of rejoicing? Is it not even you in the presence of our Lord Jesus Christ at His coming? For you are our glory and joy" (1 Thessalonians 2:19-20).

This will probably be a soul-winner's crown for those who have used their influence for the glory of God.

There will be a crown of life

James writes,

> Blessed is the one who perseveres under trial because, having stood the test, that person will receive the crown of life that the Lord has promised to those who love him. (James 1:12, NIV)

This crown is specifically promised for the man or woman who has resisted temptation and has patiently endured tests and trials. There are people who suffer from physical infirmities or bad marriages or poverty or emotional trials that are no fault of their own. Others, at this very moment, are suffering for their testimony of Jesus Christ in different parts of the world.

God says, "I have a special crown for you who have endured difficult situations and consistently resisted temptation."

There will be a crown of righteousness

Shortly before his execution in a Roman dungeon, the apostle Paul wrote these words to his young friend, Timothy:

> The time of my departure is at hand. I have fought the good fight, I have finished the race, I have kept the faith. Finally, there is laid up for me the crown of righteousness, which the Lord, the righteous Judge, will give to me on that Day, and not to me only but also to all who have loved His appearing. (2 Timothy 4:6-8)

This is a crown that will be given specifically to those who have served God and have a heart for heaven.

Do you long for the return of Jesus Christ? Then there is a crown waiting for you. There is also a crown waiting for you if you have remained faithful to the Lord and finished the race He set out before you.

So make every day of your life count, my friend. Keep one foot in heaven and keep another foot on earth, and be ready to meet your God.

He's coming soon.

And those aren't my words, they are His.

9

The Reality of Hell

Not long ago on a Christian television show, the interviewer asked me why I spoke so much about eternity.

"When I've watched you preach on your TV program or at a crusade," he said, "I've noticed whatever topic you're dealing with, you always come back to eternity.

"So why do you do that?" he asked me. "Why do you always come back to the eternal in your messages?"

After thinking about it for a moment, I answered, "I guess when you get down to it, it's the most important thing there is."

As a pastor I want to teach the Word of God and help people grow in their faith as followers of Jesus. I want them to learn how to know God's will, resist temptation, build a great marriage, walk in integrity, and all those things we talk about as pastors and teachers. But when it's all said and done, the most important thing to me is intercepting people on their way to hell and pointing them toward heaven instead.

I want people to change their eternal address.

That is why I do what I do.

Most people believe in some kind of heaven and also believe they're going there. Statistics show that for every American who believes he or she is going to hell, there are 120 who believe they'll end up in heaven.

That is a direct contradiction, however, to what Jesus said.

> Enter by the narrow gate; for wide is the gate and broad is the way that leads to destruction, and there are many who go in by it. Because narrow is the gate and difficult is the way which leads to life, and there are few who find it. (Matthew 7:13-14)

No matter how fervently we might wish it otherwise, Jesus teaches that most people today are not headed to heaven. If we believe the Bible we have to accept this simple fact. Most people are actually headed to hell, though none of us like to hear that.

It's interesting to me that even though many in our culture don't believe in a literal hell, people will use the word to punctuate their sentences.

Someone will say, "All hell just broke loose." Or maybe, "He really gave me hell." Or even, "You go to hell."

That last phrase is used a lot to insult someone. But at the same time, if someone had a great time somewhere they will say, "Man, we had a hell of a good time together."

I actually had a guy come up to me after a message on a Sunday morning, shake my hand, and say, "That was a hell of a speech, Reverend."

I actually laughed. I didn't know what else to do. I suppose in his own way he was trying to compliment me. I said, "Well, I was hoping it was a *heaven* of a speech." But I understood what he was saying.

It's funny how someone will say to another person, "You can go to hell," but at the same time they will say, "I don't believe a place called hell actually exists." I guess it's not quite as effective to yell at someone and say, "You can just go to a place that doesn't exist!"

Why do people say, "Go to hell"? Because deep down inside, even if you are a nonbeliever, you *know* there is a hell.

Hell is a real place, but because people are uncomfortable with that idea they make jokes about it. Did you know there is an actual town in Michigan called Hell? Can you imagine? It was founded in 1841 by a man named George Reeves, who had discovered a low, swampy place in southeast Michigan and didn't know what to name it. Someone said to him, "What do you want to call it?" And he replied, "I don't care. Name it Hell, if you want to."

And so they did. Hell, Michigan.

People feel free to joke about the topic of hell. Comedian Woody Allen said, "Hell is the future abode of all people who personally annoy me."

But there is a hell. A real hell. And it's no joke.

The fact of the matter is that Jesus Christ spoke more about hell than all of the other prophets and preachers of the Bible put together. Most of the teaching we have on the topic of hell was given to us by Christ Himself.

That fact surprises some people. They will say, "Really? Wasn't Jesus the very personification of love and mercy and grace? Why would He talk about hell?"

For that very reason! It's precisely because He was and is the personification of love and grace and mercy that He doesn't want any man or woman uniquely made in His image to spend eternity in this place called hell. And Jesus, being God, knows about it because He has seen it with His own eyes. As a result, He carefully, sternly, and repeatedly warns us about its existence.

It has been estimated that of the forty parables that Jesus told, more than half of them dealt with God's eternal judgment and hell. Make no mistake about it, there is a real hell for real people.

J. I. Packer said, "An endless hell can no more be removed from the New Testament than an endless heaven can."[45] It is there.

It's interesting to me how the concept of judgment in the afterlife becomes more or less popular, depending on the time in which we are living. I think belief in hell probably went up after 9/11, because when some great evil takes place, people tend to believe in a place of final retribution. But when things aren't going as badly, and the memory of mass murderers fades a little, then a belief in hell actually starts to trail off.

Years ago John Lennon famously sang, "Imagine there is no heaven. It is easy if you try. No hell below us. Above us only sky."

Dear John: We can "imagine" all we want, but it won't change eternal realities. There is a heaven. And there is a hell.

The Second Death

The Bible actually teaches there are two deaths: one physical and one spiritual. Furthermore, Jesus warned that we are to fear the second death more than the first! In Revelation 20:14 we read, "Then Death and Hades were cast into the lake of fire. This is the second death." In Revelation 21:8 (NLT), the One who sits on the throne says,

> But cowards, unbelievers, the corrupt, murderers, the immoral, those who practice witchcraft, idol worshipers, and all liars—their fate is in the fiery lake of burning sulfur. This is the second death.

The second death is hell, which is eternal separation from God. Puritan Thomas Watson wrote, "Eternity to the godly is a day that has no sunset; eternity to the wicked is a night that has no sunrise."[46]

The Bible describes hell in different ways.

1. Hell is pictured like a garbage dump

One picture we have of hell in the Bible is that of a garbage dump. But not like any garbage dump we have ever seen. I don't know if you have ever taken your own trash to the dump and looked around at all the rubbish and castoff items. You'll see an old refrigerator and a television set and maybe even part of a car sticking out of the garbage. You think how hard people must have worked at one time to obtain those items, and now here they are, moldering in a landfill.

But the dump in New Testament days, also known as Gehenna, was far worse than that. You would not only throw your trash and rubbish there, but it was a place where people could toss in dead bodies as well, and it was constantly smoldering and burning. You can imagine what a horrific place this was.

So Jesus took the picture of Gehenna, the dump, if you will, and used it to describe hell.

2. Hell is pictured like a prison

One of the clearest pictures Christ gave of hell was that of being incarcerated. He told a parable of a king's servant who was sent to jail for cruel and unforgiving behavior, then added this warning: "This is how my heavenly Father will treat each of you unless you forgive your brother or sister from your heart" (Matthew 18:35, NIV).

I don't know if you have ever been to prison. I receive letters on occasion from people in prison who listen to our radio broadcast.

When we were doing a crusade in South Dakota, I had the honor of receiving a special blanket from some Christian Native Americans there. The man who gave me the blanket first heard the gospel on our radio broadcast in prison and came to Christ. Now he is serving the Lord and preaching the gospel. That was an encouraging thing to hear.

In this prison called hell, however, there will be no opportunities to repent or to find release. It will be too late for that.

3. Hell is pictured like a fire that never stops burning

The most well-known picture of hell given to us in Scripture is that of a fire that never stops burning. That brings us to a story in Luke 16, where Jesus spoke of hell as an unquenchable fire.

The Story of Lazarus and the Beggar

Jesus told many parables or stories to make His points clear, but I don't believe that the account in Luke 16 is a parable. I think it's a true account of real people and real events.

Why do I believe that? Because Jesus used actual names in the story, and He doesn't do that in His parables. So you might describe this as a behind-the-scenes look into the invisible world. If you have wondered what happens on the other side when believers and nonbelievers pass into eternity, here is a glimpse into those realms by Christ Himself. (We've touched on some aspects of this earlier, but let's go into a little more detail.)

There was a certain rich man who was clothed in purple and fine linen and fared sumptuously every day. But there was a certain beggar named Lazarus, full of sores, who was laid at his gate, desiring to be fed with the crumbs which fell from the rich man's table. Moreover the dogs came and licked his sores. So it was that the beggar died, and was carried by the angels to Abraham's bosom. The rich man also died and was buried. And being in torments in Hades, he lifted up his eyes and saw Abraham afar off, and Lazarus in his bosom.

Then he cried and said, "Father Abraham, have mercy on me, and send Lazarus that he may dip the tip of his finger in water and cool my tongue; for I am tormented in this flame." But Abraham said, "Son, remember that in your lifetime you received your good things, and likewise Lazarus evil things; but now he is comforted and you are tormented. And besides all this, between us and you there is a great gulf fixed, so that those who want to pass from here to you cannot, nor can those from there pass to us."

Then he said, "'I beg you therefore, father, that you would send him to my father's house, for I have five brothers, that he may tes-tify to them, lest they also come to this place of torment." Abraham said to him, "They have Moses and the prophets; let them hear them." And he said, "No, father Abraham; but if one goes to them from the dead, they will repent." But he said to him, "If they do not hear Moses and the prophets, neither will they be persuaded though one rise from the dead." (Luke 16:19-31)

Jesus mentions the name of the beggar, Lazarus. The wealthy man in the story is described as "a certain rich man."

One man owned everything yet possessed nothing.

The other owned nothing but inherited everything.

One went to comfort, the other went to torment.

The believing man, Lazarus, was ushered by the angels into the presence of God into a place called paradise.

By the way, prior to the arrival of Jesus and His death and resurrection, when a person would die in faith they went to a place called "paradise" or to "Abraham's bosom," as the King James Version describes it. When Jesus was crucified and the man on the cross next to Him came to His senses and asked the Lord for mercy, Jesus said to him, "I assure you, today you will be with me in paradise" (Luke 23:43, NLT).

So that thief who had been crucified next to Jesus went into a place of waiting, a realm of bliss and comfort called paradise. That was before Jesus had been raised from the dead. But the Bible says that after His death and resurrection, a believer who dies goes straight to heaven and into the presence of God. The apostle Paul told us that to be absent from the body is to be present with the Lord. (See 2 Corinthians 5:6-8.)

One other thing about that thief on the cross: You might describe what happened to him as a deathbed conversion. And I hope this gives a measure of encouragement to you to never stop praying for friends and loved ones who are still outside of Jesus Christ. Time and again, I've heard glorious stories of people who have come to the Lord right before passing into eternity.

Sometimes we know someone who died, and we fear they are in hell right now. I've heard people say, "That person is in hell."

The truth is, you and I don't know who is in hell. We're in no position to say. Now I do think we can authoritatively say who is in heaven. If someone has put their faith in Christ, we can say, "They're with the Lord now." And the Bible assures us of this. But who are we to say what may or may not have happened to an individual in those final seconds before leaving this life?

I know this: If someone cries out to Jesus in repentance with their last breath or last fading thought, God will forgive them and accept them into heaven. No one wants to save a person more than the Lord Jesus Christ.

But what happens if a person truly rejects God's salvation to the very end? We have a picture of that in this story Jesus told in Luke 16.

Tormented

> The rich man also died and was buried. And being in torments in
> Hades, [or hell] he lifted up his eyes and saw Abraham afar off,
> and Lazarus in his bosom. (Luke 16:22-23)

The sin of this man was not his wealth; the sin of this man was that he had no time for God. You might say that he was possessed by his possessions. The Bible says he fared sumptuously and was clothed in purple and fine linen.

In this culture, purple was the color of royalty. Clothing makers would crush a special worm and use the dye to produce this luxurious garment, only worn by the richest of the rich. And this man was clothed in purple and fine linen from head to foot. The account also tells us that this man "fared sumptuously *every day*." That's another way of saying he had a daily, nonstop banquet going on. He was apparently really into food and had unlimited resources to eat whatever he wanted.

It was a different story for the beggar lying out by the rich man's front gate. His name was Lazarus, and he was weak, covered with sores, and severely impoverished—to the point of starvation. Apparently he had been living off the scraps from the rich man's table—when he could get them.

In those days, people didn't eat with a knife and fork. They didn't use utensils at all. They would pick the food up with their hands using bits of bread, and then they would wipe their hands on pieces of bread and throw them on the floor for the dogs to eat.

That was Lazarus's diet. We are also told that he was carried to the rich man's estate and laid at his gate, which would imply that he was either disabled or so weak and sick that he couldn't walk.

Surely the rich man saw Lazarus's situation. He could have invited him to his table, or at the very least, sent a proper meal out to him. But he cared nothing about Lazarus. His mind was filled with "looking out for number one" and having his nonstop feast of pleasing himself.

But then death came.

And death is the great equalizer.

When the rich man died, it probably made all the papers. It was a big deal for a few hours. Then the poor man died, and it didn't even make a ripple on earth. No one really cared about him. But God did! And Lazarus was ushered into paradise by angels.

It was now time for the rich man to face the repercussions of living a life that had no room for God. And he was going to find out that it wasn't so glamorous on the other side.

Malcolm Forbes, one of the world's wealthiest men, said shortly before his death, "The thing I dread most about death is that I know I will not be as comfortable in the next life as I was in this one."[47]

I have no idea where Mr. Forbes was at spiritually, but for the sake of a point, if you don't know God, you can be sure it won't be as comfortable on the other side.

What Do We Learn from This Story?

1. People in hell suffer

The fact that this man spoke of torment indicates that suffering is a very real thing in the hereafter. In fact, the word *torment* is used four times in the text of this story. People in hell are fully conscious, and they are in pain. It doesn't say that this man went to purgatory. There is no such thing as a place called purgatory. Nor was he reincarnated as a higher or a lower life form. Once you pass from this life you pass into eternity in either heaven or hell. This man was in hell.

2. Once you are in hell, you can't cross over to heaven

Sometimes people will say, "When I stand before God, I've got the gift of gab, and me and the Man Upstairs will sort this out."

But there will be no more sorting out. It will be too late for that; once you are in eternity, there is no changing things.

It's different now. While there is life, it is still possible to change things—including your eternal destination! There are no chances after death, but thousands before.

The Bible says, "It is appointed for men to die once, but after this the judgment" (Hebrews 9:27).

Physical death is a separation of the soul from the body and constitutes a transition from the visible world to the invisible world. For the believer it is entrance into paradise, into the presence of Jesus. For the nonbeliever, it marks his entrance into Hades. Physical death is not the end of existence; it is only a change in the state of existence.

3. When you are in hell, you are conscious and fully aware of where you are

In hell you will know what you knew on earth, but far more. You will be cognizant of where you came from and where you are, just like this man, who speaks about his five brothers in verse 28. "I have five brothers," he says, "And someone needs to testify to them so they don't come to this place of torment."

In a way this man was blame shifting. It's as though he were saying, "Hey, I really didn't know about this. No one warned me!" Abraham, however, corrects him in verse 29: "They have Moses and the prophets. Let them hear them." And the man replies, "No, father Abraham; but if one goes to them from the dead, they will repent" (verse 39).

Really?

Well, one man actually did come back from the dead. His name was Lazarus too, but it wasn't the same Lazarus in this story. This Lazarus was a personal friend of Jesus', and the Lord raised him from the dead after he'd been in the tomb for four days.

But even though the miracle was verified by many people, it only made the religious leaders of the day more determined than ever to kill Jesus—and Lazarus, too, if they could manage it. And they were speaking this way even though they acknowledged, "This man certainly performs many miraculous signs" (John 11:47, NLT).

So here was a dead man who came back to life. But still the religious leaders refused to believe.

Even more to the point, Jesus Christ Himself rose again from the dead and was seen by as many as 500 people at one time. Did everyone believe? No. Really only a small percentage of the people made that choice. So the rich man's argument that someone coming back from the dead would cause his brothers to believe just wasn't true.

The Great White Throne

So after death, the nonbeliever goes to a place of torment. But that isn't the end of it. There is still a judgment yet to come, known as the Great White Throne—a terrible final judgment for nonbelievers only.

> Then I saw a great white throne and Him who sat on it, from whose face the earth and the heaven fled away. And there was found no place for them. And I saw the dead, small and great, standing before God, and books were opened. And another book was opened, which is the Book of Life. And the dead were judged according to their works, by the things which were written in the books. The sea gave up the dead who were in it, and Death and Hades delivered up the dead who were in them. And they were judged, each one according to his works. Then Death and Hades were cast into the lake of fire. This is the second death. And anyone not found written in the Book of Life was cast into the lake of fire. (Revelation 20:11-15)

Who will be at the Great White Throne Judgment?

Answer: Everyone who has rejected God's offer of forgiveness through Jesus Christ. Notice that there are no exceptions. Verse 12: "I saw the dead, small and great, standing before God, and books were opened."

God is no respecter of persons. The fact that a person may have been a king or a queen, an emperor or president, a prime minister or rock star doesn't matter. Everyone standing before that throne is in the same position, and each person has to give an account of his or her life.

Actor Robert De Niro was asked the question, "If there are pearly gates and you stand before God one day, what will you say to Him?"

De Niro's response was, "I will say to God that if heaven exists, He has a lot of explaining to do."[48]

No. I don't think so.

At this Great White Throne, everyone will have to give an account of the life they have lived. The big issue in this final judgment, however, won't be a *sin* issue as much as it will be a *Son* issue.

The greatest and final question in the last day will be, "What did You do with the offer of salvation in My Son, Jesus Christ?"

The apostle John put it very, very simply: "And this is the testimony: God has given us eternal life, and this life is in his Son. Whoever has the Son has life; whoever does not have the Son of God does not have life" (1 John 5:11-12, NIV).

The fact is, good people don't go to heaven. Forgiven people do. Because apart from the gift of righteousness in Jesus, no one is good enough.

Why Is a Person at the Great White Throne Judgment?

They will be there because they did not believe in Jesus and receive His offer of forgiveness and salvation.

In John 3:18, Jesus said, "He who believes in [the Son of God] is not condemned; but he who does not believe is condemned already, because he has not believed in the name of the only begotten Son of God."

If the nonbeliever is already condemned, then what is the purpose of the last judgment?

This is a very important question. The purpose of the final confrontation between God and man is to clearly demonstrate to the nonbeliever *why* he is already condemned.

If someone spoke up at that judgment and said, "Wait a second, I never knew about this," their argument would be refuted, because in Revelation 20:12, it says that the "books were opened." What are these books? We don't know for certain, but one of them may be a book of God's law. And everyone who has been exposed to the truth of God's law will be held responsible. As Romans 3:19 says, "That every mouth may be stopped, and all the world may become guilty before God."

I bring this up because some people will say, "I really don't need Jesus Christ. I just live by the Ten Commandments."

No, actually you don't.

Have you ever taken the Lord's name in vain—using it in an empty, insincere, frivolous way? Have you ever taken anything that didn't belong to you? Have you ever lied? Of course you have. The fact is, if you want to live by the law you're in deep trouble, because the Bible says, "If you offend in one point of the law you are guilty of all of it" (see James 2:10).

The law was never given to make a man or a woman righteous. The law is a moral mirror that shows us our real state before God—and its intent is to drive us into the open arms of Jesus. The law says, "You are not good enough. You need God's help."

Maybe another book opened at the Great White Throne would be a record of everything you have ever said or done. That's not so hard to believe, because in this high-tech world of ours, you're being recorded by some kind of surveillance camera almost everywhere you go. If you run a red light, you might get your picture taken, and there will be no getting out of that ticket.

If you think that mankind can do this in an increasingly effective way, don't you imagine that the Creator of the universe might have some pretty tricked-out and sophisticated recording equipment?

Actually, you can be sure of it.

The Bible tells us that everything that we do, whether good or bad, is recorded, and we will be judged for it:

> For God will bring every deed into judgment, including every hidden thing, whether it is good or evil. (Ecclesiastes 12:14, NIV)

> But I say to you that for every idle word men may speak, they will give account of it in the day of judgment. (Matthew 12:36)

The most important book of all, however, is the Book of Life. *"And anyone not found written in the Book of Life was cast into the lake of fire."*

Some people will say, "That's just not right. How could a God of love create a place called hell?"

The truth is, it is *because* He is a God of love that He created a place called hell. There are terrible injustices in this life and wrongs done that people should never get away with. And though they may escape the long arm of the law, they will never escape the long arm of God.

Justice will be done, and that justice will be final and complete.

Beyond all of that, however, hell was not made for people. Jesus said hell was created for the devil and his angels. It was never God's intention to send a person to hell, and He does everything He can to keep people out of hell.

But in the final analysis, it's our choice.

God has given to you and me a free will. I have the ability to choose, and God will not violate that. If you want to go to heaven, my friend, you will, if you put your faith in Christ. If you want to go to hell, you will. That is really your choice.

J. I. Packer wrote,

> Scripture sees hell as self-chosen. Hell appears as God's gesture of respect for human choice. All receive what they actually choose. Either to be with God forever worshipping Him or without God forever worshipping themselves.[49]

C. S. Lewis said,

> There are only two kinds of people in the end: those who say to God, 'Thy will be done,' and those to whom God says, in the end, 'Thy will be done.' All that are in hell, choose it. Without that self-choice there could be no Hell.[50]

Timothy Keller said,

> People only get in the afterlife what they most wanted. Either to have God as Savior and Master or to be their own saviors and masters. Hell is simply one's freely chosen path going on forever.[51]

In the end, we get what we most truly want.

It's not enjoyable to preach or write about these things. But if you belong to Jesus Christ, I hope that being reminded of these realities will make you want to redouble your efforts to reach people with the gospel. The Bible tells us to "rescue others by snatching them from the flames of judgment. Show mercy to still others, but do so with great caution, hating the sins that contaminate their lives" (Jude 23, NLT).

Sometimes we don't warn people about hell because we don't want to offend them. We're willing to talk about the glories of walking with Christ and how He gives us peace and joy and purpose, but the person just blows us off and says, "I don't need that. I'm happy enough as I am."

But there is a warning in the gospel too.

Yes, there is a heaven to gain, but there is also a hell to avoid.

Just a brief warning, but then the message turns positive again. God poured all of His judgment on Jesus 2,000 years ago at the cross so you and I would not have to go to a place called hell. And He will forgive you of every wrong you have ever done if you will turn to Him.

And right now would be the best time of all.

10 Angels and Demons, Part 1

There is an invisible world.

It's difficult for us to believe and accept that sometimes, because we live in the natural world. We relate to what we can see, hear, taste, smell, or touch. Even so, the Bible teaches there is an invisible, supernatural world, the realm of God and Satan and of angels and demons. And it's all around us.

Right now if we could somehow pull back the veil, it would blow our minds to see what we would see. To see the angels of God at work. To see the demons of hell at work. To see all the spiritual activity swirling around us at any given moment.

The book of 2 Kings gives us a glimpse of these unseen realities in an illuminating account of the prophet Elisha and his servant, Gehazi. They were in an Israelite town called Dothan when Gehazi got up one morning and saw to his horror that the whole town was ringed about by enemy soldiers. In a panic, Gehazi ran to wake up his master with the news.

"What are we going to do?" he wailed.

We can imagine Elisha sitting up in bed and wiping the sleep out of his eyes, trying to digest this information. Apparently it didn't take him long, because we read these words:

> So he [Elijah] answered, "Do not fear, for those who are with us are more than those who are with them." And Elisha prayed, and said, "LORD, I pray, open his eyes that he may see." Then the LORD opened the eyes of the young man, and he saw. And behold, the mountain was full of horses and chariots of fire all around Elisha. (2 Kings 6:16-17)

"Open his eyes . . ."

And if our spiritual eyes could be opened for a moment or two, we, too, would see the angelic forces of God, surrounding us and protecting us. Right along with Elisha we would say, "Those who are with us are more than those who are with them."

A recent *Time* magazine article revealed that a whopping 69 percent of Americans believe in the existence of angels, and 48 percent believe they have their own guardian angel. And 32 percent even said they had felt some kind of angelic presence in their life at some point. These statistics show us again that in a broad sense, we are a spiritual people and believe in an unseen, supernatural world.[52]

Many of us believe in angels because we've sensed an angelic presence in some close brush with death. We've lived through a moment where we could have been easily killed—in an accident on the job or maybe in a car or motorcycle. And when it was over, after our pounding heart slowed down a little, we couldn't help wondering, *Did an angel intervene on my behalf?*

Questionable Sources

Many, if not most, Americans have picked up a lot of our information and impressions about angels from television and Hollywood.

And that's not good.

Over the years, Hollywood has hijacked the topic of angels, which has led to some significant distortions (to say the least).

We might think of the angel Clarence, trying to earn his wings by helping Jimmy Stewart in the holiday favorite *It's a Wonderful Life*. Or maybe we caught several episodes of that old TV program *Touched by an Angel*. In a movie called *The Preacher's Wife*, Whitney Houston's character is visited by an angel portrayed by Denzel Washington. In the movie *City of Angels*, Nicholas Cage plays an angel who falls in love with Meg Ryan. In the end, he decides to give up his rights as an angel and become a human.

As a result of these portrayals, we may have acquired strange ideas that angels are exalted humans or have to earn their wings, or any number of off-the-wall beliefs, to the point that we really don't know what we believe about angels.

In fact, there is only one reliable source of information on God, Satan, angels, and demons, and that is Scripture. And as it turns out, the Bible actually has quite a bit to say about these things.

Angels on Task

The activity of angels, especially in the lives of believers, is constant. We may not necessarily be aware of the presence of angels or be able to predict how and where they might appear, but the Bible says that we can count on the fact that they're there—and perhaps nearer to our daily lives and doings than we might have imagined.

In Psalm 34:7 (NLT), "For the angel of the LORD is a guard; he surrounds and defends all who fear him."

Did you know there are at least 300 references to angels in the Old and New Testaments? In these passages, God pulls back the curtain a little and allows us to see angels at work in the lives of believers.

A good example is when Simon Peter was arrested for preaching the gospel in the book of Acts, chapter 12. The passage tells us that the church was earnestly praying for him. In answer to the church's fervent prayers, God dispatched an angel to deliver the imprisoned apostle. Peter, however, was so deeply asleep that the angel had to practically shake him and punch him to wake him up and get him moving. After that, the heavenly rescuer led Peter right through the prison doors and gates (that opened automatically for them) and out into the street, a free man.

That's the way it is in example after biblical example. When we cry out to God in a time of danger or distress, He might choose to dispatch an angel to help us.

I love the story in the book of Genesis where Jacob is on his way home and scared spitless about meeting up with his estranged brother, Esau. The Bible says, "Jacob went on his way, and the angels of God met him. When Jacob saw them, he said, 'This is God's camp.' And he called the name of that place Mahanaim [or, two camps]" (Genesis 32:1-2).

If we could only see, we would understand that we're *always* in God's camp.

Angels are amazing creatures, immortal, and sometimes traveling between heaven and earth. In Luke 20:36, Jesus said of people who have gone on to heaven, "Nor can they die anymore, for they are equal to the angels and are sons of God, being sons of the resurrection."

Angels have a special work to accomplish in the lives of believers. We know that because Hebrews 1:14 tells us, "Are they not all ministering spirits sent forth to minister for those who will inherit salvation?"

Many of us who have been believers for years have heard story after story of the work of angels in believers' lives.

First-Person Accounts

I'm reminded of a contemporary account from Billy Graham's classic book, *Angels: God's Secret Agents.* In that book, Billy tells the story of John Patton, who was a missionary to the New Hebrides islands. On one particular night, Patton and his wife were in their home at the mission station and got word of an imminent attack by people who were indigenous to that region and wanted to kill them.

Knowing this, John and his wife began to pray. Hours passed, however, and all was peaceful; no attack ever came. The next morning there was no sign of their enemies, and the missionaries wondered what had happened.

A year or so later, the chief of the tribe that had wanted to kill the Pattons received Jesus Christ as his Savior. On one occasion John was having a conversation with this chief and said, "I have to ask you what happened that night when you were coming to kill us. Why didn't you follow through on it?"

The chief replied, "What do you mean, why didn't we go through with it? Who were all of those men there with you?"

"There were no men there," Patton replied.

But the chief would have none of it. "We didn't attack," he said, "because there were hundreds of big men in shining garments with drawn swords, circling the mission station."

And in that moment, John knew that he and his wife had been guarded by a contingent of angels.[53]

I would even take this subject of encounters with angels a step further. It's entirely possible that you have personally met an angel. We are told in Hebrews 13:1-2, "Let brotherly love continue. Do not forget to entertain strangers, for by so doing some have unwittingly entertained angels."

Now if I knew I was entertaining an angel, I would definitely take good care of him, wouldn't you?

"Hi. I'm an angel from God. Can you take me to lunch?"

"Yes, certainly. Where would you like to go?"

But what if the Lord sent someone to me who wasn't the kind of a person I would necessarily want to hang around with? What if he sent an unattractive or a difficult person, of the sort I wouldn't normally be inclined to help?

I've often thought about that.

While angels aren't human and have never been human, they sometimes take on human form, appearing as young men. By the way, there is no instance in the Bible of an angel appearing as a woman. It's funny, because our culture loves to use that word *angel* in a feminine sense. We'll say, "Oh, she is as pretty as an angel," or, "She sings like an angel." And often in religious art through the years, angels have been portrayed as female. In the Bible, however, when they take on a human form, it's always male.

I've always liked Billy Graham's book title, identifying angels with the designation of "God's secret agents." In other words, they're an elite fighting force, like the Navy Seals. When the Seals are dispatched on a mission, they go in, take care of business, and you rarely hear about it. It's not publicized. You don't know the names of the Seals that did thus and so. You may read about the success of a given mission, but you never learn any of the details.

Like the Seals, angels are sent out on missions all the time. They are "ministering spirits" who protect, deliver, guide, and bring messages from God. You don't need to engage them, and you don't need to try to communicate with them. Just step back and let them do their jobs, the work that God has called them to do.

I think we would be stunned beyond words if we could see how often (and how many) angels become involved in our day-to-day lives.

As you're no doubt aware, 3-D movies have made a big comeback. Not long ago, Cathe and I went to see an animated 3-D movie with our daughter-in-law and our granddaughter, Stella. When we put those 3-D glasses on Stella and she saw those things coming at her from the screen, she started screaming, pulled off the glasses, and wouldn't watch the movie.

My wife and my daughter-in-law took her out to the lobby, but I wanted to stay and watch the movie! I was totally engrossed.

What if we could put on 3-D glasses or 4-D glasses that would allow us to see into the spiritual dimension and watch angels and demons at work? It would be glorious, yes, but also terrifying.

In fact, if an angel appeared before you at this very moment, your temptation would be to worship him, because he would be so glorious and magnificent. That's exactly what happened to the apostle John on the island of Patmos. (And this is a guy you'd think would know better!)

The book of Revelation tells us that when John encountered one of God's angels, he fell at the angel's feet to worship him. But the angel quickly warned him, "Do not do that! I am your fellow servant, and of your brethren who have the testimony of Jesus. Worship God!" (Revelation 19:10).

This is a particularly interesting passage, because it underlines the fact that angels don't like to draw attention to themselves. They seek to shift the focus back to God, where it always belongs.

Tread Very Carefully

Even so, our culture has what you might call an obsession with angels. Go into any bookstore, and you see book after book about them. Just recently I went to Amazon.com and typed in the keyword *angel*. It seemed to me that a lot of the books that came up had an unbiblical approach to this topic.

The trouble with being so interested in contacting angels and talking to angels is that you might end up with the wrong kind of angel—a fallen one, otherwise known as a demon. That's why the apostle said, "But even if we, or an angel from heaven, preach any other gospel to you than what we have preached to you, let him be accursed" (Galatians 1:8).

Why would an angel bring a message contrary to the gospel? Because he would be a fallen angel. Satan, the devil himself, is a fallen angel. He used to be a magnificent, powerful, high-ranking angel who had access to the presence of God, but he rebelled against the Lord and became the adversary of God and humanity. However, Scripture tells us that he's kept his old clothes; he can still appear as an "angel of light" (2 Corinthians 11:14).

If the devil were to appear to you today (God forbid!), he would not have red skin, horns, and a pointed tail, nor would he be carrying a little pitchfork. That is a caricature. The real devil, originally named Lucifer, or "son of the morning," was a magnificent being. (More about that in the pages to come.)

So we must be very, very careful. When people tell you they've had contact with angels, they might very well be listening to the wrong kind of angel, opening themselves up to dangerous demonic influence.

How Many Angels Are Out There?

More than we could probably even count.

In the book of Daniel, the prophet speaks in terms of "a thousand thousands," and "ten thousand times ten thousand" (Daniel 7:10). The book of Revelation uses the same terminology.

Angels are not only numerous, they are very powerful. Psalm 103:20 tells us they "excel in strength." Angels aren't as powerful as God, but they are vastly more powerful than people. And it would appear that some angels are mightier than others.

There are also ranks among the angels. In 1 Peter 3:22, we read that Jesus Christ has gone into heaven and is at God's right hand "with angels, authorities and powers in submission to Him" (NIV). That same ranking, I would assume, also applies to fallen angels. Paul warns us, "We do not wrestle against flesh and blood, but against principalities, against powers, against the rulers of the darkness of this age, against spiritual hosts of wickedness in the heavenly places" (Ephesians 6:12).

The angels of God are organized under the command of the Lord Jesus Christ; the fallen angels are organized under the command of Lucifer, the fallen angel.

There are only three angels that we know for sure by name. One is Michael, the other is Gabriel, and the third is Lucifer, who became Satan. We'll look at Lucifer more closely in the next chapter.

Michael

Michael is identified in the New Testament book of Jude, verse 9, as "the archangel." Does that mean there are no other archangels? Possibly. The term archangel occurs twice in the New Testament, and in both instances it is used in the singular and is preceded by the definite article *the*. As in, *the* archangel. So there may only be one.

It's interesting that he will play a unique role in the rapture of the church. In 1 Thessalonians 4:16-17, we read:

> For the Lord Himself will descend from heaven with a shout, with the voice of an archangel, and with the trumpet of God. And the dead in Christ will rise first. Then we who are alive and remain shall be caught up together with them in the clouds to meet the Lord in the air.

We also know that Michael is called in when lower ranking angels need help. There is a fascinating story in Daniel chapter 10, where the prophet was praying, and the Lord dispatched an angel with an answer to his prayer. After quite a delay, the angel finally showed up and said these words:

> Then he said to me, "Do not fear, Daniel, for from the first day that you set your heart to understand, and to humble yourself before your God, your words were heard; and I have come because of your words. But the prince of the kingdom of Persia withstood me twenty-one days; and behold, Michael, one of the chief princes, came to help me. . . ." (verses 12-13)

To paraphrase: "Daniel, I have to tell you why there seems to be a delay in the answer to your prayer. I was dispatched from heaven twenty-one days ago with an answer, but I was opposed by a powerful fallen spirit identified as the prince of Persia. I couldn't handle him, so Michael came and overpowered that demon entity, and I was free to then come and bring you the answer to your prayer."

What a stunning account! And it underlines the fact that there is ranking among angels and that some are more powerful than others. (Michael, it seems, is *very* powerful.) But it also reminds us that when we pray, our prayers may unleash an invisible spiritual battle, and the so-called delay to your prayer is due to angelic battles going on behind the scenes.

Please hear this: When you are praying for someone's salvation, when you are praying for a prodigal son or daughter to repent, *don't give up.* You have no idea what is happening behind the scenes, in the spirit world, as you pray. Don't assume that God is saying no to your prayer because the answer doesn't come quickly. He might be saying no today, but maybe He will say yes tomorrow, or the day after. Just keep praying!

God's delays are not necessarily His denials.

We also know that Michael ultimately overcomes Satan himself, as revealed in Revelation 12, where the apostle John speaks about a war in heaven:

Then war broke out in heaven. Michael and his angels fought against the dragon, and the dragon and his angels fought back. But he was not strong enough, and they lost their place in heaven. The great dragon was hurled down—that ancient serpent called the devil, or Satan, who leads the whole world astray. He was hurled to the earth, and his angels with him. (verses 7-9, NIV)

So ultimately, Michael the archangel will overcome Lucifer the fallen angel.

Gabriel

Now Gabriel, though maybe not an archangel, is certainly a high-ranking angel. Gabriel appears in both the Old and New Testaments. In Daniel, he appears to the prophet with a revelation of the future. At the beginning of the new covenant, he appears to Zechariah and tells him he is going to be the father of the last of the Old Testament prophets—John the Baptist, the direct forerunner of the Messiah.

Gabriel was also given the privilege of appearing to a young girl named Mary living in Nazareth, to tell her she would be the mother of the Messiah. Can you imagine getting *that* mission?

Cherubim and Seraphim

We don't know very much about these awesome beings, but they, too, are angels. Interestingly, after Adam and Eve had been ejected from the Garden of Eden for eating the forbidden fruit, God placed cherubim and a flaming sword outside the garden to guard the way to the tree of life.

We read about the seraphim in Isaiah 6:1-3, where it says,

In the year that King Uzziah died, I saw the Lord seated on a throne, high and exalted, and the train of his robe filled the temple. Above him were seraphs, each with six wings: With two wings they covered their faces, with two they covered their feet, and with two they were flying. And they were calling to one another: Holy, holy, holy is the LORD Almighty; the whole earth is full of his glory. (NIV)

Now, as you are reading these descriptions of God's mighty angels, you might be thinking to yourself, "Okay. Fine. But what does all this actually have to do with me and my life?"

Actually, more than you might imagine.

Takeaway Truths About Angels

Angels can reveal God's purposes

You may remember that angels were dispatched to Abraham to reveal to him the judgment that was about to fall on the cities of the plain. And in the New Testament, I already mentioned how an angel was sent to Zechariah to tell him he would be the father of John the Baptist, and also to Mary and Joseph, declaring God's purposes and giving them special instructions.

Angels have come to help bring us to salvation

There is a fascinating story in the book of Acts where an angel came to Cornelius, a Roman centurion who did not know the Lord yet, but was open to the things of the Lord. In that instance, the angel revealed to this Roman officer that he needed to meet Simon Peter, who would give to him the gospel.

Have you ever read that story and asked yourself, *Why didn't the angel do that himself? Why didn't this very knowledgeable and ultracompetent envoy from heaven just straight-out tell him? Why didn't he give Cornelius the gospel, instead of linking him up with a Christian who was miles away?*

Why? Because the primary mission of angels is not to preach the gospel. That is our job. They will help us do it, and they might even guide us in our efforts to do it. But God chooses to primarily reach people through people.

Now if I were God, I don't think I would do it that way. It would seem more efficient to me to just use angels. Angels would always command attention, would always get their facts straight, and wouldn't get distracted or beat around the bush.

But I'm not God (you can be thankful for that), and for whatever reason, He has made a different choice. He reaches people through people, with angels working behind the scenes. In this story, the angel was there to direct Cornelius to go to Peter so he could hear the gospel.

Another example of angelic direction is in Acts 8 when an angel came to Philip and said, "Go to the desert." And when Philip obeyed and went to that designated place in the wilderness, he came across the path of an Ethiopian official in a chariot, who had come all the way to Jerusalem seeking knowledge of God and was now on his way home. And after Philip presented the gospel to him, the man came to faith in Christ.

Angels can protect us

Daniel was a senior advisor to King Darius, the Mede. With great wisdom and integrity, he had been advising the kings of Babylon and Medo-Persia for many years. Abundantly blessed by God and in high favor with the king, Daniel also had some enemies—people who were envious of his success.

Politics never change very much, do they? The first thing these enemies of Daniel tried to do was dig up a little dirt on his life, so they could discredit him and undermine him. So they had a meeting and started looking for ways to bring Daniel down. What were his inconsistencies? What were his weak spots and vulnerabilities? They turned loose the best dirt-diggers, private detectives, and tabloid reporters in the kingdom.

And they came up with *nothing*. A big zero. This was a man of true integrity, without any hidden skeletons in his closet.

Finally they decided, "If we're going to bring this guy down, there's only one way to do it. It has to be concerning him and his God." They concluded this because they knew Daniel had a rock-solid habit of praying three times a day. It was no secret! He would get down on his knees, open up the shutters of his house, and call on the Lord.

They said, "Let's get a law passed that says no one can pray to any god except the king, and if you violate this law, you are thrown into a den of lions. It has to work! Because we all know Daniel's going to keep right on praying."

The king, untroubled by anything approaching humility, thought it was a great idea and signed it into law. In doing so, however, he had no idea he was signing his friend Daniel's death warrant.

So Daniel heard the message: Anybody who prays to any god beside the king will be fed to the lions. And he said, "Really? That's interesting. Now, if you'll excuse me, it's time to go pray."

He prayed to the Lord just as they knew he would, so he was arrested and sentenced to be executed. There was no way out of this situation apart from God.

Let's pick up the story in Daniel chapter 6.

So the king gave the command, and they brought Daniel and cast him into the den of lions. But the king spoke, saying to Daniel, "Your God, whom you serve continually, He will deliver you." Then a stone was brought and laid on the mouth of the den, and the king sealed it with his own signet ring and with the signets of his lords, that the purpose concerning Daniel might not be changed.

Now the king went to his palace and spent the night fasting; and no musicians were brought before him. Also his sleep went from him. Then the king arose very early in the morning and went in haste to the den of lions. And when he came to the den, he cried out with a lamenting voice to Daniel. The king spoke, saying to Daniel, "Daniel, servant of the living God, has your God, whom you serve continually, been able to deliver you from the lions?"

Then Daniel said to the king, "O king, live forever! My God sent His angel and shut the lions' mouths, so that they have not hurt me, because I was found innocent before Him; and also, O king, I have done no wrong before you." (verses 16-22)

I'm thinking that Daniel—in a den full of hungry lions—had a good night's sleep. The king, however, with all his musicians and luxury and comfort hadn't been able to sleep at all. Better to be in a lion's den with Jesus than anywhere else without Him! Better to be in the valley of the shadow of death with Christ walking next to me than in the finest home with all of the money this world has to offer. I would rather be anywhere with the Lord than anywhere else without Him.

Maybe you find yourself in something like a lion's den right now. You're surrounded by hostile people, find yourself up against overwhelming odds, or you're walking through a time of great difficulty. Yet the Lord is with you in your dark, confined space, as surely as He was with Daniel. And His angels will protect you until it's time for you to head home to heaven.

When Daniel got that sentence of "death by lions," he probably thought to himself, *What's the worst that could happen? If I get torn apart by lions, I go to heaven to be with my Lord. If I live, I continue to serve the Lord.*

The words of David in Psalm 31:14-15 may have very well come to Daniel's mind in that moment:

> But as for me, I trust in You, O LORD;
> I say, "You are my God."
> My times are in Your hand.

As it turned out, it wasn't Daniel's time just yet. So the Lord sent His angel to shut the lions' mouths.

Sometimes animals have more sense than people. Those lions probably took one look at the angel and said, "We're not messing with him. Better to skip this meal."

Angels can give us guidance

I'm reminded of the story of Balaam and his donkey, in Numbers chapter 22. Apparently Balaam was a prophet for hire, and the king of Moab had a big job for him. The Moabite ruler wanted Balaam to curse the Israelites as they were passing through the wilderness on their way to the Promised Land.

The Lord spoke to Balaam and said, "Don't you dare curse those people. They belong to Me." But Balaam was determined to get the money and was soon on his way, riding on his donkey in the wrong direction to do the wrong thing. That's where we'll pick up the story:

> Balaam got up in the morning, saddled his donkey, and went off with the noblemen from Moab. As he was going, though, God's anger flared. The angel of God stood in the road to block his way.

Balaam was riding his donkey, accompanied by his two servants. When the donkey saw the angel blocking the road and brandishing a sword, she veered off the road into the ditch. Balaam beat the donkey and got her back on the road.

But as they were going through a vineyard, with a fence on either side, the donkey again saw God's angel blocking the way and veered into the fence, crushing Balaam's foot against the fence. Balaam hit her again.

God's angel blocked the way yet again—a very narrow passage this time; there was no getting through on the right or left. Seeing the angel, Balaam's donkey sat down under him. Balaam lost his temper; he beat the donkey with his stick.

Then God gave speech to the donkey. She said to Balaam: "What have I ever done to you that you have beat me these three times?"

Balaam said, "Because you've been playing games with me! If I had a sword I would have killed you by now."

The donkey said to Balaam, "Am I not your trusty donkey on whom you've ridden for years right up until now? Have I ever done anything like this to you before? Have I?"

He said, "No."

Then God helped Balaam see what was going on: He saw God's angel blocking the way, brandishing a sword. Balaam fell to the ground, his face in the dirt. (Numbers 22:21-31, MSG)

Yes, there are angels involved in our lives. And sometimes they may stop us from doing the wrong thing or guide us to do the right thing.

I welcome that. I'll take all the help I can get to please the Lord and do the right thing.

Do we have guardian angels? We may. We are told by Jesus that we should not look down on the little ones, meaning the children. He said, "For I say to you that in heaven their angels always see the face of My Father" (Matthew 18:10). So it may be that at least children have guardian angels. And I'm sure we all know some children who *need* guardian angels, because they're always getting into trouble. In fact, they may have worn out a few angels along the way.

But believers aren't always protected from death and injury, are we? What about the times when the lion's mouth isn't closed? What about when someone doesn't narrowly miss that brush with death? What about when death takes us unexpectedly? Does that mean the angels missed their opportunity or were asleep on the job?

No, it means they have another mission now.

Angels did not determine the time when I was born, nor will they determine the time when I'm going to die. That is up to God. Up until the time of our passing, the role of the angel is to guide, to protect, or possibly redirect us. But when the time has come for us to enter into eternity, the role of the angel is to give us an escort into the presence of God.

Escorting Us to Heaven

In Jesus' story of Lazarus and the rich man in Luke 16, we're told how a poor beggar passes out of this life and enters heaven. Jesus said, "The time came when the beggar died and the angels carried him to Abraham's side" (verse 22, NIV).

Death knocks at every door and is no respecter of persons.

Do you have that hope? Do you know for certain that you will go to heaven when you die? Prior to leaving on a recent trip, I was called to visit with a man who had terminal cancer. I had been told he might not make it another week. I had actually thought about visiting with him after I got back from my trip, but I decided I'd better get out there before I left, even though I felt under some time pressure.

So I went to see him. I could tell he was failing physically, yet he remained alert and aware, and we talked at length. There was no question of hiding his condition from him. In fact, he told me himself, "I don't have much longer." So I talked to him about heaven. He had already placed his faith in Jesus, but I wanted to be sure that he was ready.

Finally I said, "Would you like to pray with me right now?" He said yes, and we prayed. He prayed earnestly and with great passion. And after we were done praying, I comforted him with the promises of God. Finally I said, "I will come back and see you Saturday." But then I got the call late Friday night that he had died.

He took his last breath and may very well have seen God's majestic, beautiful angels arriving to escort him into the presence of God.

And he was ready.

Are you?

11 Angels and Demons, Part 2

Demons are fallen angels.

As hard as it may be to conceive or believe, there was a rebellion in the angelic world with many of the angels turning against God and becoming evil. The book of Jude speaks of "angels who did not keep their positions of authority but abandoned their proper dwelling" (Jude 6, NIV).

A high-ranking angel named Lucifer led this rebellion of one-third of the angels against God. There are multiple references to this in the Bible. We read of "Beelzebub, the ruler of the demons" in Matthew 12:24 and "the dragon and his angels" in Revelation 12:7. Jesus said that hell itself was prepared for the devil and his angels (see Matthew 25:41).

So what is the objective of a demon? What has a demon come to do? Their objectives seem to be twofold: to seek to hinder the purposes of God and to extend the power of Satan.

When we say, "I was tempted by the devil the other day," chances are it wasn't the devil himself.

We need to understand that the devil is not God's equal. Though he is a powerful spirit being, Satan's power is nowhere near being the equal of God, which means he can only be in one place at one time. God, however, is *omnipresent*, meaning He is everywhere at once. When you and I are tempted, then, it's probably the activity of one of Satan's demons, doing his dirty work for him.

The apostle Paul spoke about his heart's desire to visit with the church in Thessalonica, but told them, "Therefore we wanted to come to you—even I, Paul, time and again—but Satan hindered us" (1 Thessalonians 2:18). To another group of believers, he spoke of a physical affliction, which he described as a "thorn in the flesh." He went on to say that it was "a messenger from Satan to torment me" (2 Corinthians 12:7, NLT). Through these and many other passages we note there is an army of demons who will oppose us as we seek to do the work of God.

Why Is There a Devil?

As I mentioned in the last chapter, many of us visualize the devil as a cartoonish caricature rather than a living, powerful, spirit being. As a result, we may not take him as seriously as we ought to.

C. S. Lewis gave this insightful statement about the devil and his demons:

> There are two equal and opposite errors into which our race can fall about the devils. One is to disbelieve in their existence. The other is to believe, and to feel an excessive and unhealthy interest in them. They themselves are equally pleased by both errors, and hail a materialist or a magician with the same delight.[54]

It's true; the devil is perfectly content if we don't believe in him. He may even be thinking, *Hey, this is great. I will manipulate your life, and you don't even believe I'm there. That's a good deal for me.* On the other extreme, you can have an unhealthy interest in him and demonic powers. There are some people who see demons behind every rock, and everything is about the devil all the time. That's just as unhealthy as the first error.

The truth is, we need a balanced, biblical view of who Satan is. Why? Because, frankly, he loves the attention. The devil is the ultimate egotist.

But we ask the question, where did the devil come from? What are his tactics? What are his strengths? What are his weaknesses? What can he do? What can't he do? Let's seek to answer some of those questions from Scripture.

Where Did the Devil Come From?

How could a God of love create someone as horrible as the devil?

The very question itself sounds like an accusation, obviously implying it was a bad decision on the part of God.

But God did not create the devil as we know him today.

The Lord created a spirit being, a mighty angel known as Lucifer, or "son of the morning." Lucifer, however, exercised the free will God had given him and rebelled against his creator. In so doing, he chose to be God's adversary and became Satan. The devil, then, was not created by God. The devil became what he is by his own volition.

On the other hand, God certainly allowed it.

When did this happen? We can't know for sure, but in Genesis 1:31 we read that "God saw everything that He had made, and indeed it was very good." By the time we get to Genesis 3, we encounter the serpent, who is tempting Eve. Something must have happened, then, between Genesis 1 and 3 that led to this vast angelic rebellion.

But it didn't start that way.

Lucifer was once a high-ranking angel. A radiant, beautiful being. In the book of Ezekiel, we have a fascinating description of Lucifer's fall:

"You were the seal of perfection, full of wisdom and perfect in beauty. You were in Eden, the garden of God; every precious stone adorned you: carnelian, chrysolite and emerald, topaz, onyx and jasper, lapis lazuli, turquoise and beryl. Your settings and mountings were made of gold; on the day you were created they were prepared. You were anointed as a guardian cherub, for so I ordained you. You were on the holy mount of God; you walked among the fiery stones. You were blameless in your ways from the day you were created till wickedness was found in you. Through your widespread trade you were filled with violence, and you sinned. So I drove you in disgrace from the mount of God, and I expelled you, guardian cherub, from among the fiery stones. Your heart became proud on account of your beauty, and you corrupted your wisdom because of your splendor. So I threw you to the earth; I made a spectacle of you before kings. By your many sins and dishonest trade you have desecrated your sanctuaries. So I made a fire come out from you, and it consumed you, and I reduced you to ashes on the ground in the sight of all who were watching. All the nations who knew you are appalled at you; you have come to a horrible end and will be no more." (28:12-19, NIV)

Have you ever seen a really beautiful girl or handsome guy who *knows* how attractive they are? Everything they do sort of draws attention to themselves. They've never met a mirror they didn't like, and the world just seems to revolve around them. Every conversation ultimately ends up being about them.

That is what Lucifer was like. He was this magnificent spirit being who was clearly a wonder to behold. And that very beauty became his downfall, as he allowed his perfection to become the cause of his corruption. Lucifer, you see, wasn't satisfied with worshiping God. He wanted a piece of the action. He wanted to be worshiped himself, and this "guardian cherub," once an exquisite angel of God, lost his former exalted position in heaven.

Lucifer became Satan when he fell to the earth. In Isaiah we read,

How you are fallen from heaven,
O Lucifer, son of the morning!
How you are cut down to the ground,
You who weakened the nations!

For you have said in your heart:
I will ascend into heaven,
I will exalt my throne above the stars of God;
I will also sit on the mount of the congregation
On the farthest sides of the north;
I will ascend above the heights of the clouds,
I will be like the Most High.
Yet you shall be brought down to Sheol,
To the lowest depths of the Pit.
(Isaiah 14:12-15)

Jesus says, "I saw Satan fall as lightning from heaven."[55] And as we have noted, when Satan fell he did not fall alone, but took one-third of the angels with him.[56]

That's the bad news. The good news is that-two-thirds of the angels are still with us. We have more angels than he has! But even more importantly, we have the Lord Jesus Christ on our side.

Even though he has fallen, however, Satan still has access to heaven. How do we know this? Because we read in the book of Job how the angels came to present themselves before the Lord, and Satan was among them. God directed His remarks to the devil himself:

"Where have you come from?" the LORD asked Satan. And Satan answered the LORD, "I have been patrolling the earth, watching everything that's going on." (Job 2:2, NLT)

That is just so creepy, isn't it? He is watching everything, checking things out, and his intent toward mankind in general and Christians in particular is all evil all the time.

The Bible describes the devil as a roaring lion, seeking whom he may devour.[57] He's like a hungry beast of prey looking for his next meal—and ready to pounce.

Have you seen some of those wildlife TV shows, where they film a pride of lions checking out a herd of antelope? The big cats are just hanging out in the sunshine, soaking up the rays, watching the antelope in the distance, and kind of sizing them up.

You can almost read their thoughts. *Let's see, which one am I going to eat today?* Inevitably, there's an antelope that's a little slow, and he falls behind the rest of the herd. He has V-I-C-T-I-M written all over him. And the lion says to himself, "That looks like lunch to me, because it's a hot day, and I really don't want to work too hard." Suddenly, he lunges, catches up to the dawdling antelope, and drags it down.

It's an analogy of the way the devil and his demons watch human beings. (Remember his words? *"I have been patrolling the earth, watching everything that's going on."*) He watches. He waits. He looks for weakness. He probes vulnerabilities. He strategizes on the best way to bring someone down. That is his basic agenda.

And by the way, he's at it 24/7. He never takes a vacation. Don't you wish he did? Wouldn't it be great if I could announce to you, "Guess what I just found out? Satan is taking August off every year. We can have August devil-free."

But no. Our adversary the devil doesn't take a month off—or a week, or a day, or an hour. He is always busy with his well-organized network of demon powers, helping him to accomplish his purposes.

What is the devil's purpose? We could cite any number of things, but here is the endgame, as summarized by Jesus Himself: "The thief's purpose is to steal and kill and destroy" (John 10:10, NLT).

Satan may come with some enticing temptation—something that dazzles you or thrills you or has an element of temporary enjoyment in the beginning. But the endgame, the ultimate result, is to steal, kill, and destroy.

Names of the Evil One

When Jesus was casting demons out of people, the Pharisees falsely claimed He did it by the power of *Beelzebub*, the prince of the demons. The name Beelzebub meant "lord of the flies," and the Jews later changed it to the "lord of the dunghill." So that is what Satan is the lord of: the dunghill.

Satan is also identified as the *prince of this world*. Jesus said, "Now is the time for judgment on this world; now the prince of this world will be driven out. And I, when I am lifted up from the earth, will draw all people to myself" (John 12:31-32, NIV).

Prince of this world? Isn't that a little surprising, hearing Jesus give Satan that title? No, that is exactly what Satan is at this present time. When Jesus was in the wilderness, being tempted by the devil, the evil one showed Him all the kingdoms of the world in a moment of time and said, "All this authority I will give You, and their glory; for this has been delivered to me, and I give it to whomever I wish. Therefore, if You will worship before me, all will be Yours" (Luke 4:6-7).

Effectively, the enemy was saying, "Jesus, I know why You have come. You have come to purchase back that which was lost in the Garden of Eden. But I'm going to make You an offer You cannot refuse. I will give You what You want. Right now! It is all Yours, if you will give me the momentary satisfaction of worship. I want You to worship me."

Of course, Jesus resisted that temptation. But it highlights an interesting point. When Satan claimed authority over the kingdoms of the world, *Jesus did not refute this*. Why? Because it is true . . . for now.

Until Jesus returns to earth as King of Kings and Lord of Lords, Satan is the *prince of the power of the air*. He is also identified as the god of this world. So he is the one that controls so much of our culture today.

Have you ever wondered why things are as dark as they are? It's really no great mystery. There is an evil mastermind behind it all. We are talking about a spirit power that infiltrates culture, government, the entertainment world, religious institutions, and the lives of men and women. Day after day, he continues to pull people down with him into temptation, sin, corruption, and death.

Ah, but the devil is clever. If someone isn't attracted by one of his lures, he says, "Okay, so you're not into that particular bait. No problem. I've got lots more where that came from."

If the "prince of darkness" image proves to be a turnoff, he also has the ability to mimic some of his former beauty and can come to us as "an angel of light."[58]

Sometimes a person will say, "I'm not into all of that darkness and immorality. I want to learn spirituality. I want to be a religious person."

The devil says, "Really? I've got that covered too. Check out my New Age mysticism. Check out all the tolerant, multicultural beliefs I can offer you. I can do a customized package for you, with a little of this and a little of that. All roads lead to God, right?"

No, not right. The devil lies about this and a lot of other things as well. Jesus points this out to us in John 8:44 when He says,

> You belong to your father, the devil, and you want to carry out your father's desire. He was a murderer from the beginning, not holding to the truth, for there is no truth in him. When he lies, he speaks his native language, for he is a liar and the father of lies. (NIV)

Sometimes the devil can just outright lie and a person will immediately swallow the falsehood. He will say to someone, "Right isn't actually right. In fact, it is wrong that is right." And the individual will respond, "Oh, really? That's interesting. Didn't know that. Okay, I believe it." Other people are a little more discerning, so he will candy-coat his lie with enough truth to make it appealing.

How long has he been employing that technique? Only since the beginning of time!

The First Big Lie

Right from the get-go, Satan has employed his tactic of mixing just a little bit of truth with a deadly dose of outright falsehood. It worked so well in the Garden of Eden that he's been using it ever since.

> Now the serpent was more cunning than any beast of the field which the LORD God had made. And he said to the woman, "Has God indeed said, 'You shall not eat of every tree of the garden'?"
>
> And the woman said to the serpent, "We may eat the fruit of the trees of the garden; but of the fruit of the tree which is in the midst of the garden, God has said, 'You shall not eat it, nor shall you touch it, lest you die.'
>
> Then the serpent said to the woman, "You will not surely

die. For God knows that in the day you eat of it your eyes will be opened, and you will be like God, knowing good and evil."

So when the woman saw that the tree was good for food, that it was pleasant to the eyes, and a tree desirable to make one wise, she took of its fruit and ate. She also gave to her husband with her, and he ate. Then the eyes of both of them were opened, and they knew that they were naked; and they sewed fig leaves together and made themselves coverings. (Genesis 3:1-7)

Right off the bat we can see where things began to go wrong.

Eve was in the wrong place at the wrong time listening to the wrong voice. Why in the world was she hanging around *the one place God told her to avoid?* God had clearly said to stay away from the fruit on a particular tree, so out of all the lush, beautiful trees in the garden (and who knows how vast it was), she decided to shade herself under that particular tree.

And guess who was waiting for her there?

It's like telling a little child, "Whatever you do, don't open that cookie jar." You know very well what that child will eventually do. And we are exactly the same way.

Then she listened to the wrong voice. She could have had all the conversation she wanted with God Himself or her husband, Adam. But she chose to listen to a snake instead.

Oddly enough, I was something of a snake fanatic as a child. I really don't know why, but I loved snakes in those days and collected all kinds of them. I had corn snakes and gopher snakes and king snakes and even boas. I thought constantly about snakes, read books about snakes, and talked about snakes. (Yes, I know. I had a strange childhood.) I wanted to grow up to become a herpetologist one day, someone who studies reptiles.

So I kept cages stacked on cages with snakes in them.

My mom, however, hated snakes.

One day she was in the house and saw that one of my snakes had escaped and was slithering across the front room floor. Since it seemed to be heading for the sliding glass patio door, she simply slid the door open and let it slide out of the house to freedom.

"Aw, Mom!" I said later. "That was my best snake!"

Why she put up with all those snakes in the house, I have no idea.

One time I told her that I wanted a particular kind of snake that was at a nearby pet shop. So we got in our baby blue Ford Starliner and went to the shop to check out this new creepy crawler.

I bought the snake and put him in my little terrarium in the trunk, and we drove home. When we opened the trunk, however, my new pet was AWOL. He had somehow escaped into the car.

My mom said, "I am never driving that car again."

Nevertheless, she had to drive it a couple of weeks later, knowing that the snake might still be in it . . . somewhere. She was very reluctant but reassured herself by reasoning that the snake had probably escaped by that time.

Pulling up to a red light at an intersection, she suddenly felt a cold coil drop onto her ankle. The snake! She threw open the door, jumped out and ran into the intersection, screaming, "There's a snake in the car!"

A police officer happened to be nearby and came over to her.

"Ma'am, what is wrong?"

"There's a snake in the car!"

He went over to the car to look and spotted what had given her such a fright. One of the hoses under the dashboard had come loose and fallen on her ankle.

She said, "I am never driving this car again!" And this time she meant it. She gave me the car, and it all worked out pretty well for me! (I wish I had held on to that car, as it really is a collectable now.)

Snakes are escape artists and very clever. They seem to be able to get out of (or into) the tightest of places. In other words, if you're living in an area where there are snakes, it pays to be cautious.

I've learned something else about snakes. Did you know the venom of a baby rattlesnake is more potent than that of an adult? Have you ever seen a baby rattler? They're actually kind of a cute, because everything is miniaturized, right down to the little rattle.

But make no mistake about it, the bite of a baby rattler will kill you.

In the same way we will say, "This is just a little baby sin. Hardly worth worrying about. It's just a small compromise. It really isn't a big deal. I can do this little thing one time, and it won't lead to anything else. I can handle this."

Watch out! An unguarded strength is a double weakness. Don't ever say, "I will never fall in this one area." Don't you believe it or let down your guard! Because that is the very area where Satan may trip you up.

Proverbs 16:18 says, "Pride goes before destruction, and a haughty spirit before a fall."

Frankly, you don't know what you might be capable of in a given set of circumstances. You need to keep your guard up at all times, because it is these little deals we make with the devil—the small, seemingly harmless compromises—that lead to bigger and more devastating things later.

Satan is smart. Don't underestimate him. Stay alert (as the New Testament says again and again) and watch your thoughts.

Please note, however, that it is *not* a sin to be tempted. As Martin Luther is reported to have said, "You can't stop a bird from flying over your head, but you can stop it from making a nest in your hair."

In other words, the sin is not in the bait, it's in the bite. Just because bait was dangled before you doesn't mean you have done anything wrong. In fact, if someone tells me they're never tempted, I have to wonder what's wrong with them. The very fact that you *do* struggle with temptation from time to time is an indication that you're moving forward spiritually and that the devil would like to bring you down. So if you have faced temptation and attack lately, it may very well mean you're doing something *right*.

Packaging Sin

Satan certainly understands humankind after all these years and all his experience of dealing with us. As a result, he knows how to make things look very, very appealing. In the Genesis passage we read earlier, it says, "The woman saw that the tree was good for food, that it was pleasant to the eyes, and a tree desirable to make one wise. . . ."

In other words, it had a lot of eye appeal.

That fruit looked good.

By the way, the Bible never says that it was an *apple*. Just speaking personally, an apple wouldn't have tempted me at all. Now a nice ripe peach or nectarine maybe. . . . But I suggest it was a piece of fruit like you have never seen before. There was something unbelievably attractive about it. Maybe it glowed or pulsated, and Eve was drawn to it. *Wow, what's this?*

When she approached the tree, Satan was ready and had his lines down cold. He knew what he would say to her. If she ate of this fruit, she would become a goddess and know as much as heaven knew. In fact, wasn't it just a little bit strange that God was holding out on her, keeping something back from her? If God really loved her, He would let her have this marvelous fruit, wouldn't He?

Satan will say the same thing to us: "If God really loved you, He would let you do whatever you want to do. If God really loved you, He would allow you to chase after whatever passion interests you. If God really loved you, He wouldn't have allowed this to happen to you." That is what he was doing with Eve. He was challenging the Word of God, and he was challenging God's love for her.

It worked, and Eve fell.

We, however, must resist.

The apostle James says, "But resist the devil and you'll find he'll run away from you" (James 4:7, PHILLIPS). The temptations will come, they will never stop coming, and they will come in unexpected ways at unexpected times as Satan adapts his strategies.

We simply have to be ready. We have to be able to say of our adversary, "For we are not unaware of his schemes" (2 Corinthians 2:11, NIV).

Imagine you're playing tennis with someone, and you are rallying for serve. So you're hitting the ball back and forth across the net, and as you are, you're taking note of your opponent's game—sizing him up. You might say to yourself, "Ah-hah. He's not very strong off his backhand." Or you might notice that he's not very effective when he has to rush the net. So after a while, you develop a strategy of how to play him and how to take advantage of his weak areas. Then you'll start scoring some points, because the object is to defeat your opponent and win the game.

It's the same way with the devil. He will say, "Oh, I see he's strong in this area. I'll try something else." Or, "She seems to lack confidence in that area—I'll go after it harder."

That's why we've always got to keep our guard up. The devil never takes a day off, and neither can we take a day off from spiritual warfare. The Christian life is not a playground, it's a battleground. We are either winning or losing, advancing or retreating. And the stakes are very, very high.

So let's keep our eyes open and our minds protected. Because the Bible tells us that we are to bring every thought into the captivity of the obedience of Jesus Christ.[59]

Strategies from Hell

So Satan attacks us, and here is how his strategy works.

First he will come as the enticer. Then he will come as the accuser.

As the enticer, or the tempter, he will whisper in your ear, "You deserve a break today. You work so hard, and you're such a committed Christian. You're doing a great job and have been really strong. In fact, you are so strong it really wouldn't even matter if you compromised in this little area or gave in a little over here. What difference could it make? Anyway, it will be fun. (And it's about time you had a little fun, don't you think?) Besides, it's no big deal. Everyone else is doing it. Go ahead! I won't tell anyone if you won't. Come on, just this once!"

So you say, "Well, okay . . . I'll do it." And you do.

Almost immediately, the devil comes back to you and says, "You pathetic hypocrite. Look at you! You call yourself a follower of Jesus after what you just did? Don't even think about showing your face in church again! And don't open that Bible. Oh man, that would be so hypocritical for you to open the Bible. And don't pray. Don't you dare call out to God. That would be so wrong."

And sometimes we listen to this stuff and fall right into his strategy. Yes, he is certainly the tempter. But he is equally adept as an *accuser*. The Bible says he is "the accuser of our brothers and sisters, who accuses them before our God day and night" (Revelation 12:10, NIV).

So what about this thing called guilt?

When you sin, you will feel guilt. And that is a good thing. Guilt simply means your conscience is working. The time to be concerned is when you *don't* feel guilt. The time to be concerned is when you can sin against God again and again and feel no remorse or sense of wrongdoing. The Bible says in the book of Hebrews, "Whom the LORD loves He chastens."[60] That means that when you as a son or daughter of God goes astray, the Holy Spirit will convict you of your sin and say, "That is wrong." He will call you on it, because He loves you. *"Don't do that. That is wrong. Stop it now."* Just like a father or mother would reprove a child.

When my sons were growing up, it was my responsibility to correct my own children, not someone else's children—though I would like to have done that at times. You see a child talking back to his mom and just being naughty, and you feel like saying, "Let me step in here." But you can't do that. That's not your privilege. But it is your responsibility to bring correction to your own sons and daughters.

In the same way, God disciplines His own children. If you are without discipline, if you can do things that you know are wrong and not feel any remorse, I think you have to wonder whether you are truly a child of God. But if you feel busted the moment you cross the line and come under the conviction of the Spirit, I say, "Hallelujah!" Your conscience is working. And the Spirit is working in your life, correcting you and changing you from the inside out.

Guilt is meant to lead us to a correct response. And when we have responded appropriately, turning from that sin and seeking the Lord's forgiveness, the guilt can go away, because it has served its purpose.

It's very important that we learn the difference between the legitimate conviction of the Holy Spirit and the devil's accusations, which are meant to damage or destroy us. The devil will use your sins in a hateful way to drive you away from the cross. The Holy Spirit will convict you of your sins in a loving way to bring you to the cross.

Let me say it again. Satan will always try to keep you from the cross. The Holy Spirit will always bring you to the cross.

Here's how it works. You have sinned, and you know you have sinned. You say to yourself, *Oh no! I can't believe I just did that.* The devil says to you, "Run. Go. Get away. Get by yourself and sulk or maybe despair a little. But don't go to God." The Holy Spirit, however, says, "Yes, you have sinned. But repent now. Get back into fellowship with the God who loves you." So right there on the spot you say, "Lord, I'm sorry. I know that I was wrong. I repent of that sin. I ask You to forgive me right now. In Jesus' name."

And then, after you have asked God for forgiveness, you don't need to keep going over and over it again. You don't need to keep berating yourself or kicking yourself or calling yourself names.

Why? Because your God has a big eraser. And if He has used it in your life, then be thankful! Your sin is not only forgiven, but it is forgotten. We know that because God has said, "Their sins and their iniquities will I remember no more" (Hebrews 8:12, KJV).

The devil, however, will try to push you into despair over your failures. He will try to use your sins to drive a wedge between you and your heavenly Father.

Don't listen to him.

Not then, not ever.

As I pointed out, he is a liar and the father of lies.

When you think about it, both Judas and Peter betrayed the Lord on the same night—Judas for thirty pieces of silver and Peter before the servant of the high priest. I believe that if Judas had wanted it, Jesus would have forgiven him and restored him.

In the Garden of Gethsemane, when Judas came to identify Jesus as the one the authorities were looking for, he did so by kissing Him.

Jesus said to him, "Why have you come?"

Jesus was God. He knew all things, and He knew very well what Judas was doing. I believe that in that moment, however, Jesus was offering His disciple a final chance for repentance and forgiveness.

Judas, however, plunged on ahead with his evil plan and betrayed Jesus. Sometime later, however, the enormity of what he had done dawned on him. Although he was filled with regret, we never read that he actually repented or turned back to the Lord. Instead, he listened to the voice of the one who "kills, steals, and destroys" . . . and went out and hung himself.

For his part, at a crucial moment, Simon Peter had denied even knowing the Lord—not once, not twice, but three times. Scripture says he uttered an oath to that effect, which essentially means, "I swear to God I never knew Jesus."

And then the rooster crowed, he made eye contact with the Lord Jesus, and he went outside to weep. After that, however, he stayed with his Christian friends, turned back to the Lord, and Jesus forgave and restored him. Judas listened to the wrong voice and ended up destroying himself; Peter listened to the right voice, did the right thing, and went on to great kingdom exploits.

We're all going to sin; it's not a matter of *if*, it's a matter of *when*. The Bible tells us very clearly, "If we claim to be without sin, we deceive ourselves and the truth is not in us" (1 John 1:8, NIV).

The question is, what will we do when we sin? Will we listen to the wrong voice and do wrong, destructive things, or will we listen to the right voice and find healing, hope, and full restoration? The wrong voice, the devil, would drive us from Jesus, from church, from fellowship, from the Word of God, and from everything that could help us. But if we listen to the right voice, the voice of the Holy Spirit, He will direct us back to the Word of God, to church, to our Christian friends, to the Lord in prayer, and to the great joy of an intimate relationship with the living God.

It's our choice.

Let's choose wisely.

Part 3

Living the Life

12

The Four Ws of Evangelism

It was 1971, and I had just come to faith on my high school campus. As a brand-new Christian, I'd heard that I was supposed to be sharing my faith in Christ with others. And even though I'd only been a believer for a short time, I told myself, *I know enough now to go out and tell others about Jesus.*

Sometimes ignorance is bliss.

So one afternoon, armed with my Bible and a copy of the *Four Spiritual Laws*, I went down to Huntington Beach alone to see if I could talk to someone about the Lord.

Walking along, I saw a lady about the age of my mom sitting on the beach by herself, and I thought, *Maybe she will listen to me. She'll be kind to me because I'm so young.*

At that point in my life, I had shoulder-length hair and a full beard, so I'm not sure what she thought of me when I walked up to her and, with shaking voice, began talking to her.

"Hi," I said. "Do you mind if I talk to you a little bit about Jesus?"

She looked up at me. "No, I don't mind," she replied. "Go right ahead."

That was my first surprise. I had expected to be rejected out of hand. Sitting down in the sand beside her, I pulled out my copy of the *Four Spiritual Laws* and simply began reading it to her, page by page. Even as I read, however, I kept thinking, *Greg, you're such an idiot. This will never work. Who do you think you are, talking to a woman old enough to be your mom about Jesus? Do you really think your pitiful attempt at sharing your faith will convince her of her need for Christ?*

Thoughts like these bombarded me as I worked my way through the booklet. But I kept on reading. Glancing up once or twice, I saw that she was looking at me. *This isn't going well at all,* I thought. *I can hardly wait until I'm done.*

I got to the very end of booklet and read the final question: "Is there any good reason why you shouldn't accept Jesus right now?"

And she said, "No."

No? I couldn't believe my ears. "Are you saying you want to accept Jesus?" I asked, incredulous.

"Yes," she replied.

Oh man, now what? I had planned for failure, not success. Nevertheless, in the most reverent tone I could muster, I said, "Let's bow our heads for a word of prayer together," and she promptly closed her eyes. Frantically, I began searching the tract for a prayer—any prayer. Finally I found one on the last page and led her to pray it with me, phrase by phrase.

Even as we were praying, I found myself thinking, *This can't really be happening. This isn't going to work.*

When we were done praying, however, she said, "Something just changed inside of me."

"Yes," I said, "and something just changed inside of me, too." I had realized, for the first time, that God could use someone like me—with all my inexperience and limitations—to reach people for Jesus.

Thinking Again About Evangelism

How much do we really have to know before we start speaking to people about our faith in Christ?

I think many of us have made this thing called "evangelism" way too complicated. I'm not suggesting we start telling others about Christ when we have no real understanding of what the Bible teaches. Obviously, we need a little teaching and instruction to get us ready. Having said that, however, I think most Christians know more than enough to begin sharing their faith with others.

Most of us are simply afraid to try.

It's my belief that God can use you to win others to Jesus Christ. Why would God command us in Scripture to share the gospel if we had no chance of being effective at it?

Proverbs 11:30 tells us, "The fruit of the righteous is a tree of life, And he who wins souls is wise." In the book of Daniel we read, "Those who are wise shall shine like the brightness of the firmament, and those who turn many to righteousness like the stars forever and ever" (Daniel 12:3).

In this chapter, we're going to talk about the *who, where, why,* and *what* of evangelism.

Let's start with the "who."

Who?

Go therefore and make disciples of all the nations, baptizing them in the name of the Father and of the Son and of the Holy Spirit, teaching them to observe all things that I have commanded you; and lo, I am with you always, even to the end of the age. (Matthew 28:19-20)

These are the words of the Lord Himself, given to His followers, just before He ascended into heaven.

In the original language, it's easier to see that these words are addressed to everyone. It could be translated, "Every one of my followers, you are to go into all of the world and preach the gospel."

This task, then, isn't just for the so-called professionals. This is for all of us. This is for preachers and Sunday school teachers, missionaries and construction workers, students and surfers, businessmen and housewives, secretaries and mechanics. Just fill your own name in the blank. It's for you, and it's for me. No one is exempt.

Another thing we note in the original language is that this was a *command*. Jesus is *not* saying, "I know you are all so busy, but as a personal favor to Me, would you mind going into all the world with the gospel?" No, He clearly says, "I *command* you to do this."

As my sons were growing up, I would often tell them what to do. I wouldn't say, "Would you please—just for me—take out the trash?" No, as their dad, I would simply tell them to do this or that. And most of the time they would!

Why did I say it that way? Simply put, to get things done. We had a household to run, and each of us had a part to play. As a parent, I was responsible to see that as my boys grew up, they knew how to help, contribute, and carry their own weight. Besides that, we had a relationship. I could speak to them that way because of the relationship of intimacy we already had as father and sons. They had no problem with getting simple marching orders from their dad; they expected it.

In the same way, God doesn't say, "Could you please help Me out a little and see if you could talk to a few people?"

No, He has the authority to say, "Do this." After all, He created us, purchased us, and redeemed us, paying our ransom with His own blood. We belong to Him. He is our *Lord*.

Matthew 28:19-20, then, is not the Great Suggestion. It is the Great Commission. If I am a disciple, this is what I will be about during my lifetime here on earth. I'm to go out and make disciples of others. And if I am not making disciples of others, one has to wonder if I am really the disciple He wants me to be.

For many people, however, the Great Commission has become the Great *Omission*. They simply don't make it a part of their lives.

The fact is, I believe that if we *aren't* looking for opportunities to share the gospel, it's a sin.

Someone might say, "What? A sin? No, Greg, a sin is when you break a command. A sin is when you fall short of God's glory."

That's true. But there are not only sins of commission, there are also sins of *omission*.

I'm reminded of the story about the little boy in Sunday school class. The teacher was talking about sin and said, "I want to talk about sin today. Can anyone can tell me what the sin of *commission* is?"

A little girl in the front said, "I know," and the teacher called on her. "The sin of commission," the girl said, "is when you do what you shouldn't do."

"That's right," said the teacher. "Now, can someone tell me what the sin of *omission* is?"

A little boy in the back of the room was waving his arm back and forth, and the teacher called on him. "Yes, son. What is the sin of omission?"

"The sin of omission," he said, "are the sins you want to do, but haven't gotten around to them yet."

Well, not exactly . . . In reality, the sin of omission is not doing what you know very well that you *should* do. The Scripture is clear when it tells us in James 4:17 (NIV), "If anyone, then, knows the good they ought to do and doesn't do it, it is sin for them."

So I can actually be sinning when I don't respond to the prompting of the Holy Spirit to share the gospel with an individual He has pointed out to me.

"Okay, Greg," you say, "now you're trying to lay a guilt trip on me."

I'm really not. In fact, what I want to communicate most in this chapter is the sheer joy of engaging another with the message of salvation in Jesus. There's no thrill that can match it.

The hardest part about evangelism is just getting started. But once you launch out and the Lord begins speaking through you, it can be one of the most exhilarating and satisfying experiences in life. You will say to yourself, *I was born for this.* Just to think that God Almighty would speak through someone like you or me is an unspeakable privilege.

The fact is, it's an honor to tell others about Jesus. Right from the start, it's a message that was designed to be shared—not hoarded. You and I were blessed to be a blessing.

In Proverbs 11:25 (NLT), Solomon wrote, "Those who refresh others will themselves be refreshed." It is refreshing to help other people learn and understand the gospel message. When we keep taking in and absorbing good teaching and strong, biblical messages but never give anything out, our knowledge can become stale and lose its vitality.

So the choice before us is really this: We can evangelize or we can fossilize.

Statistics tell us that 95 percent of Christians have never led another person to Christ. You say, "Well, Greg, we're not all called to be evangelists." That may be true, yet we are called to *evangelize*.

Where?

Assuming, then, that we are the "who," *where* do we start this process? Where do you and I start to reach the whole world for Jesus Christ? The world, after all, is still a pretty big place.

It must be a little like eating an elephant. Where do we start with that? One bite at a time. And that's where we start to reach the world . . . one person at a time.

We know that Jesus said, "Go into all the world and preach the gospel," but let's personalize and localize His command. Instead of saying, "Go into all the world," we might say, "Go into your neighborhood and preach the gospel."

Go into your school . . .

Go into your workplace . . .

Go into your family circle . . .

Unless you happen to live in a cave somewhere in the Himalayas, you have a sphere of influence; you have a group of people who will listen to what you have to say. Go into *that* world. That is the world God has called you to.

Note for a moment the words that Jesus used after He commanded us to make disciples of all nations. He said, "Teaching them to observe all things that I have commanded you . . ." (Matthew 28:19-20).

Jesus not only tells us to make a proclamation, but He also instructs us to teach people to observe things that He has commanded. Our endgame, then, as believers is to lead people to Christ and then help them get on their feet, spiritually. We're not only to win people, but to help them mature in Christ. And then we go out and do the process again . . . and again . . . and again.

Here is something I would give anything to get across in this book: When you are engaged in helping others come to Christ and grow spiritually, it will revolutionize your Christian life.

So many of us, however, are very focused on ourselves, caught up in our own needs, concerns, and struggles. But here is a truth I've seen demonstrated again and again: If you would stop thinking about yourself so much and begin to have concern for and try to reach someone who is literally separated from God and on their way to hell, you would find your own life incredibly refreshed.

This may be a poor analogy, but I'm reminded of the difference between going to Disneyland with children and going with other adults. The simple fact is, going to the Magic Kingdom with grown-ups can be disappointing. Adults are too often cynical, critical, and generally complain about everything.

"Can you believe how expensive this is?"

"Do you remember the old days when Walt was alive, and the tickets were so-and-so?"

"When I was a kid, you didn't have to spend all day waiting in line."

"Where do you get something decent to eat around here?"

Blah-blah-blah. Whine-whine-whine.

That's what it's like to go with adults. But when you go with children, it's completely different. I recently went back to Disneyland for our granddaughter Stella's fourth birthday, and I can tell you this: the way to see Disneyland is through the eyes of a child. Seeing it all through her eyes transformed the experience into something that really did seem magical.

In the same way, when there is a new believer in your life in the first bloom of faith—discovering truths of God for the first time— not only is it glorious for them, but it is a *huge* blessing to you.

So here is Dr. Greg's prescription for spiritual dryness: Go out and try to win people to Christ and help them grow spiritually. That is the Great Commission.

Why?

Why are we to do this? Why doesn't God just poke His face out of the heavens and say, "Hello, humanity. I am God. You are not. Believe in Me now or you will be judged. What do you say?"

Or here's another option: Why doesn't He just send an army of bright, powerful angels to proclaim the gospel?

He certainly could have done either of those things, or even both—or something else that we have never even thought of. But that isn't what He has chosen to do. For reasons known to Himself, the Lord has primarily chosen to reach people through people. People just like you and me.

Romans 10:14-15 says,

How then shall they call on Him in whom they have not believed? And how shall they believe in Him of whom they have not heard? And how shall they hear without a preacher? And how shall they preach unless they are sent? As it is written:

"How beautiful are the feet of those who preach the gospel of peace, who bring glad tidings of good things!"

Acts chapter 8 tells the story of a foreign dignitary who had visited Jerusalem and was on his way back to Ethiopia. He was the national treasurer of that nation, working for Queen Candace, and a very powerful man. After journeying all the way to Jerusalem in search of God, he was now on his way home, disappointed. He hadn't found God, but rather a dead, lifeless religion. Nevertheless, he had managed to obtain a scroll of the book of Isaiah the prophet. Putting his chariot into cruise control (what can you run into in the middle of the desert?), he read from the scroll as he traversed the wilderness road on the way home.

As it happened, he was reading out loud from Isaiah 53, which just happens to be a passage that talks about the suffering of the Messiah. Meanwhile, the Lord had led a disciple named Philip to approach this man in the chariot and talk to him.

The Holy Spirit said to Philip, "Go over and walk along beside the carriage."

Philip ran over and heard the man reading from the prophet Isaiah. Philip asked, "Do you understand what you are reading?"

The man replied, "How can I, unless someone instructs me?" And he urged Philip to come up into the carriage and sit with him.

The passage of Scripture he had been reading was this: "He was led as a sheep to the slaughter. And as a lamb is silent before the shearers, he did not open his mouth. He was humiliated and received no justice. Who can speak of his descendants? For his life was taken from the earth."

The eunuch asked Philip, "Tell me, was the prophet talking about himself or someone else?" So beginning with this same Scripture, Philip told him the Good News about Jesus.
(Acts 8:29-35, NLT)

Before the day was over, that man from Ethiopia became a believer, was baptized, and went on his way back to Africa with joy in his heart and a spring in his step.

Here is what you need to understand: There are people in your circle, in near proximity to you, who are also seeking God. There are people who are ready to listen and believe, if only someone will take the time to explain things to them and show them the way.

I remember when I was a teenager, before I knew the Lord, and I was partying and doing drugs and basically throwing my life away. One of the places I liked to hang out was called the Fun Zone, in Newport Beach, California. I remember leaning up against a wall, watching people go by, and trying to look really tough.

Christians would come along sometimes, handing out their little Bible tracts. They would see me leaning on the wall, scowling, and probably didn't know what to make of me. One of them would thrust a tract at me and quickly back off.

I can remember saying in my heart, *Talk to me. Don't be put off by my tough-guy façade. It's all fake, but I'm too proud to say I need help. I'm too proud to say, "Tell me about Jesus."* More than anything else, I wanted these Christians to engage me, reach out to me, speak to me, draw me out. Mostly, however, they just thrust their little booklets at me, and I would stuff them in my pockets. I didn't throw them away. I kept them. I took everything everyone gave to me.

Back at home, I had a drawer full of all kinds of religious literature. Every now and then I would pull it out, empty it on my bed, and try to sort through it all. It seemed so confusing to me. And no wonder! I had tracts from Christians and literature from Mormons, Jehovah's Witnesses, Krishnas, you name it. Looking through all of that stuff, I would say to myself, "What does all of this mean?"

I was like that Ethiopian man in the chariot, reading with a hungry heart but not understanding. What I needed was someone to show me the way.

The fact is, anyone with a basic knowledge of the faith could have easily explained the gospel to me. I suggest to you there is a world full of people out there just like I was, who are waiting for someone like you to step out, take a risk, and say, "I'll go ahead and give it a go."

What's the worst-case scenario? That someone would reject you? That someone might say, "No, I'm not interested." Yes, they could very well say that. But then again, they might be interested. They might say, "Please tell me."

Why? Because God has primarily chosen to reach people through people. And the number-one way to do this is through verbal communication.

In other words, actually talking to someone.

"Well," someone will say, "I believe in lifestyle evangelism. I'll just live out my faith by the way I treat people and the way I do my job, and people will see that."

That's good. I'm all for that. But God wants you to live it *and* to speak it. Yes, He wants you to "earn the right" to discuss spiritual things with people by the way you conduct yourself, but He also wants you to verbally engage them. He wants you to actually initiate a conversation and speak out for what you believe, not just wait for someone to come up and ask you.

Here's the big question. Do we really believe what the Bible says? Because if we do, it means that if a person doesn't know Jesus Christ they will go to hell when they leave this life. Do we actually believe that? If we do, how can we be so cavalier or casual about sharing our faith? How can we be so apathetic or uncaring if we really believe what we say we believe?

Sometimes we may even find ourselves looking at nonbelievers as the enemy. But they are not the enemy, they are trapped by the enemy, who is the devil. They are captives of sin, just as we were before Jesus Christ set us free.

In 2 Timothy 2:24-26, Paul counsels us with these words:

> God's servant must not be argumentative, but a gentle listener and a teacher who keeps cool, working firmly but patiently with those who refuse to obey. You never know how or when God might sober them up with a change of heart and a turning to the truth, enabling them to escape the Devil's trap, where they are caught and held captive, forced to run his errands. (MSG)

Nonbelievers, you see, are in bondage and under the power of the enemy. They may not understand that, but you do. So you need to pray that God will open their spiritual eyes and they will see their need for Jesus.

What?

Just what is it, then, that we are to go into all of the world and preach?

Morality?

Responsibility?

Our political viewpoint?

No, those things, important as they may be, aren't our primary message. Our message is the gospel. And if you embrace the gospel, I believe that you will become a moral, more responsible person.

But I don't preach morality. I preach that God can change a person no matter how they have lived or what they have done.

First . . . the bad news

The word "gospel" means *good news*. But to fully appreciate the good news, I must also understand the bad news.

We've all heard those good-news-bad-news jokes. Like the doctor who said to his patient, "I have some good news and some bad news."

"What's the good news?" the patient asks.

The doctor replies, "You only have three weeks to live."

Staggered, the patient gasps, "If that's the *good* news, then what in the world is the bad news?"

"Well," the doctor admits, "I've been really busy. I should have told you a couple of weeks ago."

Oh . . . that *is* bad.

But the truth is, before a person can fully appreciate the good news, he or she needs to have a handle on the bad news. We tell people the Good News that Jesus gave His life for them and will forgive them of all their sin. That's true. But the bad news is that all of humanity has sinned against God and offended Him, whether we have done it in ignorance or on purpose. Romans 3:23 says, "All have sinned and fall short of the glory of God." And in 1 John 1:8 we read, "If we say we have no sin, we deceive ourselves, and the truth is not in us."

In fact, one of the reasons God gave us the Law, the Ten Commandments, was to show us that we are sinners. Some people will say, "I live by the Ten Commandments. That's all the religion I need." But the fact is, nobody lives by them. Everyone has broken them. For that matter, most people don't have a clue what the Ten Commandments are.

Sometimes when I'm talking to someone who claims the Ten Commandments as their religion, I recite a commandment or two for them. I'll say, "Let's talk about that a little bit. One of the commandments says, 'You shall not steal.' Have you ever stolen anything in your life? Another says, 'You shall not bear false witness.' Have you ever lied about anything? Another states, 'You shall have no other gods before me.' Have you ever had someone or something that has been more important to you than God?"

"Well, yeah, maybe once or twice."

Here's the problem, then. James 2:10 (TLB) tells us that "the person who keeps every law of God, but makes one little slip is just as guilty as the person who has broken every law there is."

So the truth is, no one lives by the Ten Commandments.

The commandments weren't given to make us righteous; they were given to show us our need for Jesus. They are like the moral mirror: When I look into the law of God, I realize that I fall hopelessly short of His standards. The commandments were given to open my eyes, to shut my mouth, and to convince me of my need for Jesus. The commandments were given to say, "Listen, friend, you need Jesus."

Some people believe (though not as many as a generation or two ago) in the "innate goodness of man." They say, "I believe man is basically good. I believe in human kindness. I believe that for every drop of every rain a flower grows."

Are you kidding me? Have you read the newspaper this morning? Have you looked at the real world?

Not long ago I read a true story about a man named Fred. He had decided to walk across America to "prove that most people along the way are good and decent people." He got as far as the Georgia-South Carolina border when he was robbed and pushed off a bridge.

He'd been walking across a bridge when a faded red pickup pulled up next to him. The driver leaned out and said, "Are you the guy walking across America?"

"Yes, I am," Fred replied.

"Good," said the stranger. "Give me your wallet." Then, after relieving Fred of all his money, he pushed him off the bridge. Fred fell one hundred feet, but miraculously survived. When he was interviewed later, Fred said ruefully, "This could have happened two months from now, and I wouldn't feel so bad. But I only got through one state!"

Wise up, Fred. People are *not* basically good.

"Now wait a second, Greg," someone might object. "Are you saying there aren't any good people out there?"

Not at all. In fact, I have met many good people all across the world. I'll take it a step further. I have met nonbelievers who are kind, generous, and walk with real integrity. Truthfully, I have met some non-Christians who were nicer than many Christians I know.

I'm not denying that there are nonbelievers out there who are great humanitarians, and men and women who have shown admirable courage, selflessness, and sacrifice in their lives.

What, then, is the Bible saying when it declares, "There is none righteous, no, not one"?[61] It is simply pointing out the fact that no one is good enough to please God. There is no one—not even one—who meets the righteous demands of God. Even the best of us fall short.

And then . . . the good news

We all fall short. That's the worst of the bad news, but it's at that very point that we encounter the Good News of Jesus Christ. He is the only one qualified to bridge the gap between a holy, flawless, perfect God and unholy, flawed, sinful humanity.

Paul wrote,

> And all of this is a gift from God, who brought us back to himself through Christ. And God has given us this task of reconciling people to him. For God was in Christ, reconciling the world to himself, no longer counting people's sins against them. And he gave us this wonderful message of reconciliation. (2 Corinthians 5:18-19, NLT)

This is why Jesus Christ's being the only way to God is a non-negotiable. It's not, "You have your way, I have my way, and she has her way." No, He is *the* way. The only way. He declared this fact with crystal clarity when He said in John 14:6, "I am the way, the truth, and the life. No one comes to the Father except through Me." Acts 4:12 (NIV) boldly declares: "Salvation is found in no one else, for there is no other name under heaven given to mankind by which we must be saved."

You say, "Why?"

Because only Jesus died on the cross and rose again from the dead. The Bible says "For [God] made Him who knew no sin to be sin for us, that we might become the righteousness of God in Him" (2 Corinthians 5:21).

Jesus took upon Himself the sin of the world.

So here is the gospel message. The bad news is that you are separated from God, and there is nothing you can do to earn God's favor. The bad news is that morality or "living a good life" will never get you into heaven, and you are in deep trouble. The good news is that God loved you so much that He sent His Son Jesus, who lived a perfect life and went to the cross and died in your place. He became sin for you. And if you will believe in Jesus, you can be forgiven.

What is the essential gospel message? C. H. Spurgeon defined it this way: *Jesus died for me.*[62]

The Power of the Simple Gospel

We could talk here about apologetics–defending our faith–and any number of helpful strategies, systems, and techniques for sharing our faith.

But in all of those good arguments and methodologies, we dare not miss the bottom line. Our primary message must always be "Jesus Christ and Him crucified." The Bible reminds us that "the message of the cross is foolishness to those who are perishing, but to us who are being saved it is the power of God." Paul said, "I am not ashamed of the gospel of Christ, for it is the power of God to salvation for everyone who believes" (1 Corinthians 1:18; Romans 1:16).

There is power in the gospel. Never forget that. There is power in the simple story of the life, death, and resurrection of Jesus. Don't complicate it. Don't add to it. Don't take away from it. Don't apologize for it.

Just proclaim it and stand back and watch what God will do.

My job isn't to convert anyone. I have never converted anyone, and I never will. Only God can change a heart and life. Only the Holy Spirit can produce that work of transformation in the heart of a man or a woman or a boy or a girl.

What's our job?

Our job is to simply herald the message. Our job is to take the gospel seed and throw it out there as far as we can get it—to as many people as we can get it to. And then to pray for results and leave it all in the hands of God.

13 Secrets of Spiritual Growth, Part 1 The Word of God

It was G. K. Chesterton who said, "Christianity has not been tried and found wanting. It has been found difficult and not tried." [63]

The problem isn't that "I tried and it didn't work." It's more like, "Well, as I looked at what it really meant to be a Christian, I decided I didn't want to do that."

Why do some succeed spiritually and others fail?

Short answer: *Because they choose to.*

If you want to walk with God, if it's truly your heart's desire, you'll go for it. If, on the other hand, you're apathetic about it, you won't be inclined to go for it—all the good teaching, literature, and careful follow-up in the world won't change that. But if you have a real desire to know and serve God, by His grace you'll do just that.

"But Greg," someone might protest, "it sounds like you're implying that our Christian walk is a result of human effort."

Not at all.

Nevertheless, I am saying there are things only God can do, and there are things only I can do. For instance, Philippians 2:12 says, "Work out your own salvation with fear and trembling." Please note that it doesn't say to work *for* your own salvation, because that's already a gift that's been given to us by the Lord. No, it says, "Work *out* your own salvation."

What does that mean?" The Amplified Bible renders the verse like this: "Work out (cultivate, carry out to the goal, and fully complete) your own salvation with reverence and awe and trembling (self-distrust, with serious caution . . .)."

Here's how it reads when we put Philippians 2:12 and 2:13 together:

> Work out your own salvation with fear and trembling; for it is God who works in you both to will and to do for His good pleasure.

There is the whole picture laid out for us. I am to live out my salvation and carry it to the goal with a healthy dose of self-distrust and serious caution; I am also to remember that it is God who gives me the strength to live the life He has called me to live.

Only God can do certain things. Only I can do certain things. Only God can convict me of my sin, and only God can convert me. Only I, however, can repent of my sin. Only I can make that choice to follow Jesus Christ. So there is a part that God wants to do, and there is a part that I need to do.

But here's the incredible good news: God, by the power of the Holy Spirit, has given you everything you need to live the Christian life. Could I spell that significant word for you? E-V-E-R-Y-T-H-I-N-G. Here's how it reads in 2 Peter 1:3 (NIV): "His divine power has given us everything we need for a godly life through our knowledge of him who called us by his own glory and goodness."

It was Alexander MacLaren who said, "He that has the Holy Spirit in his heart and the Scripture in his hands has all he needs."[64]

It makes me think of a car with a powerful engine. You've got all the horsepower you could ever need under that hood; you just need to put the key in the ignition, hit the gas, and watch what happens!

So we come to this life of following Jesus, and we wonder how to accomplish it. We live in a culture, of course, where we get everything fast and easy. And then we come to the Bible and we encounter words we're not all that comfortable with—words like discipline and obedience. We read in Psalm 46:10, "Be still, and know that I am God." We also read about stepping out in faith and trusting God.

Some of those things sound like work or taking some risk, and we don't want to do that. We want to get on a spiritual fast track—a Christian express lane—and find the easy way to do it.

It's like dieting. We want to be in good shape, but we want it to happen overnight. We want to take that pill they advertise on TV that melts the pounds away overnight while we're asleep. Or do you remember the ads for that ab machine that you simply wrap around your waist and let it do all the work? No muss, no fuss, no crunches or sit-ups. And you wake up in the morning with six-pack abs!

We live in an instant society, and we want everything right now. Instant messaging on our smartphones, instant knowledge of the most obscure facts on Google, instant music and movie downloads, and instant maps and directions at our fingertips. With each passing day, technology makes our world run faster, and we are incredibly spoiled.

My point is simply this: In a culture where we get news on demand and all kinds of information in real time, we come to the Bible and say, "Okay, where's the shortcut? What's the fast way to do this?" The truth is, however, we need to learn about *discipline* and *obedience* as we search out and apply ourselves to the truths of God's Word—even if it means that some of us need to change our way of thinking.

The points that follow may seem simple and basic to you. So be it. Yet for those who walk this pathway, there is life, enrichment, joy, fulfillment, and spiritual prosperity. As Solomon wrote, "People who accept discipline are on the pathway to life, but those who ignore correction will go astray" (Proverbs 10:17, NLT).

The rest of this chapter will discuss the first principle of being successful spiritually.

You Must Read, Study, and Love the Word of God

"This Book of the Law shall not depart from your mouth, but you shall meditate in it day and night, that you may observe to do according to all that is written in it. For then you will make your way prosperous, and then you will have good success." (Joshua 1:8)

Years ago a young man named Billy Sunday received Christ into his life. An older believer gave him some advice he never forgot. He said,

"William, there are three simple rules I wish you would practice. And if you do, no one will ever write the word 'backslider' after your name. Number 1: Take 15 minutes every day to let God talk to you. Number 2: Take 15 minutes every day to talk to God. Number 3: Take 15 minutes every day talking to someone else about the Lord." [65]

Simple advice? Yes, but think how your life would change if you did those three things every day without fail.

How, then, does God talk to us? God speaks to us primarily through his Word, the book we call the Bible. And by the way, you will never, never outgrow or get beyond this. Psalm 119:159, 160 says,

See how I love your commandments, LORD. . . . The very essence of your words is truth; all your just regulations will stand forever. (NLT)

It was Spurgeon who said, "Nobody ever outgrows Scripture. The Book widens and deepens with our years." [66] That is true. You don't outgrow your need to study the Bible any more than you outgrow your need to eat food.

Can you imagine anyone saying something like this? "Yes, I used to be into that whole eating thing. Every day. Three times a day. Sometimes even with snacks in between. But I don't need that anymore. I've moved beyond that."

Or what about someone who would say, "Breathing? Oh, yeah, I used to breathe with the best of them. Inhale. Exhale. Inhale.

Exhale. On and on. There's nothing wrong with it, but it was kind of a phase in my life. I'm not into breathing anymore."

The trouble is, if you're not into eating and breathing, you're aren't into *living* either.

In the same way, if you're not into the regular study of the Bible, you will find yourself crashing spiritually. It's not enough to just go to church once or twice a week, read good Christian books, and listen to great Christian radio broadcasts. Those things are all wonderful and have their place. But nothing will ever take the place of your opening up your Bible and reading it every single day. God Himself will personally speak to you through the pages of the Bible.

"Well," you say, "I'm not much of a reader."

Then *become* one.

"But Greg, I never read that much growing up."

Neither did I. I remember the first time I went to church and heard the pastor say, "Turn in your Bibles to Romans chapter 3, verse 1." I remember thinking, *What? What page number is that?* It would have made more sense to me if he had said, "Turn over to channel 3," rather than turn over to chapter three. I never really read at all as a boy. But as I opened up God's Word, it began to change my life.

I remember when I received my first Bible, right after I had accepted Christ. I accepted the Lord on a Friday on my high school campus, and I really wasn't quite sure what I had done. All I knew was that something radical had happened to me. But no one followed up on me or really took the time to explain to me what it meant to be a Christian. So when I got back to school on Monday morning, I was startled when some guy saw me across campus and yelled out, "Hey, brother Greg!"

Brother Greg? What was that? I looked at him and then realized it was one of the Jesus freaks. But why was he calling me "brother Greg"? He seemed really loud to me and had a big gold cross hanging around his neck. He came over to me with a big smile on his face, and said, "Brother Greg! Praise the Lord."

I remember thinking, *How am I supposed to reply to that?*

"Bro," he said.

"Yes?"

"I have something for you."

"Really? What's that?"

"It's a Bible, bro."

He pulled out this huge old Bible and pushed it into my hands. It was as big as an unabridged dictionary. And to add insult to injury, it had a cross on the front made out of Popsicle sticks glued together.

"Bro. Here."

"Oh. Popsicle sticks on a Bible. Thanks a lot. That's great. Really great."

Really, I just wanted him to go away. I was embarrassed, and I didn't know what to do. I certainly didn't want to pack that super-sized Bible around campus all day. I had an old jacket on that day with huge pockets, and I tried to shove my new Popsicle stick Bible into one of them. It didn't quite fit, so I ripped the pocket open and shoved it in so that no one would see it.

I hadn't seen my old friends for a few days, and I didn't want to tell them I had accepted Christ. One of the guys lived in a house near the campus, so I walked over there at lunchtime. It was something a group of us did every school day. We'd go to his house and get loaded. (That was our vernacular for coming under the influence of drugs.) And then we would go back to class and hallucinate for the rest of the day.

We called that "fun," but really it was a miserable life. Nevertheless, that's what I did, because I didn't know any better. As I approached the door, I realized I still had my Bible and didn't want to take it in the house. So I hid it in some bushes by the front door and went inside.

"Hey, Greg, what are you doing?"

"Nothing."

"Where have you been?"

"Nowhere."

"What's been going on?"

"Nothing."

They were all looking at me in a strange way. But why? How could they have known what happened to me?

Then one of them said, "Hey, you want to get stoned?"

"No."

"Why not?"

"I just don't want to."

"Greg, what's wrong with you?"

"Nothing."

They all kept staring at me. Suddenly the door opened and this guy's mother came in, holding up my Bible in plain view.

"I found this out in the bushes," she said. "Who does this belong to?" She held up the Bible with the cross in Popsicle sticks for everyone to see. And somehow everyone in that room knew that Greg and that book went together. They looked at the Bible. They looked over at me.

"That's mine," I said.

One of my friends said, "What is that?"

"It's a Bible."

"A what?"

"It's a *Bible*."

"A what?"

"A BIBLE. A BIBLE!" I grabbed it. "It's *my* Bible."

One of my friends said in a mocking tone, "Oh, praise the Lord, brother Greg. Are we going to be Christians now?"

"No," I said, "we're going to hit you in the mouth. That's what we're going to do." You see, I hadn't read 1 Corinthians 13 yet. This was all new to me.

My friends started mocking me, laughing at me, and making fun of me. And that's when I made a discovery. I realized they weren't my friends at all. I also realized the big book I held in my hand—Popsicle sticks and all—was the Word of God, and I wanted to find out what it had to say.

So I went home that night and started reading it.

I remember being amazed at how it resonated with truth. How it spoke to me. How it related to what I was facing as a 17-year-old kid back in 1970. And here's the amazing thing: It will still resonate every bit as much with a 17-year-old kid today. Or a person who is 78 years old. Whatever your age, background, or literacy level might be, it's the Word of God, and if you want to grow spiritually, you need it in your life. This is the user's manual you've been searching for, and you'll never find a better one. Spell out the word Bible in an acrostic and you have B.I.B.L.E. *Basic Instructions Before Leaving Earth*.

Start reading it, and you'll be amazed to find a personalized message tailored just for you and your present situation.

Psalm 19 tells us five important things we need to know about the Bible—things that will help every one of us in our spiritual growth.

> The law of the LORD is perfect, converting the soul;
> The testimony of the LORD is sure, making wise the simple;
> The statutes of the LORD are right, rejoicing the heart;
> The commandment of the LORD is pure, enlightening the eyes;
> The fear of the LORD is clean, enduring forever;
> The judgments of the LORD are true and righteous altogether.
> More to be desired are they than gold,
> Yea, than much fine gold;
> Sweeter also than honey and the honeycomb.
> Moreover by them Your servant is warned,
> And in keeping them there is great reward.
> (Psalm 19:7-11)

The Word of God is sufficient for our needs

The law of the LORD is perfect . . . (verse 7)

That phrase *the law of the Lord* is a Hebrew term that simply means the Scriptures. We could just as easily substitute "the Word of God" or "the Bible." The Bible is perfect. The Word of God is perfect.

Where are you going to turn in a time of crisis? When tragedy hits? When disaster strikes? When you don't know where to go? *People* magazine? Your favorite website? The morning newspaper? The evening news? Hardly. What you need is something that will give you strength and direction in your time of crisis. And that will come from the Word of God.

Robert McCheyne said, "One gem from the ocean of the Bible is worth all of the pebbles from earthly streams."[67] That is so true. Just a pebble from the ocean of God's Word can make all the difference in the world. How many people across the world, through generation after generation, have found comfort from Scripture in their times of confusion, affliction, or sorrow? One person wrote, "He who rejects the Bible has nothing to live by. Neither does he have anything to die by."

I can tell you from personal experience that I have put the Word of God to the test. Through the months of grieving for my son, Christopher, I have trusted in what the Bible has said. It has sustained me through the darkest hours and given me direction, hope, and comfort when I needed it most.

Little platitudes or clever sayings just won't cut it when you're in trouble or suffering, but the Word of God speaks to any and every situation. I urge you to get a good foundation in this Book, because it's only a matter of time until hardship, affliction, or even tragedy will strike you. That's not being negative; it happens in every life, without exception. But if we have a foundation in the Word of God, we'll be ready for it when it comes. Don't wait until you're in the midst of a crisis and try to catch up on all the spiritual help and insights you never had time for. Start now. Get that foundation now and take the teachings of Scripture to heart.

Trends, theories, styles, and philosophies come and go. But the Word of God is never out of style and will never be out of date. This morning's newspaper will be lining the birdcage in just a matter of time, but the Word of God will always be relevant. As the prophet said, "His mercies begin afresh each morning" (Lamentations 3:23, NLT).

"The law of the Lord is perfect . . ."

That word translated "perfect" here could also be translated *whole, complete, sufficient.* The Bible is sufficient. I don't need to add to it or take away from it. In 2 Timothy 3:16, Paul writes: "All Scripture is given by inspiration of God." Or literally, "It is God-breathed." That means that the Bible is God's infallible Word. The original autographs, that is, the first copies, were without errors. There are no mistakes and there are no contradictions.

Even with a recent discovery like the Dead Sea Scrolls, where an older version of some writings were discovered in the back of some caves in the Middle East, we find that the words are virtually the same. The Word of God is perfect. It has stood the test of time, and we can depend on it. It is God's gift to us.

The Word of God transforms us

The law of the LORD is perfect, converting the soul;
The testimony of the LORD is sure, making wise the simple. (Psalm 19:7)

This phrase *converting the soul* could be translated, "It revives us. It restores, transforms, and changes us."

If you don't need to be changed, then maybe you don't need the Bible. If you've got it all together and don't have any questions, don't have any conflicts, and feel that your life is perfect, then I guess you don't need the Bible. But if you're like the rest of us, and you're aware of your weakness, your inadequacies, and your need for God, then you will be thankful to know that the Word of God is perfect. It can transform you, helping you to become the person God has called you to be.

But it's not just enough to read it. You must process it. And then you must obey it, doing what it says. The apostle James wrote these words:

Don't fool yourself into thinking that you are a listener when you are anything but, letting the Word go in one ear and out the other. Act on what you hear! Those who hear and don't act are like those who glance in the mirror, walk away, and two minutes later have no idea who they are, what they look like. (James 1:22-24, MSG)

Imagine you're at a party, and you feel like you're looking pretty good. But then you notice people looking at you out of the corner of their eye, touching their faces, or maybe smiling or laughing at you. But why are they laughing when you haven't said anything funny? Later, when you go into the restroom and check yourself in the mirror, you notice you have something stuck to your face—maybe a noodle or a piece of spaghetti. And somehow you hadn't noticed it or felt it.

So what do you do? You clean off your face and go back out again.

But what if you simply looked in the mirror and said, "Isn't that interesting? That's never happened to me before." And then you went right back out into the public without doing anything about that weird noodle hanging off your face.

That would be crazy. That wouldn't make any sense at all.

It's the same way when I come to the Word of God. It clearly tells me something about my life, exposing an error in judgment or showing me something I need to do. If I just shrug my shoulders and ignore God's Word, I'm like a fool who looks at his reflection in a mirror but doesn't heed what he sees.

The Word of God gives us incredible wisdom

The testimony of the LORD is sure, making wise the simple. (verse 7)

The Hebrew word translated "simple" here comes from a root which means "an open door." It's the idea of a person who has a mind like an open door—everything comes in and everything goes out. Have you heard of In-N-Out Burger? This is like an in-and-out brain. It goes in one ear and flies out the other.

It's the kind of person who would say, "I believe Jesus is the Son of God," but would also say, "I believe in UFOs, and I'm certain Elvis is still alive." It's a person who is basically open to anything. As a result, they have difficulty holding on to real truth when they encounter it. But the Word of God can make a person like that— a simple-minded person—into someone who is wise and sees the world through God's eyes.

The Word of God is right

The statutes of the LORD are right, rejoicing the heart. (Psalm 19:8)

In Hebrew, this means that the Bible has set out the right path for us to follow. We don't have to lose our bearings in the fog of human opinion. We don't have to let our fickle emotions lead us about. We have a more sure foundation—the very Word of God. That is why it's important to read through books of the Bible verse by verse and chapter by chapter. And as I read these verses every day, I ask myself questions like this: *Is there any sin identified here for me to avoid? Is there a promise here that I might claim? Is there a victory to gain? Is there a blessing to enjoy?*

Sometimes people will ask me the question, "What do you do if you come to a verse in the Bible you don't agree with?"

Answer: I change my opinion, because I'm in the wrong.

Now we've all known people who take a verse out of its original context and try to make it say something God never intended it to say. But if we read through a book of the Bible, keeping the truths in context and using an accurate Bible translation, we can depend on what God is saying to us.

If you have believed something differently than the clear teaching of the Word of God, then you need to change your opinion. The objective is to conform your thinking to what the Bible teaches, rather than trying to conform the Bible into your philosophy or way of thinking.

We are told in Romans 12 that we are to be transformed by the renewing of our minds. The problem we have today is that people are trying to change or adjust God's Word to suit their own lifestyle or choices. It doesn't work that way. The Word of God is *right*, and if you aren't in alignment with it, you are *wrong*, and you need to change.

The Word of God makes us happy

The statutes of the LORD are right, rejoicing the heart. (Psalm 19:8)

Luke 11:28 (NLT) says, "Blessed [or happy] are all who hear the word of God and put it into practice."

Did you know you can have a happy life without sin? A happy life without sex outside of marriage? A happy life without drugs and alcohol? A happy life without selfishness? God is not out to ruin your life; He wants it to be fulfilled. When you are living as a follower of Jesus Christ, the happiness doesn't stop when the party's over and everyone has gone home.

Some people, of course, have the opposite view. Their idea is that God is out to make life miserable, and "out in the world" is where they will be liberated and have all of the fun.

In fact, it's the very opposite.

The world will bring you misery, bondage, and regret. It is the freedom of following Christ and living by the Word of God that will bring true and lasting happiness. You have God's Word on it:

> Blessed is the one
> who does not walk in step with the wicked
> or stand in the way that sinners take
> or sit in the company of mockers,
> but whose delight is in the law of the Lord,
> and who meditates on his law day and night.
> That person is like a tree planted by streams of water,
> which yields its fruit in season
> and whose leaf does not wither—
> whatever they do prospers.
> (Psalm 1:1-3, NIV)

The psalm continues on and in verse 4 (NIV) says, "Not so the wicked!"

In other words, it's not that way with the unbeliever. They are blown about like wind-driven chaff.

So I have a choice. I can follow God's Word and live a happy and fulfilled life, or I can disobey it and reap the consequences. If you want to be successful spiritually, you must love and study the Word of God.

And you must memorize Scripture as well. Psalm 119:11 says, "Your word I have hidden in my heart, that I might not sin against You."

It's funny how people react to the Bible, isn't it? Do you take your Bible out in public? It freaks some people out—especially if you have one of those big, black, "old school" Bibles. You can get Bibles now that don't look like Bibles at all—or you can even read Scripture on your iPhone, and people will think you're checking your e-mail. But when you pull out the big book with black leather, ribbons, and gold pages, they know exactly what it is, and people will react to what they see.

I can think of times when I've been on a plane, pulled my Bible out of my briefcase, and it was as if I'd pulled out a live snake. People will back off a little as if it's going to attack them.

People will react even if they swear up and down that they don't believe the Bible, because deep down, they know there's some kind of power there they don't understand.

I love it when someone says to me, "The Bible is full of contradictions."

"Really?" I say. "Are you sure of that?"

"Oh yes."

"Well, here's a Bible," I say, holding it out to them. "Why don't you show me one?"

"Get that thing away from me!"

"Just show me a contradiction. You said this Book was full of them."

"Well . . . they're in there."

"Where?"

"Um, well, you know . . . somewhere."

It's not enough, however, to carry a Bible around or talk about the Bible. You need to *internalize* the Word of God in your life. Colossians 3:16 says, "Let the Word of God dwell in you richly." A popular paraphrase words it like this: "Let the Word of Christ . . . have the run of the house. Give it plenty of room in your lives" (MSG).

God wants His Word to permeate every area of your life, with no exceptions. He wants it to be a part of your business ethic, your social life, your marriage, and your family. He wants it to guide you in the way that you raise your children, conduct your friendships, and respond to the government. He wants it to show you what your priorities in life ought to be. And the only way you are going to live in the richness of this timeless counsel is by reading and studying the Bible, learning it, internalizing it, and memorizing it.

The Word of God is a guidebook to life

Some people love to study maps and pore over them, but I'm not one of those people. Maps often confuse me, and I avoid them whenever I can. God's Word, however, is a map I can understand and follow.

It is the Bible that tells us we are separated from God by our sin. It is the Bible that tells us that while we were yet sinners, Christ died for us. It is the Bible that tells us that Jesus both died and rose again from the dead. And it is the Bible that tells us that Jesus stands at the door of our life and knocks, and if we will hear His voice and open the door, He will come in.

I mentioned earlier that the Bible is the instruction manual that we have all been looking for. If you're like me, you don't like to read instruction manuals. I'll buy some gadget and instead of reading about how to operate it, I will immediately start pushing buttons. Sometimes, of course, you push a button you weren't supposed to push, and then you have to consult the owner's guide to try and undo the damage.

In the same way, we launch into life and say, "I'll just figure this thing out as I go along. I'll just start making decisions and see where I end up."

But mistakes in life can hurt people deeply and land us in situations we never intended. In our distress and anguish, we say, "What do I do now?" And finally we open up God's Instruction Manual for Life and find out what we should have been doing all along.

We also learn there is help, forgiveness, grace, and practical counsel within its pages. In fact, it is not only a guidebook for life, it is a road map to heaven. No other book in all the world, in all of history, compares with this Book that so many people have on their shelves, but so few ever open its pages and experience its wonders.

14

Secrets of Spiritual Growth, Part 2
The Priority of Prayer

Why is it that some Christians succeed while others who make that profession of faith miserably fail? Why is it that some seem to run the race of life and cross the finish line with flying colors, while others just collapse in a heap?

Why?

Because of choices. Decisions that people make each and every day. It comes down to this: We make our choices and our choices make us. The fact is, our lives overflow with choices. From the moment you get up in the morning till the time you lay your head down on your pillow at night, you have made hundreds, perhaps even thousands, of choices.

That's why it's hard to go into certain restaurants where the menu is like a phone book. How can you ever decide on something? There are too many options.

My favorite hamburger place only has a few options. Hamburger. French fries. Soft drinks.

Maybe a milkshake. That's about it. You don't have to waste a lot of mental energy trying to figure out what to order.

Some simple choices, of course, don't seem to mean very much. Other choices mean everything. In fact, there are choices that will determine our destiny.

When it comes to your spiritual life, here's how that process works out: If you want to grow spiritually, if you want to succeed, you will. If you don't care that much about it, you won't. It's not random or the luck of the draw. People grow spiritually because they make the right choices to do the right things.

We will either go forward as a Christian or we will go backwards. We will either progress or regress. We will either gain ground or lose ground.

And by the way, if you stand still, you *will* lose ground.

If we want to make headway in our life in Christ, we need to make a daily commitment to grow spiritually. To progress. To learn. Not just to "hold our own" or "dig in." We need to gain ground every day.

What we want to do, then, is to live a life that will honor the Lord and stay away from things that will drag us down spiritually. Second Timothy 2:22 (NLT) tells us to "run from anything that stimulates youthful lust. Instead, pursue righteous living, faithfulness, love, and peace. Enjoy the companionship of those who call on the Lord with pure hearts."

Spiritual growth, then, is based on doing what is good and not doing what is bad.

In the last chapter, we saw that if we want to grow spiritually we must love, study, and read the Word of God. That's essential. It's a no-brainer. Joshua 1:8 says, "This Book of the Law shall not depart from your mouth, but you shall meditate in it day and night, that you may observe to do according to all that is written in it. For then you will make your way prosperous, and then you will have good success."

But that's not all.

You also need to pray.

Prayer Points

As he put pen to parchment in his lonely prison cell, the apostle Paul did some thinking about his friends at the church in Ephesus. He had developed a deep relationship with the church and wanted the best for their lives. Unsure of his own future, he wanted these men and women to succeed in their walk with Christ through the years. And he understood very well that one of the greatest keys to their success—in good times or times of great testing and trial—would be their prayer life.

In Ephesians 6:18 (NIV), Paul urges the Ephesians—and all of us to this day—to "pray in the Spirit on all occasions with all kinds of prayers and requests. With this in mind, be alert and always keep on praying for all the Lord's people."

Always keep on praying

In other words, wherever we are and whatever we are doing, God wants us to be people of prayer. You can pray publicly or privately, verbally or silently, and any position is acceptable! You can pray kneeling, standing, sitting, lying down, and even driving. (Keep your eyes open while you're driving, of course.)

We have been teaching our little granddaughter Stella to pray before meals, and we will say, "Stella, let's pray. Close your eyes, now." So she dutifully closes her eyes. One time I opened my eyes to see what she was doing, and she was reaching for the food with her eyes closed!

There is some value in closing your eyes in prayer as a means of filtering out some of the distractions of life. But in the end, it doesn't really matter. You can pray anytime, anywhere, in the midst of most any activity.

Sometimes we may think that God will hear our prayers better if they are offered in a place of worship. Again, that's not true. He hears our prayers wherever we offer them.

Look at some of the places people prayed in the Bible. Daniel prayed in a den of lions. David prayed in a cave and also in the wilderness. Peter prayed on top of the water—and also *in* the water as he began to sink! Jonah prayed from the stomach of a fish. So it seems to me that wherever you are, God will hear your prayer.

Pray without ceasing

The key is that we should pray frequently. As Ephesians 6:18 tells us, we are to pray "on all occasions." Morning. Noon. Afternoon. Evening. The middle of the night. Bottom line, the Bible tells us to "pray without ceasing . . . for this is the will of God in Christ Jesus for you" (1 Thessalonians 5:17, 18).

Pray everywhere

The Bible tells us in 1 Timothy 2:8, "Pray everywhere, lifting up holy hands."

Pray *everywhere*. Should I ask the blessing of God on my meal when I'm out in public? Absolutely. We've all experienced that awkward moment when you're out dining with family or friends who aren't believers, and your meal arrives. You wonder, *Should we pray?* Because normally, that's what you would do as a believer or as a Christian family. But what if it offends or turns off the nonbelievers present?

You know what I say? *Pray anyway.*

Often, I will initiate that prayer. I will simply say, "Let's pray."

I don't say, "Do you mind if I pray?" and give them the option of saying yes. If they don't want to pray, that's fine; I figure they can just watch me for a few seconds as I pray. And here's the great thing about prayer: When you pray, you have the floor. By that I mean that when you're praying, other people will generally listen. So you can say, "Lord, thank You for this food. You have provided it. . . ." And then just go on from there.

I would recommend that you keep it short. Why? Because everyone wants to eat! The food is right there, steaming and fragrant before you. You don't want to offer the plan of salvation in your prayer at that point or intercede for missionaries around the world. There are other times to do that. Just give a quick, heartfelt word of thanks for God's provision of the food and pray in Jesus' name.

In the Bible, you will find that prayers in public tended to be shorter, while prayers in private were longer. I think that we often do the reverse: We don't have much to say to the Lord in private but get a little verbose and eloquent when we have to pray out loud.

Just keep it simple. But don't miss the opportunity.

Sometimes we have the luxury of taking our time and praying like the prophet Daniel prayed, three times a day before his open window. At other times, however, all we have time to do is shoot up a quick prayer—like an arrow pointed to heaven. The Bible tells us how Nehemiah prayed a prayer like that. He was a counselor to Artaxerxes, king of Persia, standing in the king's presence, when suddenly an opportunity opened up for him to bring up the plight of his fellow Jews who were back in conquered Israel.

Should he do it? Was he risking his life? Nehemiah didn't have time to go home, get on his knees, open the window, and pray to the Lord as Daniel had. He only had a moment. Should he speak? Should he remain silent? Shooting up a quick prayer, he went on to tell that powerful king everything that was on his heart. And the king responded with kindness and generosity. (See Nehemiah 2:1-8.)

It will be that way for us sometimes. We will find ourselves in a situation where we must make a decision immediately, and there isn't time to lay out all the details before the Lord.

The boss calls. The police knock on your door. Your friend calls you in great need. The doctor comes in the room, looking grim. You find yourself in an emergency of some kind, and you have to make a decision or respond. So you say, "Lord, help me," or "Lord, enable me," and you take that next step.

You can pray a prayer like this with your eyes wide open. You don't even have to verbalize it at all, unless you want to. God is there. God knows. God hears. God has a complete grasp on all the details—including a million angles you never thought of.

The main thing is to pray.

Pray continually

There is a sense in which we can pray continuously all day long. The Bible tells us that Elijah went into the court of King Ahab, a wicked man, and said, "As the Lord God of Israel lives, before whom I stand . . ." (1 Kings 17:1). In other words, Elijah was aware of the fact that wherever he went, he stood in the presence of God.

The fact is you are never alone. Wherever you go, God is with you—and you can commune with Him, fellowship with Him, pray to Him, and hear from Him. That's the idea of continuous prayer: being in fellowship and communion with the Lord.

Why Should I Pray?

1. Jesus told me to

Jesus said in Luke 18:1, "Men always ought to pray and not lose heart." And He not only told me to pray, but He left me an example of prayer. Jesus was constantly praying. Here was God in human form, walking our planet, breathing our air, and yet feeling the need to be in constant communion with His Father. He prayed during the day. He prayed at night when the disciples were sleeping. He prayed early in the morning, before anyone else was up.

We know that while He was in Gethsemane, in the most agonizing hour of His life to that point, He prayed, "Father, if it is your will, take this cup away from Me."[68] And as He hung on the cross of Calvary, His first statement was, "Father, forgive them, for they do not know what they do." [69] Later He prayed, "My God, My God, why have You forsaken Me?"[70]

When Jesus raised Lazarus from the dead, we read that He spoke first to His Father, saying, "'Father, thank You for hearing Me. You always hear Me." But He said it out loud for the sake of those that were standing here, "So that they will believe You sent Me." Then He shouted, "Lazarus, come out!"[71]

When He fed the five thousand people, we read that He looked up toward heaven and asked God's blessing on the food. We read that the mothers brought their children to Jesus so He could lay His hands on them and pray for them.

So here's my point. *If Jesus felt the necessity to pray constantly, day and night, how much more should we?*

2. Prayer is God's appointed way for obtaining things

"Obtaining things," of course, isn't the only reason—or even the primary reason—we pray. (Although that might come as a surprise to some.)

Having said that, prayer most certainly is God's way of giving things to you that you need in your life. The New Testament tells us bluntly, "You do not have because you do not ask God" (James 4:2, NIV).

Think about that. There are things God may want to give to you, do for you, and say to you, but He hasn't given you those things because you haven't asked Him.

Why is it that I never know the will of God for my life?

Could it be because you haven't asked?

Why is it that I'm never able to lead other people to Christ?

Could it be because you haven't asked?

Why am I always just barely scraping by with my finances?

Could it be because you haven't asked?

Why do I keep getting sick? Why can't I shake this infection?

Could it be because you haven't asked?

Now, I'm not suggesting here that God will always give you everything that you ask for or that He will heal every person who asks for His touch.

But He will heal some. Maybe it will be you. Have you asked Him to?

What have you got to lose? Yes, the Lord may very well say no, or perhaps wait. But He might also say yes. So go ahead and pour out your heart to Him in prayer and tell Him all your hopes and desires.

3. Prayer is the way by which God helps us overcome our anxiety and worry

Life is full of troubles. We have concerns about our future, our health, our family, and our finances. The list goes on and on. Sometimes circumstances or events enter our lives that scare us or even terrify us.

So I have a suggestion for you. Instead of worrying, *pray*. It has been said, "If your knees are shaking, *kneel* on them."

If you have no worries in your life at all, I'd recommend that you check your pulse, because you may not be alive. Everyone worries from time to time. I'd be a hypocrite if I didn't admit here that I worry at times too. I don't say that proudly, and my worrying certainly isn't a virtue. In fact, it can be a sin, where I am failing to trust my heavenly Father as I ought to.

The Bible's remedy for all of us in times of anxiety or concern is to pray. In Philippians 4:6-7, Paul gives us these strong words of encouragement:

> Don't worry about anything; instead, pray about everything. Tell God what you need, and thank him for all he has done. Then you will experience God's peace, which exceeds anything we can understand. His peace will guard your hearts and minds as you live in Christ Jesus. (NLT)

Notice, however, what these verses do *not* say. We don't read, "Don't worry about anything; pray about everything, and God will take your problems away."

No, but what He does promise us is His peace—right in the middle of everything. And it is a peace (as it says in the old King James Bible), which "passeth all understanding."

Maybe God will take your problem away. That may be part of His plan. Then again, maybe He won't. Because sometimes you will pray and pray and the problem will still be with you. But here is what happens: He gives you perspective right in the midst of it. You get a better view of what's going on, who God is, and who you are. You will see your problem for what it is.

If you have a big God, you have a relatively small problem. But if you have a big problem, it might be that your God is too small. In other words, you aren't seeing God in His glory, wisdom, and power.

There are times when I'm hit with anxiety over the reality that my son Christopher is no longer with us. I feel overwhelmed at times, and what should I pray? That God would bring him back? I don't think that's very likely. So here is what I pray, "God, help me. I need You."

It reminds me of what David prayed in Psalm 61:2: "From the end of the earth I will cry to You, when my heart is overwhelmed; Lead me to the rock that is higher than I."

When I pray like that, God gives me His peace and the strength to get through what I am dealing with. And He will do the same for any person who will call upon Him.

I will tell you this: I pray a great deal because I *need* to.

I need prayer to get through the day. I need prayer to get up in the morning. I need prayer to get through the afternoon, and I need prayer to go to sleep at night. I'm not ashamed to say those things. I pray because I need God's help.

Time after time, He gives me the help, strength, perspective, and comfort that I need. And He will give those things to you as well, if you ask Him.

4. Prayer helps us ready ourselves for the return of Jesus Christ

One modern translation translates the words of Jesus to His disciples like this:

> Watch out! Don't let your hearts be dulled by carousing and drunkenness, and by the worries of this life. Don't let that day catch you unaware, like a trap. For that day will come upon everyone living on the earth. Keep alert at all times. And pray that you might be strong enough to escape these coming horrors and stand before the Son of Man. (Luke 21:34-36, NLT)

Jesus told us that no one, apart from His Father, knows the day and hour of His return to earth. He said, "Take heed, watch and pray; for you do not know when the time is" (Mark 13:33).

How can we overstate the importance of prayer to a believer's life? If you want God to speak to you, *pray*. If you want Him to provide for you, *pray*. If you want help with your worry, *pray*. If you want to be ready for His return, *pray*.

But sometimes we pray, and we don't like the outcome. Someone may say, "God never answers my prayer."

Really? What do you mean by that?

"Well, I have prayed for such-and-such to happen, but it never happened. God doesn't answer my prayers."

What we tend to forget is that no is just as much of an answer as yes.

If God in His wisdom replies to our request with no or not now, that doesn't mean He hasn't heard us—or that He hasn't answered. We might not like His answer, but we can't really say He "doesn't answer our prayers."

Here is something to consider, however. If the *request* is wrong, God will say, "No." If the *timing* is wrong, God will say, "Slow." If *you* are wrong, God will say, "Grow." But if the request is right and the timing is right and you are right, God will say, "Go."

So here is the question. Is there something we can do to cause God to say go more often? Is there something we can do to see our prayers answered more often in the affirmative? My answer to that question is yes, I believe there are some things that we can do. We'll look closely at those things in the next chapter.

It may surprise you to find that the suggestions grow out of the most familiar prayer of all.

15

Secrets of Spiritual Growth, Part 3
A Pattern for Prayer

The Lord's Prayer, in Luke 11, is the most well-known prayer in all of the Bible and one that many have committed to memory. The Bible itself, however, never calls this prayer "the Lord's Prayer." Frankly, this is not a prayer Jesus would have ever prayed for Himself. He would never need to say, "Forgive us our sins, as we forgive those who have sinned against us."

This wasn't a prayer for Him, it's a prayer for us. He gave us this prayer because the disciples had said, "Lord, teach us to pray." (If you want to listen in on the *real* Lord's Prayer, you can find it in John 17. It's a prayer that only Christ could have prayed.)

Here again are the familiar words:

> Now it came to pass, as He was praying in a certain place, when He ceased, that one of His disciples said to Him, "Lord, teach us to pray, as John also taught his disciples."
>
> So He said to them, "When you pray, say:

Our Father in heaven,

Hallowed be Your name.

Your kingdom come.

Your will be done

On earth as it is in heaven.

Give us day by day our daily bread.

And forgive us our sins,

For we also forgive everyone who is indebted to us.

And do not lead us into temptation,

But deliver us from the evil one.

(Luke 11:1-4)

The gospel of Matthew adds the familiar closing: "For Yours is the kingdom and the power and the glory forever" (6:13).

I want to point out to you that the disciples said, "Teach us to pray." They didn't say, "Lord, teach us *a prayer*," or, "Lord, teach us the prayer to pull out when things get really bad." That's how some people treat the Lord's Prayer. When crisis hits, they rattle off the words, *"Our-Father- who-art-in-heaven-hallowed-be-Thy-name."*

Some consider this prayer like the emergency equipment you find behind glass panels in a big building. *"In case of emergency, pray this prayer."*

No, there's nothing wrong with saying this prayer verbatim. It's a beautiful, powerful prayer from the Lord's own lips. But it wasn't given to us merely as a prayer to pray. It was given as a model or template for prayer.

Matthew also tells us Jesus said, "In this manner, therefore, pray" (6:9). So it is a structure for our prayers.

It's also something more.

If you and I follow the pattern that Jesus gives us in this prayer, if we take to heart each element that He provides for us here, we will find that more and more of our prayers will be answered with a yes.

How will we get more of our prayers answered in the affirmative? Let's consider some of the strong principles growing out of these familiar words.

How to Get Your Prayers Answered in the Affirmative

1. You must realize who it is you're praying to

"Our Father in heaven . . ."

When I approach God in prayer, I am speaking to the all-powerful, all-knowing Creator of the universe.

The very first words of this prayer are very important. Notice that Jesus did not teach us to pray, "Our Creator in heaven," "Our Sovereign in heaven," or even "Our God in heaven."

He is all those things of course—Creator, Sovereign, and God. But that's not what Jesus said. He said, "In this manner, therefore, pray, 'Our Father in heaven . . .'"

Do you realize what a revolutionary idea that was for a first-century Jew to hear? The Hebrew people were raised with a great awe and respect for the God of Israel. They would approach God through the high priest who would offer sacrifices on their behalf. To actually call God "Father" would have been unthinkable. In fact, one of the reasons they crucified Jesus was because He so boldly named God as His Father.

But now Jesus, the Lamb of God who has died in our place and taken away the sin of the world, has opened up a new relationship between us and God the Father. Now we can call Him "Father" too.

After the Lord was newly risen from the dead, He spoke these tender, incredibly encouraging words to Mary Magdalene, "Don't cling to me . . . for I haven't yet ascended to the Father. But go find my brothers and tell them, 'I am ascending to my Father and your Father, to my God and your God' " (John 20:17, NLT).

He is my Father now. I can call Him that because I have been adopted into God's own family. In the book of Romans, Paul writes, "For you did not receive the spirit of bondage again to fear, but you received the Spirit of adoption by whom we cry out, 'Abba, Father.' The Spirit Himself bears witness with our spirit that we are children of God" (Romans 8:15-16).

Abba, Father. That reference takes our intimacy with God a step further, because "Abba Father" means "Daddy" or "Papa." It's a more affectionate term. There is tenderness and intimacy there.

I don't know what kind of dad you have or had growing up. Maybe you had a father who was distant, cold, or harsh. He never affirmed you or spoke an encouraging word to you. Perhaps he was austere, mean, or downright abusive. Then again, you may not be able to remember a father at all; he was someone who walked away from your family and became a distant stranger. As a result, when you think about your Father in heaven, you find yourself attaching the weaknesses or negative qualities of your earthly father.

But God isn't like your earthly father.

God the Father loves you unconditionally.

God the Father will be there for you—no matter what.

God the Father will never abandon you.

God the Father loves you with an everlasting love.

He is *"my Father"* in heaven. Don't let Satan cloud or steal away that great reality from your life.

The next phrase, *"Hallowed be Your name,"* literally means, "set apart be Your name." May Your name be glorified. To say words like these means that as a follower of Jesus Christ I want to honor His name and live a holy life.

Because of this commitment, I need to question my interests and pursuits, asking myself, "Is this for His glory?" Can I write "hallowed be Your name" over what I am about to do? Can I write "hallowed be Your name" over my career choice? Can I write "hallowed be Your name" over my choice of a boyfriend, girlfriend, husband, or wife? Can I write "hallowed be Your name" over the programs I watch on TV or the movies I go to or the music I listen to? Can I write "hallowed be Your name" over the things I'm engaged in?

If not, then I should change.

I should realize that my life needs to be "set apart" from anything that would reflect negatively on the name and reputation of my heavenly Father and my Lord Jesus Christ.

2. You must pray according to the will of God

"Your kingdom come.
Your will be done
On earth as it is in heaven."

We can offer all kinds of requests to God, but what is the primary objective of prayer? Here it is: *To line my will up with the will of God.* True praying is not overcoming God's reluctance; it is laying hold of His willingness. Remember this: Prayer is not getting my will in heaven; it is getting God's will on earth.

Our goal, then, is to pray, "Lord, what do You want? I want to pray according to your will." Over in the book of 1 John, the apostle writes,

> Now this is the confidence that we have in Him, that if we ask any-thing according to His will, He hears us. And if we know that He hears us, whatever we ask, we know that we have the petitions that we have asked of Him. (1 John 5:14)

There is nothing outside the reach of prayer except that which lies outside of the will of God.

When I pray, then, I ask God for what seems right to me, but I always add the words, "Nevertheless, not my will, but Yours be done."

I actually heard a preacher once say, "Never pray, 'Not my will but Yours be done.' Instead, you should pray, *my* will be done."

That's crazy. Not to mention unbiblical.

The longer I live, the more thankful I am that God said no to many of my foolish prayers. With 20/20 hindsight, I can now see how disastrous it might have been for me and my family if God had answered all of my requests with a yes. He knew what was best for me then, and He still does now.

Now I pray, "Lord, you know my heart and all my desires. I'm ask-ing for this thing, but You know best. I want Your will in this, because I know Your will is best."

When I'm praying for a sick person, I will often say, "Lord, we ask You to touch and heal this person right now. We ask this in faith."

But then I will always add, "But Lord, You might have a purpose we don't know about, so let Your will be done here."

"That's a cop-out!" some would say.

That's not a cop-out. That is an acknowledgement that I don't know everything, but God does. And I am asking Him to use executive privilege and do what He wants to do where He wants to do it, because God's will is better than my own.

If you want God to say yes to you more often when you pray, you must align your will with God's will.

When you pray, "Your kingdom come. Your will be done on earth as it is in heaven," you are effectively saying something like this: "Lord, here I am as finite person, coming before You as an infinite God. With my limited understanding, I am saying, 'Here is the course You ought to follow. Here is what I would like You to do.' At the same moment, however, I am also saying that if this somehow falls short of Your bigger plan or purpose for my life, then *Your* kingdom come, *Your* will be done."

When we pray, "Your kingdom come" we are praying for the will of God or the rule of God on earth. We are anticipating the day when Jesus Christ returns to Planet Earth and establishes His kingdom.

We are praying, "Lord, may Your kingdom rule in Washington D.C. May Your kingdom rule in the Democratic Party and the Republican Party. May Your kingdom rule in our state capitol and in our city hall. We are looking for the day when there is a righteous rule on earth, because we know government is not the answer. The kingdom of God is the only answer. Lord, come rule and reign on this earth!"

It's interesting that the word *come* in the phrase *Your kingdom come* speaks of a sudden, instantaneous event. It is the same as when the apostle John prayed, "Even so, come, Lord Jesus!"[72]

In other words, "Lord, not only am I asking You to come and rule on the earth, but I am asking You to come and do it soon."

This is also, however, a *personal* request. I am asking for the rule of God's kingdom in my own life. But consider this: You can't pray,

"Your kingdom come" until you are prepared to pray, "*My* kingdom go." Are you willing to do that? Until we give God permission to supplant or even dismantle our personal kingdom—our own wants, desires, priorities, plans, and goals—we can't really pray, "Your kingdom come" with any integrity.

When I pray this phrase in the Lord's Prayer, then, I'm praying something for the whole world, and I'm also praying something for myself.

It's also an evangelistic prayer. I am saying, "Lord, I want to see Your rule and reign in the life of others as well." One of the most important ways God's kingdom is brought to this earth happens each time a new soul is brought to salvation in Jesus Christ.

3. Your petitions must follow your submission

"Give us this day our daily bread."

If we wrote the Lord's prayer, we would move this phrase to the front. We would say, "Our Father in heaven, hallowed be Your name. Give us this day our daily bread. . . ." It's as though we were praying, "Hello, God. How are You? Here's what I need. Here's my grocery list. Gotta go now. Amen."

There is nothing wrong with bringing your petitions before God. But that is not how the prayer is structured. No, here is the correct flow: "My Father in heaven, hallowed—set apart—be Your name. Your kingdom come. Your will be done on earth as it is in heaven. Now, Lord. . . . give me this day my daily bread."

Here is what we sometimes wonder: *Why is it that this all-knowing, all-powerful, omnipresent God who created the entire universe would care about you and me as individuals?* As Job said, "What is mankind that you make so much of them, that you give them so much attention?" (Job 7:17, NIV). Why would God care about my needs—and even my wants? Why would He commit Himself to providing my daily bread?

Why? Because He loves us, and He wants to bless us.

Our God is generous, not stingy.

Maybe the better picture of generosity would be that of a grand-parent, rather than a parent. As a grandfather, I've been known to "overindulge" my granddaughters. That analogy, of course, breaks down pretty quickly. But here's my point. It is not hard for me to do something for my children or my grandchildren. I love doing things for them. It's my delight.

And Jesus said of our heavenly Father, "So don't be afraid, little flock. For it gives your Father great happiness to give you the Kingdom" (Luke 12:32, NLT).

In the same way, God says to us, "I want to pour out My blessings upon you so you won't have room enough to receive them."[73] He wants to show you His love.

Yes, I am taught to pray, "Give me this day my *daily* bread." But notice that it doesn't say, "Give me this month my monthly bread." If God provided for you monthly, you would probably call upon Him monthly. No. It is "Give me this day my daily bread." God arranges things in such a way that I will have to be dependent upon Him on a daily basis.

Here is something else the phrase *Give us this day our daily bread* implies. It is acknowledging that everything you have comes from God. Yes, you can work hard, save diligently, and invest wisely. You can buy your own food and clothes and pay for your house or your car or whatever else. But here is what you need to remember: It all came to you from God. It's all a gift from His hand.

We need to remember that. Deuteronomy 8:18 says, "And you shall remember the LORD your God, for it is He who gives you power to get wealth." The point is simply this: *God gave you all these things, so acknowledge that fact.*

"Lord, everything I have is from You. This food on the table. My health. My ability to earn money. My children. My grandchildren. My career. My talents. It's all from You, Lord, and I acknowledge that and give You glory for it. Now, Lord, will You please keep providing for Me, for I am dependent on You."

4. You must confess your personal sin

"And forgive us our sins . . ."

If you want to see your prayers answered in the affirmative, you must confess your personal sin. As a model for all of our prayers, the

Lord's Prayer teaches us to ask for cleansing and forgiveness on a regular basis. The word *sins* here is literally the term *shortcomings*. In other words, "Forgive us, Lord, for what we owe You, for the wrong we have done."

Some people don't think they necessarily need forgiveness all that often. They quickly review the day in their minds and say to themselves, "I don't know if I really sinned today, so maybe I don't need to talk to the Lord about that."

But what if you sinned today and didn't realize it? What if you did something or spoke words that hurt your wife, your child, or one of your friends or coworkers? Sometimes we're not always aware of sins that we commit. But the Lord is certainly aware of those things.

For that matter, there are different ways that sin can be defined. Sin isn't merely a transgression or the breaking of one of God's laws. Sin is also "falling short of a mark." In fact, the Bible tells us that "everything that does not come from faith is sin" (Romans 14:23, NIV).

If, then, I do something without the certainty it has the blessing of God, it can be a sin for me. In the same way, there are sins of *omission*, where you and I neglect to do something we know we ought to do. Again, the Bible says, "Therefore, to him who knows to do good and does not do it, to him it is sin" (James 4:17).

Whether we are immediately conscious of our sin or not, then, we can assume that we fall or walk into sin on a regular basis—probably more than we realize. As the apostle put it so succinctly: "We all stumble in many ways" (James 3:2, NIV).

Have you ever noticed that when you wear white pants you always spill things on them? At least that's my experience. Why is that? It just seems inevitable that if I put on a nice clean pair of white pants in the morning, by that evening I'll have stains on them. Is it because I'm more clumsy or careless when I wear white? I don't think so. The sad truth is that I probably spill stuff all the time but just don't notice it so much on my dark jeans. But there's no hiding mustard or ketchup or dirt on bright white pants. White *displays* the stains. They stand out in sharp relief.

In the same way, when we come into the presence of God and see Him for who He is, we see ourselves for who we are.

Here's the bottom line: We need to pray for cleansing and forgiveness whether we're aware of our need or not. The Bible says, "If we say that we have no sin, we deceive ourselves, and the truth is not in us" (1 John 1:8). In fact, I would take it a step further and say the more you grow spiritually, the more aware you become of your own personal sin. It has been said, "The greater the saint, the greater the sense of sin and the awareness of sin."

As we noted earlier, when Isaiah suddenly found himself in the Lord's awesome presence, he immediately became aware of his own sins and shortcomings. He wrote, "I saw the Lord sitting on a throne, high and lifted up, and the train of His robe filled the temple." And almost immediately after this, he wrote, "Woe is me, for I am undone! Because I am a man of unclean lips, and I dwell in the midst of a people of unclean lips; for my eyes have seen the King, the LORD of hosts" (Isaiah 6:1, 5).

Isaiah could have said, "I just saw the Lord. I'm the greatest prophet alive!" But no, he didn't boast of his own glory in God's presence. He became overwhelmed with the sense of his own sinfulness.

So we need to pray regularly, "Lord, forgive me of my sins." Why is that important? Because if you don't confess your sin, your prayers won't go any higher than the ceiling! Sin—and even contemplating sin—will shut down your prayer life cold. Psalm 66:18 (KJV) says, "If I regard iniquity in my heart, the Lord will not hear me." That word *regard* in this verse means "to cling to" or "hold on to." In other words, if I hold on to sin in my life, it will bring my prayer life to a screeching halt. Underlining that fact, the Bible says: "Your iniquities have separated you from your God; and your sins have hidden His face from you, so that He will not hear" (Isaiah 59:2).

If I'm not aware of what sin I may be guilty of, I can pray along the lines of David's prayer in Psalm 139:23-24:

> Search me, God, and know my heart; test me and know my anxious thoughts. See if there is any offensive way in me, and lead me in the way everlasting. (NIV)

5. You must forgive others

"And forgive us our sins, for we also forgive everyone who is indebted to us."

If you want your prayers answered in the affirmative, you must forgive others. Forgiven people are forgiving people.

Let me take it a step further. An unforgiving Christian is an oxymoron. An oxymoron, of course, is one of those self-contradictory terms we read now and then.

"They were found missing." Were they found, or missing?

"There was a deafening silence." Really? How could it be both?

"It's a minor crisis." If it's one, it can't be the other.

"Genuine imitation." That's a contradiction in terms!

I would put "unforgiving Christian" in that same category. If we are truly in Christ, then how could we act in the opposite way that He does? The fact is, we are all flawed, fallible people; we will sin against others, and others will sin against us. Husbands will offend their wives, and wives will offend their children. Not necessarily intentionally, but they will. Family members will offend one another. Friends will offend one another.

How do we respond? We must simply say, "I forgive them for that. I'm choosing to simply let this go. I don't want those things to keep me from communion and fellowship with my God."

"Hold on, Greg," someone says. "That person really did me wrong. That person has really hurt me. I have every right to be angry and bitter." Yes, you might have a valid case against that person who wounded you. But if you are harboring anger and hostility and vengeful thoughts toward someone, *you* are the one who is being hurt the most.

Why? Most importantly because you are cutting yourself off from fellowship with God. Ephesians 4:32 says, "Be kind to one another, tenderhearted, forgiving one another, *even as God in Christ forgave you*" (emphasis added).

Did *you* deserve to be forgiven? Did *I* deserve to be forgiven? Absolutely not. Does the person who offended you deserve your forgiveness? Maybe, maybe not. But you are to forgive that person anyway. We should forgive as God in His love and grace forgave us.

How important is this? Consider what Jesus said in the Sermon on the Mount: "So if you are standing before the altar in the Temple, offering a sacrifice to God, and suddenly remember that a friend has something against you, leave your sacrifice there beside the altar and go and apologize and be reconciled to him, and then come and offer your sacrifice to God" (Matthew 5:23-24, TLB).

Forgiving people in your life who have hurt you is one of a Christian's most important priorities. You can't read those verses in Matthew any other way.

6. As much as possible, you must avoid the place of temptation

"And do not lead us into temptation, But deliver us from the evil one."

As one woman put it, "Lead me not into temptation, I can find the way myself." [74] We do a pretty good job of that, don't we?

We all know of places we can go where we'll be tempted. We all know of people we can hang around with who drag us down and open us up more to enticement. By the same token, we also know of places we can go that will strengthen us spiritually (like church) and people we can hang around with who will build us up and make us want to sin less. So as much as possible, stay out of the way of temptation. When Jesus teaches us to pray, "Deliver us from evil"(KJV), it could be better translated, "Deliver us from the evil one."

In other words, "Lord, help me to not get too close to the fire. Help to be smart about this."

In the book of Jeremiah, the Lord said, "The human heart is the most deceitful of all things, and desperately wicked. Who really knows how bad it is?" (17:9, NLT). It's amazing how we can rationalize sin in our lives. If someone else does the same thing, it's wrong. But somehow, it's okay for us. We have these little double standards that we work up in our minds in an attempt to excuse ourselves. That's why the Lord said the heart "is the most deceitful of all things."

Do you have some area of your life that troubles you a little, where you wonder if this is something you ought to do as a Christian or not? Pray about it and bring it into the clear light of the presence of Christ.

Could you ask God's blessing on that activity? Could you comfortably take the Lord along with you as engage in this?

"Lord, bless us tonight as we go out and party and get drunk."

"Lord, please be with my girlfriend and me as we have sex outside of marriage."

"Lord, please grant me success as I sue my Christian brother."

"Father, please smile down on me as I divorce my husband because I met a cuter guy."

See how stupid that sounds? We would never verbalize prayers like those. And yet somehow, our minds can rationalize away activities that we might have once criticized or condemned in others.

I dare you to pray about these activities in the clear light of the presence of Jesus Christ. It might lead you to reconsider how you move forward.

This brings us to our last principle on how to have your prayers answered in the affirmative.

7. You must not give up!

And so I tell you, keep on asking, and you will be given what you ask for. Keep on looking, and you will find. Keep on knocking, and the door will be opened to you. (Luke 11:9, NLT)

Jesus told his disciples a story to show that they should always pray and never give up. (Luke 18:1, NLT)

Going back to Luke 11, Jesus had told His men another story on the same theme:

"Suppose you went to a friend's house at midnight, wanting to borrow three loaves of bread. You say to him, 'A friend of mine has just arrived for a visit, and I have nothing for him to eat.' And suppose he calls out from his bedroom, 'Don't bother me. The door is locked for the night, and my family and I are all in bed. I can't help you.' But I tell you this—though he won't do it for friendship's sake, if you keep knocking long enough, he will get up and give you whatever you need because of your shameless persistence.

"And so I tell you, keep on asking, and you will receive what you ask for. Keep on seeking, and you will find. Keep on knocking, and the door will be opened to you. For everyone who asks, receives. Everyone who seeks, finds. And to everyone who knocks, the door will be opened." (Luke 11:5-10, NLT)

Often in prayer we will ask God for something once or twice and then simply give up. What we should remember, however, is that sometimes God is not saying no. He may instead be saying, "The timing isn't right. I will do this for you later, but not now." So keep praying. Keep asking. Don't give up.

Really, God isn't anything at all like the ill-tempered, stingy friend who didn't want to get out of bed to get his friend some bread. The passage isn't saying that we will only get God to respond to us by constantly badgering Him. No, Jesus is using this story as a *contrast* to our heavenly Father.

We come to a Father who wants to answer our prayer, who wants to open the door at midnight, who wants to give good gifts to His children, whose ear is open to our prayers.

So don't give up so easily. As the Scripture says, keep on asking, keep on seeking, and keep on knocking on the door. The Lord's language is unusually compelling, because the three verbs used here—ask, seek, and knock—indicate an ascending intensity.

To *ask* means to request assistance. It would be like being in the hardware store and looking around for someone to help you find something. You would say, "Excuse me. Could you help me?" But maybe that employee is busy talking on his cell phone or counting widgets in a bin. If you really want help, you would have to step it up a little.

That brings us to the next word. To *seek* denotes asking with some action. So you might tap that preoccupied hardware clerk on the shoulder, get some eye contact, and say, "Excuse me. Sorry to interrupt, but I really need some help right now. Could you assist me?"

The final word, *knock*, speaks of asking plus action plus persevering. In the hardware store, this might mean that you risk making a little scene, because you're simply not going to take no for answer.

Not long ago when I was in New York City, I went out to dinner on a Friday night with twenty-two people in a very noisy Italian restaurant in Little Italy. It was so loud I couldn't even hear myself think. And as I sat down at the table, I saw that I didn't have any silverware. I kept trying to catch the waiter's eye, but I couldn't get him to notice me. So I turned to my friend Mike, who is a native New Yorker and knows how to speak to fellow New Yorkers.

Understanding my plight as a polite West Coast person, Mike stood up and yelled, "HEY! WE NEED SOME SILVERWARE OVER HERE!" Mike knew how to work the system, and I got my silverware.

Even the most timid or polite among us know that sometimes a person has to step up to the plate and get a little aggressive to make his or her wishes known. Did you ever think about that in conjunction with prayer?

"Well," someone might say, "I don't want to insult God."

Listen—you are *not* insulting God when you are praying according to His will. You are pleasing God.

Remember the story of the Gentile woman who approached Jesus with a request for her hurting daughter?

> A Gentile woman who lived there came to him, pleading, "Have mercy on me, O Lord, Son of David! For my daughter is possessed by a demon that torments her severely."
>
> But Jesus gave her no reply, not even a word. Then his disciples urged him to send her away. "Tell her to go away," they said. "She is bothering us with all her begging."
>
> Then Jesus said to the woman, "I was sent only to help God's lost sheep—the people of Israel."
>
> But she came and worshiped him, pleading again, "Lord, help me!"
>
> Jesus responded, "It isn't right to take food from the children and throw it to the dogs."
>
> She replied, "That's true, Lord, but even dogs are allowed to eat the scraps that fall beneath their masters' table."

"Dear woman," Jesus said to her, "your faith is great. Your request is granted." And her daughter was instantly healed. (Matthew 15:22-28, NLT)

This needy Gentile woman had said to Jesus, "Lord, would you heal my child?" And Jesus gave her the most amazing response. He said, "It's really not right to take the children's food and give it to the dogs."

What? Is that a nice thing to say to a lady asking for help for her daughter? To clarify a little, the word that Jesus used for "dogs" spoke of the family pet. So it would be like saying, "It's not right to take the children's food and give it to little Fifi."

Some people would have walked away in a huff. Not this lady. She understood the value of persistence. She said, "Well, Lord, even those little dogs get the crumbs that fall off the masters' table."

I can readily imagine Jesus looking at her with a smile and saying, "Ask what you want and I will give it to you." In that same moment, I can imagine the disciples' jaws collectively dropping to the ground. First of all, why is He even talking to a Gentile woman? And now, He's going to give her whatever she wants!? Why?

Because she passed the test.

Jesus had placed obstacles in front of her, but she cleared hurdle after hurdle. What's the point? She understood the value of persistent prayer. "This is my daughter, Lord. I love her. I'm going to keep praying for her. I intend to follow You around until You touch her and help her."

Her persistence was well-rewarded. At that point where her will aligned with His will, Jesus granted her request.

Sometimes the Lord will put obstacles in our path as well. He will test our resolve and our persistence. Will we persevere in our prayers? Will we hang in there over the long haul? Will we "always pray and not give up"?

Jesus says, "To the one who keeps on knocking, the door will be opened."

Part 4

Last Things

chapter

16 Signs of the Times

When I get up in the mornings, I always want to know what the weather will be so I'll know how to dress.

Will it be warm? Cool? Raining? Yes, I do check with the weatherman, but I have come to realize that my guess is nearly as good as the so-called expert meteorologist with all his sophisticated instruments. So often he will predict clear skies, and then it rains. Or he'll say that rain's on the way, but the sky is blue all day long.

I can guarantee a way to make it rain. Just wash your car and polish it up as nicely as you possibly can. It *will* rain. It works every time.

Actually, bald men are usually the first to know when it starts to rain. On more than one occasion my wife and I have been walking down the street, and I will say, "It's raining." She will look at me and say, "No, it isn't."

"Oh, yes it is," I will reply, and I'm usually right. Her hair is so thick she wouldn't know for a week if it was raining. But I know the moment the first little drop hits. That is sensitive instrumentation!

Did you know that Jesus spoke about predicting the weather? He once told a group of his critics:

> "You know the saying, 'Red sky at night means fair weather tomorrow; red sky in the morning means foul weather all day.' You know how to interpret the weather signs in the sky, but you don't know how to interpret the signs of the times!" (Matthew 16:2-3, NLT)

That's quite an indictment, isn't it?

Signs of the times? What He meant was, "You've learned indicators and methods that help you read the weather, but you have totally missed the indicators God has given you that show what He is doing in the world." By saying this, He is also telling us that we tend to miss the obvious signs of His soon return to this earth.

Lost in Translation?

Some signs, of course, are easier to read than others. This is especially true when you find yourself overseas facing a language barrier. Things are often "lost in translation."

I remember being in England years ago and noticing signs in many of the windows that said, "Bill Stickers Will Be Prosecuted." And I began to wonder, who is this Bill Stickers, and what exactly has he done? Why will Bill Stickers be prosecuted?

I finally asked someone, and he said, "Oh, you're a bit of an idiot, aren't you?" He told me that Bill Stickers are people who put posters up on walls and windows and such without asking permission. (Why didn't they just *say* so?)

Our ministry team has also spent quite a bit of time in Australia, where I've encountered some interesting designations for certain foods. "Rocket," for instance, is a salad. And shrimp is called "bugs." So you read in the menu, "Rocket with bugs." I said to the server, "What is this, exactly?" He explained it, but by that time I'd lost my appetite.

Even subtle changes in the language can throw you off a bit.

I came upon a collection of actual signs from around the world, written by non-English speakers attempting to use English words.[75] The resulting message may fall a bit short of what the writer intended.

In a Bucharest hotel lobby, for instance, this sign was posted in front of the lift, or elevator. "The lift is being fixed for the next day. During that time we regret that you will be unbearable."

In a Paris hotel elevator, a sign read, "Please leave your values at the front desk."

In a Belgrade hotel elevator, another sign instructed, "To move the cabin push button for wishing floor. If the cabin should enter more persons each one should press a number of wishing floor. Driving is then going alphabetically by national order."

A Hong Kong supermarket posted this notice: "For your convenience we recommend courageous efficient self-service." I kind of like that one.

In a hotel in Athens, a notice proclaimed, "Visitors are expected to complain in the office between the hours of 9 and 11 daily." (No doubt they do too.)

A dinner menu in a Polish hotel included this bizarre description of a certain dish: "Salad a firm's own make; Limpid red beet soup with cheesy dumplings in the form of a finger; Roasted duck let loose; Beef Rashers beaten up in the country people's fashion."

How about this one in an advertisement from a Hong Kong dentist? "Teeth extracted by the latest Methodists." Methodists pulling teeth in Hong Kong? Who would have known?

This one is kind of scary. In the window of a Swedish furrier, a sign read, "Fur coats made for ladies from their own skin." (I'm sure most English-speaking women would steer clear of that place!)

And then there was the detour sign in Japan that read: "Stop. Drive sideways."

Or how about this one from a Copenhagen ticket office? "We take your bags and send them in all directions." (I can think of a number of airlines that seem to have adopted that motto.)

The truth is, some signs are more clear than others. Some are easy to read and pretty straightforward, while others are more difficult.

In the pages of the Bible, God has given us "signs of the times," if we will look for them. And these signs are telling us that Jesus Christ is coming again, and soon. (He says so Himself, by the way, in Revelation 22:20.)

What are some of these signs of the times?

The regathering of the nation of Israel to its ancient homeland is a gigantic and unmistakable sign of His soon-coming. Linked closely to that important divine indicator is the Bible's warning that after the Jewish people have regathered in their homeland, their enemies will threaten to destroy them.

Anyone who follows the news, of course, will immediately think of Iran's ongoing threats to wipe Israel off the map.

Speaking of watching the news, we can look around the world on any given day and watch as events unfold just as the Bible predicted they would in "the last days."[76] What kinds of events? Things like global turmoil, an increase in earthquakes, tsunamis, the crash of the stock market, rapid changes in the global economy, the fading of the United States of America as the economic superpower, the rise of a united Europe, and the move toward a one-world currency.

Signs of the times.

Jesus told us that we are to be aware of the times and the seasons. In other words, to stay alert and keep our eyes open.

Truth for the Heart

It's one thing for people to be interested in Bible prophecy in an intellectual sort of way, trying to decipher names and places and events like some complex jigsaw puzzle. However, I think we need to approach this very significant subject with not only our minds but also with our *hearts*. By that I mean we don't want to merely consider these things in an abstract, academic way, but should instead allow God to move our hearts and change our behavior because of what we read. Someone has said that the Bible wasn't only written for our information or even our inspiration, but for our *transformation*.

When we read about the workings of God and the great events just over the horizon, it ought to stir us, creating a sense of awe in our hearts. As God revealed to the prophet Daniel what was about to unfold in the future, the prophet dropped to his knees. He was stunned and was unable to even speak. When he caught a glimpse of the future, it moved him to his very core.[77]

It should be the same for us. In fact, if we really understand what the Bible is saying about the imminent return of Jesus, it should cause us to want to live a more godly life. We read in 1 John 3:2-3,

> Dear friends, we are already God's children, but he has not yet shown us what we will be like when Christ appears. But we do know that we will be like him, for we will see him as he really is. *And all who have this eager expectation will keep themselves pure, just as he is pure.* (NLT, emphasis mine)

In other words, if you really understand what the Bible is saying about the soon return of Jesus, it should cause you to want to live a pure, godly life. You should want to be on your toes, spiritually speaking.

Some might say, "You know, I've never really understood all of that Bible prophecy stuff. Antichrist this. Millennium that. Rapture. Mid-trib. Post-trib. I don't know what it means. I can't sort it out. I'll just let the experts figure those things out."

That may be an understandable response to confusion over details about prophetic teaching, but we really don't want to ignore what the Bible has to say about these things. In fact, there is a special blessing promised for those who would hear and keep the words of this prophecy:

> Blessed is he who reads and those who hear the words of this prophecy, and keep those things which are written in it; for the time is near. (Revelation 1:3)

You want to be blessed, don't you? What is true about the study of the book of Revelation is no doubt true in principle as we look at what all of the Bible teaches about end times events.

The fact is, God must have wanted us to learn Bible prophecy, because at least 30 percent of the Scriptures is dedicated to this topic. And God wants us to know and understand that He keeps His

Word. Just as surely as He kept His Word with prophesies that foretold the arrival of the Messiah in Bethlehem, He will keep His Word about the prophesies pertaining to the return of the Messiah.

Tim LaHaye, who has written extensively on the topic of Bible prophecy, makes this statement:

> No scholar of academic substance denies that Jesus lived almost 2,000 years ago. And yet we find three times as many prophecies in the Bible relating to His Second coming as to His first. Thus the Second Advent of our Lord is three times as certain as His first coming, which can be verified as historical fact.[78]

A World in Turmoil

When Jesus described the world prior to His second coming, He painted a picture of a planet stirred by strife, war, suffering, and famine in the midst of plenty, rocked by great earthquakes, and ravished by pestilence. Luke 21 tells us:

> "There will be strange signs in the sun, moon, and stars. And here on earth the nations will be in turmoil, perplexed by the roaring seas and strange tides. People will be terrified at what they see coming upon the earth, for the powers in the heavens will be shaken." (Luke 21:25-26, NLT)

The Message puts it this way:

> "It will seem like all hell has broken loose—sun, moon, stars, earth, sea, in an uproar and everyone all over the world in a panic, the wind knocked out of them by the threat of doom, the powers-that-be quaking."

The Bible tells us that prior to the return of Christ to the earth there will be an increase in earthquakes. Luke 21:11 (NLT) says, "There will be great earthquakes, and there will be famines and plagues in many lands, and there will be terrifying things and great miraculous signs from heaven."

Of course, we have always had earthquakes—and tsunamis and hurricanes. But there is no doubt that all of these have dramatically increased in recent years. For the past five decades, every decade has increased the number of earthquakes—and not minor quakes, either. According to Hal Lindsey, they are *killer* quakes coming at a level and a frequency like we have never seen before.[79]

A recent quake in China claimed the lives of at least 69,000 people. In 2005, an earthquake in Pakistan sent 80,000 people into eternity. A massive quake in Haiti took the lives of over 200,000 men, women, and children in 2010. A killer quake and tsunami hit Japan in 2011. Many of us remember the catastrophic tsunami of December 26, 2004, caused by the fourth most powerful under-sea earthquake on record. It was an earthquake that was so power-ful it moved the entire island of Sumatra 100 feet to the southwest from its pre-quake position. And in that particular earthquake and tsunami, 290,000 people lost their lives. Many more earthquakes will come.

Jesus told us, "You will see an increase in earthquakes." We have, and that is a "sign of the time" that is difficult to miss. Jesus describes these devastating events as birth pangs or labor pains. And He goes on to say, "But all this is only the first of the birth pains, with more to come" (Matthew 24:8, NLT).

In the same way, Jesus indicates that national disasters will begin to increase in frequency and intensity shortly before His return. These things are reminders—for all who are willing to receive them—that Christ is coming back again.

A Quick Flyover

As we prepare to dig into these things, let me set forth what I believe to be a chronology of the major end times events. This will just be a quick flyover, and we'll come back later and fill in some of the gaps.

In my opinion, the next event on the prophetic calendar is what the Bible describes as *the rapture of the church*. This is spoken of in the book of 1 Thessalonians, the fourth chapter, where we read,

But I do not want you to be ignorant, brethren, concerning those who have fallen asleep, lest you sorrow as others who have no hope. For if we believe that Jesus died and rose again, even so God will bring with Him those who sleep in Jesus.

For this we say to you by the word of the Lord, that we who are alive and remain until the coming of the Lord will by no means precede those who are asleep. For the Lord Himself will descend from heaven with a shout, with the voice of an archangel, and with the trumpet of God. And the dead in Christ will rise first. Then we who are alive and remain shall be caught up together with them in the clouds to meet the Lord in the air. And thus we shall always be with the Lord. (verses 13-17)

The term *rapture* comes from the Latin word *rapturus*, which means "taken by force." In this instance, it means we will be caught up to meet the Lord in the air, and then we will be with Him forever.

Jesus, talking about this same event, said, "I tell you, in that night there will be two men in one bed: the one will be taken and the other will be left. Two women will be grinding together: the one will be taken and the other left. Two men will be in the field: the one will be taken and the other left" (Luke 17:34-36). Paul said that this event, the rapture will happen "in a moment, in the twinkling of an eye" (1 Corinthians 15:52).

Either right before or right after the rapture I believe a large force from the north, known as "Magog" in Scripture, will attack the nation of Israel. Shortly thereafter, a man will emerge on the scene whom the Bible describes as "the beast" and "the Antichrist."

Don't let that word *beast* fool you. He will be smooth, charismatic, skillful, and a marvelous communicator. He will come with economic solutions that will amaze everyone and with a peace treaty that the Arab nations and the Jews will both actually sign. And he will come with promises of great peace. In fact, he will be heralded by some as the messiah.

His very title, however, *Antichrist*, gives you an indication as to who he truly is. The prefix *anti*, of course, means "against," or "instead of." Many will hail him as the world's savior because of what he will be able to accomplish in such a short time.

So the Antichrist will come as a man of peace. He will do away with the monetary system as we know it today, and no one will be able to buy or sell without his mark. At the halfway point of the seven-year period known as the Tribulation, he will show his true colors, and something called "the abomination of desolation" will take place. This will occur after the third Jewish temple has been rebuilt in Israel, and the Antichrist will erect an image of himself and command worship.

This is a significant point of the Tribulation period, and we read about God's judgments beginning to fall upon the earth. The Antichrist begins a campaign of intense persecution against Christians and Jews. Various events unfold that ultimately culminate in the final battle known as the Battle of Armageddon, fought in the valley of Megiddo in Israel. During that climactic battle, Jesus Christ Himself returns to the earth in what we know as the Second Coming.

In the Rapture He comes *for* His church, and we are caught up to meet the Lord in the air. In the Second Coming, He comes *with* His church as He returns to earth. And then the Millennium begins. Millennium means "a thousand," and what follows is a thousand-year reign of Christ over this earth. During this glorious period, Satan will be chained up and unable to wreak havoc on the earth. At the end of the Millennium, Satan will be released briefly in a final rebellion. After he is defeated for the final time, he will be cast into the lake of fire forever. And then the New Jerusalem comes down from heaven to earth, and heaven and earth effectively become one. This will be the ultimate fulfillment of what our Lord taught us in the Lord's Prayer when He said, "Your kingdom come. Your will be done on earth as it is in heaven."

Sometimes you hear people say, "After I die, I will go to heaven and be there forever with the Lord." That is not totally true. You *will* be with the Lord forever, but one day heaven and earth will become one. There will be a new earth.

So this is an overview of things to come, and you can be certain that events will unfold exactly as the Bible has said.

"Take Heed...."

In the Gospel of Mark, we read these words:

> Then as He went out of the temple, one of His disciples said to Him, "Teacher, see what manner of stones and what buildings are here!"

> And Jesus answered and said to him, "Do you see these great buildings? Not one stone shall be left upon another, that shall not be thrown down."

> Now as He sat on the Mount of Olives opposite the temple, Peter, James, John, and Andrew asked Him privately, "Tell us, when will these things be? And what will be the sign when all these things will be fulfilled?"

> And Jesus, answering them, began to say: "Take heed that no one deceives you. For many will come in My name, saying, 'I am He,' and will deceive many. But when you hear of wars and rumors of wars, do not be troubled; for such things must happen, but the end is not yet. For nation will rise against nation, and kingdom against kingdom. And there will be earthquakes in various places, and there will be famines and troubles. These are the beginnings of sorrows. . . .

> "For in those days there will be tribulation, such as has not been since the beginning of the creation which God created until this time, nor ever shall be. And unless the Lord had shortened those days, no flesh would be saved; but for the elect's sake, whom He chose, He shortened the days.

> "Then if anyone says to you, 'Look, here is the Christ!' or, 'Look, He is there!' do not believe it. For false christs and false prophets will rise and show signs and wonders to deceive, if possible, even the elect. But take heed; see,
> I have told you all things beforehand." (13:1-8, 19-23)

What Christ has just described is the Tribulation period. When He says, "Many will come in My name, saying, 'I am He,' and will deceive many," He is not only talking about false prophets, but He is also talking about the Antichrist himself. The events of the Tribulation period are like a group of dominoes stacked closely together. And when the first one falls, the rest will fall after. You have the Antichrist, then you have war, earthquakes, and on it goes. So what we are seeing now in this present time—a killer quake here, another war breaking out there—are just glimpses of things to come.

Jesus reminds us, however, that as the time draws near, we will see an increase in the frequency of these shocking events. And when we see these things, we can know that we are getting closer and closer to the time of the Tribulation period and to the end of the world as we know it. But today's headlines, terrible as they may be, are just a small foretaste of what is to come.

Temple Talk

The backdrop for the conversation captured above in Mark 13 was the disciples' pointing out the magnificent Jewish temple. They were saying, "Just look at this marvelous temple, Lord. How magnificent it is! What do you think about that?"

The Lord's reply shocked them out of their sandals.

> And Jesus answered and said to him, "Do you see these great buildings? Not one stone shall be left upon another, that shall not be thrown down." (Mark 13:2)

The temple that so enthralled and amazed them would soon be a smoking ruin, with not one stone left standing upon another.

This was the second Jewish temple, being constructed by Herod at that point, and it had been under construction for forty-six years. In fact, it was destroyed just seven short years after it was finally completed. But while it lasted, it was certainly a magnificent structure.

If you look at the skyline of Jerusalem today, you will notice a building with a large gold dome on the top. That is known as the Dome of the Rock, and that is not what the disciples were looking at. In that day, a mighty temple stood on that site, with massive walls of huge stones and sheets of gold that flashed and glowed as the sun set over Jerusalem each night. It was considered one of the wonders of the ancient world, and it's certainly no surprise that the disciples would have been so impressed by it.

Jesus, however, made a radical and specific prediction: "Not one stone shall be left upon another."

Did the prediction come true?

Yes, it did, and exactly as He described it. In A.D. 70, just decades after Jesus shocked His followers with that prophecy, the Roman general Titus built large wooden scaffolds on that same temple, piled them high with wood and flammable items, and set them on fire. The heat from that fire was so intense that the gold on the temple melted in between the crevices. As a result, the Romans dismantled the gutted building stone by stone to retrieve the gold.

The prophecy was fulfilled exactly as Jesus had said. In fact, that is one of the many reasons why you can place trust and confidence in the truths of the Bible—the Bible is the one Book that dares to predict the future again and again and again with perfect accuracy.

Significance of Israel

One of the most vital things we need to understand as we look at Bible prophecy is the significance of the nation of Israel. In Mark 13, Jesus compares the nation to a fig tree.

> Now learn this parable from the fig tree: When its branch has already become tender, and puts forth leaves, you know that summer is near. So you also, when you see these things happening, know that it is near—at the doors! Assuredly, I say to you, this generation will by no means pass away till all these things take place. Heaven and earth will pass away, but My words will by no means pass away. (verses 28-31)

This comparison of Israel with a fig tree happens several times in Scripture. In Hosea 9:10, the Lord says, "I found Israel like grapes in the wilderness; I saw your fathers as the firstfruits on the fig tree in its first season."

Scripture makes similar comparisons in Judges 9 and Joel 1.

So here is what Jesus is saying: The rebirth of the nation Israel isn't just a sign of the last days, it is a *super* sign of the last days.

The Bible is specifically saying the Jews will be regathered in their ancient homeland of Israel.

Let's consider a brief history of the Jewish people. Her roots go back to Abraham, when God established a covenant with him and with his descendants. In Genesis 17 we read,

> When Abram was ninety-nine years old, the LORD appeared to Abram and said to him, "I am Almighty God; walk before Me and be blameless. And I will make My covenant between Me and you, and will multiply you exceedingly. . . . And I will establish My covenant between Me and you and your descendants after you in their generations, for an everlasting covenant, to be God to you and your descendants after you. Also I give to you and your descendants after you the land in which you are a stranger, all the land of Canaan, as an everlasting possession; and I will be their God." (verses 1-2, 7-8)

The Lord is very specific in saying to Abraham that the land of Canaan, later to be conquered by the Hebrew people, would be their land forever. That "land of Canaan" is essentially modern-day Israel, though at this time they don't occupy all of the land originally given to them by the Lord.

Not only did God promise this land to His people, but He also made this profound statement in Genesis 12:

> I will make you a great nation; I will bless you and make your name great; And you shall be a blessing. I will bless those who bless you, and I will curse him who curses you; and in you all the families of the earth shall be blessed. (verses 2-3)

God has blessed the world through the Jewish people. It was through the Jews that our Bible came. It was through the Jews that our Messiah came. And God has promised that those who bless Israel and bless the Jewish people will be blessed of God, while those who curse Israel and curse the Jewish people will be cursed by God.

If you don't believe that promise is true, just pull out your history books. Look at every nation that has tried to destroy the Jews and how God has dealt with them. I believe one of the reasons the Lord has so richly blessed the United States of America is because of our support for the nation of Israel. He has blessed us because we have blessed them, and if we begin to curtail or withdraw our support, it would be a tragedy and a monumental mistake.

Israel is the only true democracy in that part of the world, but even more than that, Israel is a nation specifically established by God Himself. They are still His people, and He has a plan for them in the future. This isn't a political issue. This is a *scriptural* issue that we're dealing with here.

God made a covenant with Abraham, with his son, Isaac, and with Isaac's son, Jacob. Jacob had a son named Joseph, and you may remember the story of how his brothers sold him into slavery. Through a remarkable series of circumstances, Joseph not only ended up in Egypt but became the second most powerful man in all of Egypt and was placed in charge of that nation's food supply. When a famine hit the land, Joseph's brothers, along with their father, Jacob, made their way to Egypt to receive food from Joseph's own hand.

Fast-forwarding four hundred years, the Jews had multiplied greatly, and Pharaoh was using them for slave labor. In fact, there were so many Jews in that land that he felt threatened by their numbers and began devising ways to thin their ranks. It began with a decree that every newborn Hebrew baby boy should be killed outright. Through God's providence, however, one of those baby boys was placed in a waterproofed basket and set down in the Nile River. When Pharaoh's daughter came to bathe, she found the child and took him into her home as her own.

This little boy, of course, was Moses. According to the Jewish historian Josephus, he was being groomed to become the next Pharaoh of Egypt. But Moses, being a Jew, saw the plight of his fellow Hebrews. God directed him to bring about their deliverance and the great exodus took place when all the Jews left Egypt and made their way across wilderness to the Promised Land.

It took them forty years to get there, of course. Some have said it's because men were in charge, and they wouldn't stop to ask for directions! But that's not true; the real reason for their long wanderings and going in circles was because of their disobedience to the Lord.

Eventually, however, they came to the Promised Land. Moses died just before they crossed over into Canaan, and Joshua led them in and they conquered this new land, just as God had said they would.

The promise of Abraham was fulfilled: they were in the land, and it was theirs. Through the years, however, the Jewish people turned away from the Lord and began giving their devotion and worship to manmade idols. Speaking through His prophets, God pleaded with the people to turn away from this corrupting sin before it destroyed them. But again and again they hardened their hearts and refused. Even when the Lord warned them that another nation would overtake them, destroy their cities, and take them as slaves, they still refused to listen.

Finally, because God's rebellious people would seemingly have it no other way, they were conquered by King Nebuchadnezzar. The Israelites that weren't killed outright were taken into captivity in Babylon for seventy years. At the end of the seventy years, the Jews returned to Israel and Jerusalem and began to rebuild on the ashes and the ruins.

Centuries later, when the nation was occupied by Rome, the long-awaited Messiah of Israel finally stepped onto the scene. For the most part, however, He was rejected by His own people. As the Scripture says, "He was in the world, and the world was made through Him, and the world did not know Him. He came to His own, and His own did not receive Him" (John 1:10-11).

Denounced and betrayed, Jesus was arrested by Rome, crucified on a cross, and rose again on the third day and ascended to His Father in heaven. Not many years after that, the Jewish people in the land rebelled against their Roman overlords. General Titus overcame Jerusalem, destroyed their city, burned down their second temple, and effectively scattered them to the four corners of the earth.

No Ordinary Nation

It is abundantly clear that if this had been an ordinary nation under ordinary circumstances, that would have been the end of it. No more Israel. No white-and-blue Star of David flag. No more national identity. Not now, not ever.

But Israel is not, and never will be, an ordinary nation.

For all of their wandering and rebellion through the years, the Jewish people remain (to this day) the very apple of God's eye. In His Word God had promised that, scattered as the Jewish people may have been, they would one day return to their homeland, and the nation would be reborn.

They did, and it was.

On May 14, 1948, the last British forces left Haifa, and the Jewish Agency, led by David Ben-Gurion, declared the State of Israel in accordance with the 1947 UN Partition Plan. Both superpower leaders, U.S. President Harry S. Truman and Soviet leader Joseph Stalin, immediately recognized the new state.[80]

Such a thing could have never, ever happened apart from the mighty hand of a sovereign God. He said He would take the sons of Israel from among the nations where they had gone, gather them from every side, and bring them into their own land as a nation.

And that's just what He has done.

After World War II and the horrific events of the Holocaust, Jews began to return to their homeland, and we are seeing the prophecy of Ezekiel and others fulfilled before our very eyes.

Since that day in 1948 when Israel once again became a nation, the prophetic clock has been ticking. Will the end come in our generation? Jesus said, "Truly I tell you, this generation will certainly not pass away until all these things have happened" (Matthew 24:34, NIV).

How Should These Things Affect Us?

As I've already noted, the study of Bible prophecy is more than just an interesting pastime or an academic exercise. God didn't record these things for us to sit back and say, "Well, now, isn't that interesting?" No, He gave us these prophecies to change our lives. So what should we do in light of what we have just seen? Three things.

We should wake up.

We should sober up.

We should suit up.

In 1 Thessalonians chapter 5, the apostle Paul writes,

> So then, let us not be like others, who are asleep, but let us be awake and sober. For those who sleep, sleep at night, and those who get drunk, get drunk at night. But since we belong to the day, let us be sober, putting on faith and love as a breastplate, and the hope of salvation as a helmet. (verses 6-8, NIV)

The teaching of Christ's return is a litmus test of where you are spiritually. If you are walking with God and enjoying His presence every day, hearing that Jesus could come back at any time will motivate and excite you. That knowledge will continue to nudge you to live with integrity and purity. Why? Because you want to be right with God. For the person who is not right with God, however, hearing that Jesus may appear at any moment is a frightening and alarming prospect.

Here again, then, is how the apostle Paul urges us to live in light of Christ's soon coming.

1. We need to wake up

Paul says in verse 8, "Let us not sleep, as others do." There are people today who are asleep in the church.

The truth is, people fall asleep in church all the time. Not just physically but spiritually too. You may hear the Word of God, but because you never put it to work in your life, you become spiritually lethargic. Or maybe you become a "spiritual connoisseur," with all sorts of critical comments to make about the pastor, the sermon, or the church service.

"Hmmm, well, I don't think that message was quite as good as the one two weeks ago. And I really like Pastor X better than Pastor Y. . . ."

No, we should let the truths of God's Word move us—move us to obey, move us to action, move us into a closer relationship with God. "Wake up!" the Bible is saying. "The signs of the times are all around you, and Jesus Christ is coming back again."

Does that thought bring you joy and a sense of anticipation? Does it make your heart beat just a little bit faster? C. H. Spurgeon put it this way:

> It is a very blessed thing to be on the watch for Christ. It is a blessing to us now. It detaches you from the world. You can be poor without murmuring. You can be rich without worldliness. You can be sick without sorrowing. You can be healthy without presumption. If you are always waiting for Christ's coming untold blessings are wrapped up in that glorious hope.[81]

So we need to wake up.

2. We need to sober up

Verse 8 says, "Let us who are of the day be sober."

When I was growing up, I spent a lot of time around intoxicated people. For seventeen years of my life, I was in an alcoholic home, where I witnessed people getting drunk from morning until night.

As a result, I observed all kinds of people and the way they react to alcohol. I've noticed that when many people get "under the influence," they try to act as though they are not under the influence. Invariably, however, they give themselves away.

One of the principle ways that police officers nail people who are driving while intoxicated is by observing those who are driving too slow as well as those who are driving too fast. If you see someone in the fast lane doing twenty miles an hour, that's usually a DUI, and sooner or later, he or she will get caught at it.

Jesus said in Luke 21, "Be careful, or your hearts will be weighed down with carousing, drunkenness and the anxieties of life, and that day will close on you suddenly like a trap" (verse 34, NIV).

To be sober means that you are to be clearheaded. You are to be alert, sane, and steady, with your eyes open. Don't be drunk or careless, and don't let yourself be preoccupied or overcome with cares and worries. Be awake and alert.

3. We need to suit up

1 Thessalonians 5:8 continues, "Putting on the breastplate of faith and love, and as a helmet the hope of salvation."

This is specific instruction from the apostle that we are to put our armor on in these days. My friend, we are in a spiritual battle. It's war! And if you fail to realize this or prepare for this, you're in danger of becoming a casualty. One of the signs of the end times is that people will fall away from the faith—giving heed to seducing spirits and the doctrines that demons teach.[82] There has never been a time when it was more important for us to know our Bibles and to walk closely with God. As our world draws nearer and nearer to its final curtain, there will be more and more false teaching and various vices that are designed to entrap you and pull you away from God. We need to be sane, clearheaded, and alert to the fact that Christ could come back at any time.

• • •

Wake up, sober up, and suit up.
In the Phillips translation of Romans 13, Paul writes,

Why all this stress on behaviour? Because, as I think you have realised, the present time is of the highest importance—it is time to wake up to reality. Every day brings God's salvation nearer. The night is nearly over, the day has almost dawned. Let us therefore fling away the things that men do in the dark, let us arm ourselves for the fight of the day! Let us live cleanly, as in the daylight, not in the "delights" of getting drunk or playing with sex, nor yet in quarrelling or jealousies. Let us be Christ's men from head to foot, and give no chances to the flesh to have its fling. (verses 11-14)

Are you ready for His return?
Do you know how to know if you're ready?
It all boils down to this: You know you are ready if you have a

relationship with Jesus Christ, if you are walking daily with Him, and if you are watching and waiting for His return. The understanding of Christ's imminent return should cause you to want to live a godly life and be as ready as you can be. You don't have to be perfect. No one is. But you need to be prepared and ready.

Are you?

chapter 17 Israel, Magog, and the Rapture

When I first became a Christian back in 1970, lots of people were talking about the return of Jesus Christ. The top-selling book of that entire decade was *The Late, Great Planet Earth*, by Hal Lindsey, which spoke in depth about Bible prophecy and the signs of the times.

Driving around the roads and freeways, you would see bumper stickers with slogans like "Maranatha," "Jesus is coming," "In case of Rapture this car will be left unmanned," or maybe, "Get right or get left."

There was a sense of expectancy among so many of us that we could be the generation that would see the return of the Lord.

Well, that was forty years ago, and I've gone through quite a few "Jesus is coming" bumper stickers since those days.

Was my hope displaced?

Did I get it wrong?

Did we misread the signs of the times?

Not at all. God is not late, and the Lord will return to this earth at the appointed hour that has been predetermined in the councils of eternity. But there may be a reason why Jesus didn't come when we were hoping He would in 1970.

Consider this: Millions and millions of men and women, boys and girls, have come to Jesus since 1970.

The Bible reminds us, "The Lord isn't really being slow about his promise, as some people think. No, he is being patient for your sake. He does not want anyone to be destroyed, but wants everyone to repent" (2 Peter 3:9, NLT).

It is all in the Lord's hands, of course, but I do believe that somewhere on this planet there is a particular man or a woman whom the Lord is waiting for, and when that person finally places faith in Jesus Christ, we will be caught up to meet the Lord in the air, in what we call the rapture of the church.

All around me there are signs of the times. We've already considered one of the "super signs" of the last days, which was the regathering of the nation of Israel in their ancient homeland.

That was against all odds. It was something that had no precedent in human history—that a nation and a people that had been scattered throughout the four corners of the earth would gather again where they had once been and form a nation.

Jesus said, "This generation will by no means pass away till all things take place."[83] Once the Jewish people returned to their homeland and became a nation on May 14, 1948, you might say that the prophetic clock started to tick. It is a very important date in Bible prophecy.

But the Bible not only said that the Lord would gather the Jews back to their homeland again, He said that Jerusalem would end up being a source of conflict in the end times. What's interesting to me is that on May 14, 1948, Israel did not possess Jerusalem. In fact, that didn't happen until the 1967 war when Israeli forces captured the old city and reunified all of Jerusalem. For the first time in centuries the city was under Jewish control.

That, of course, is where the rub comes in.

Jerusalem remains at the heart of the Israeli-Palestinian conflict, with many Arab leaders worldwide insisting that Jerusalem and the entire West Bank are rightly Palestinian territory and must ultimately be given back as a condition of peace.

But here's the problem with that: God gave Israel and the city of Jerusalem to the Jewish people. He made that promise to them, and they're not going to give it up again. Nor should they.

Checking the Checklist

The Bible is the one book that dares to predict the future. Not once, not twice, but hundreds of times. We can look back now and see that many of those prophecies have already been fulfilled. But not all of them! Some remain to be fulfilled, and we may be the generation where that begins to take place.

It's not a big stretch for God to predict the future. God can speak of future things as easily as you and I might discuss the past or present. In fact, God can predict the future far more accurately than you and I can recall the past.

As you may have already picked up in this book, you might say I have a few issues with forgetting things. My wife seems to remember every detail of everything. I will come home and describe something that happened to me, and she catches every detail. Then, a couple days later, I will be redescribing the events to someone else and my wife will say, "No, Greg. You've got it wrong. Here's what happened."

I will look at her say, "You weren't even there!"

"I know," she'll reply. "But I was there when you told this story the first time, and now you're leaving out some of the details."

Amazing.

As much as I may struggle to remember things with any degree of accuracy, God has perfect retention (if you want to call it that). In fact, He sees the past, present, and future *simultaneously*.

Tomorrow is like yesterday to God. Every day is before Him with equal clarity. The Lord does not forget things, nor does He learn new things.

He literally knows everything—past, present, and future.

So let's just take out our checklist of events and see what has already transpired.

- The Bible says Israel will be scattered to the four corners of the earth. Did that happen? Yes. *Check*.

- Israel will be regathered as a nation. Did that happen? Yes. *Check*.

- Israel will regain the city of Jerusalem. Has that happened? Yes. *Check*.

- Israel will be isolated from the other nations of the world. Is this happening? Yes. *Check*.

- Israel will be attacked by a nation to her north, bent on her destruction. Has that occurred? Not yet. But we could easily envision such a scenario.

Jerusalem will be at the center of the conflicts of the world. Not Rome. Not Paris. Not London. Not New York City, but the ancient, tiny little city of Jerusalem. We read in Luke 21:20 (NLT): "And when you see Jerusalem surrounded by armies, then you will know that the time of its destruction has arrived."

In Zechariah 12:2-3 (NLT) God says,

I will make Jerusalem like an intoxicating drink that makes the nearby nations stagger when they send their armies to besiege Jerusalem and Judah. On that day I will make Jerusalem an immovable rock. All the nations will gather against it to try to move it, but they will only hurt themselves.

John Walvoord, a respected expert on Bible prophecy, made this statement:

The prophesies about Jerusalem make it clear that the holy city will be in the center of the world events in the end time. The conflict between Israel and the Palestinian Arabs will focus more and more attention on Jerusalem. In all of the situations Jerusalem is the city to watch as the city of prophetic destiny prepares to act out her final role.[84]

Israel is so tiny! At one point the nation is only nine miles wide. Yet God says she will be at the center of end time events. And it is happening just as the Bible promised it would.

"Them Bones": Ezekiel's Prophesy

There is a startling passage in the book of Ezekiel, written almost 600 years before Jesus was born, that speaks to Israel's reemergence as a nation.

> The LORD took hold of me, and I was carried away by the Spirit of the LORD to a valley filled with bones. He led me all around among the bones that covered the valley floor. They were scattered everywhere across the ground and were completely dried out. Then he asked me, "Son of man, can these bones become living people again?"
>
> "O Sovereign LORD," I replied, "you alone know the answer to that."
>
> Then he said to me, "Speak a prophetic message to these bones and say, 'Dry bones, listen to the word of the LORD! This is what the Sovereign LORD says: Look! I am going to breathe into you and make you live again! I will put flesh and muscles on you and cover you with skin. I will put breath into you, and you will come to life. Then you will know that I am the LORD.' " (Ezekiel 37:1-6, NLT)

Now I have preached to some dead audiences before, but nothing like this! God says to Ezekiel, "Preach a sermon to the dry bones." Why would he want to do that?

Because God said they were going to live again.

The Lord gives us the interpretation of what the prophet says in verses 11 to 14 of Ezekiel 37.

> Then he said to me, "Son of man, these bones represent the people of Israel. They are saying, 'We have become old, dry bones—all hope is gone. Our nation is finished.' Therefore, prophesy to them and say, 'this is what the Sovereign LORD says: O my people, I will open your graves of exile and cause you to rise again. Then I will

bring you back to the land of Israel. When this happens, O my
people, you will know that I am the LORD. I will put my Spirit in
you, and you will live again and return home to your own land.
Then you will know that I, the LORD, have spoken, and I have done
what I said. Yes, the LORD has spoken!' " (NLT)

It's a picture of the regathered nation of Israel in her own land,
and it has happened just as God said it would.

In 2010, Israeli Prime Minister Benjamin Netanyahu was speaking in Poland, commemorating the 65th anniversary of the liberation of Auschwitz. Speaking on the actual site of the Nazi death
camp, the Prime Minister said these words:

After the Holocaust, the Jewish people rose from ashes and
destruction, from a terrible pain that can never be healed. Armed
with the Jewish spirit, the justice of man, and the vision of the
prophets, we sprouted new branches and grew deep roots. Dry
bones became covered with flesh, a spirit filled them, and they
lived and stood on their own feet. As Ezekiel prophesied: "Then
He said unto me: These bones are the whole House of Israel. They
say, 'Our bones are dried up, our hope is gone; we are doomed.'
Prophesy, therefore, and say to them: Thus said the Lord God: I
am going to open your graves and lift you out of your graves, O My
people, and bring you to the land of Israel."

I stand here today on the ground where so many of my people
perished—and I am not alone. The State of Israel and all the Jewish
people stand with me. We bow our heads to honor your memory and
lift our heads as we raise our flag—a flag of blue and white with a
Star of David in its center. And everyone sees. And everyone hears.
And everyone knows—that our hope is not lost.[85]

It's one thing when a pastor makes a statement like this, but when
the Prime Minister of Israel says it, it's breathtaking! I wonder if Mr.
Netanyahu also looks for clues about Israel's future from Ezekiel 38-39.

If he does, than he can hardly fail to notice that in Ezekiel 38, the
Lord speaks of a large and powerful nation to the north of the newly

established Jewish homeland, along with a number of her allies, invading Israel. This has not yet happened. So let's see what it says.

> This is another message that came to me from the LORD: "Son of man, turn and face Gog of the land of Magog, the prince who rules over the nations of Meshech and Tubal, and prophesy against him. Give him this message from the Sovereign LORD: Gog, I am your enemy! I will turn you around and put hooks in your jaws to lead you out with your whole army—your horses and charioteers in full armor and a great horde armed with shields and swords. Persia, Ethiopia, and Libya will join you, too, with all their weapons." (Ezekiel 38:1-5, NLT)

Drop down to verses 7-11:

> "Get ready; be prepared! Keep all the armies around you mobilized, and take command of them. A long time from now you will be called into action. In the distant future you will swoop down on the land of Israel, which will be enjoying peace after recovering from war and after its people have returned from many lands to the mountains of Israel. You and all your allies—a vast and awesome army—will roll down on them like a storm and cover the land like a cloud.
>
> "This is what the Sovereign LORD says: At that time evil thoughts will come to your mind, and you will devise a wicked scheme. You will say, 'Israel is an unprotected land filled with unwalled villages! I will march against her and destroy these people who live in such confidence!' " (NLT)

Magog? Now who could that possibly be? And who are these allies that march with her? It is believed by many that Magog is speaking of modern-day Russia. The reasoning goes like this: Magog was the second son of Noah's son Japheth, who according to the ancient historian Josephus, settled north of the Black Sea. Tubal and Meshech, also mentioned here in Ezekiel 38, were the fifth and sixth sons of Japheth, whose descendents settled south of the Black Sea.

These tribes intermarried and became known as Magog. They settled to the north of Israel. In Ezekiel 39:2 (NLT) God says to them, "I will turn you around and drive you toward the mountains of

Israel, bringing you from the distant north."

So all Bible directions are given in relation to Israel. And if you look to the extreme north of Israel today you will find the mighty nation of Russia.

Now here is where it really gets interesting. Look at the allies that march with Russia. We have Ethiopia (that would be modern-day Sudan), Libya, and Persia, which is modern-day Iran. These are all Islamic cultures, and they are all anti-Israel. Russia has arms deals in play right now with Libya alone. And Persia? It wasn't until March 21, 1935, that Persia changed her name to what we now call Iran, a recent ally of Russia.

So here is the alliance that God says will form against Israel, and there's really nothing about it that surprises us. It's already taking shape before our eyes.

The Rise of Iran/Persia

Did you know that Russia recently signed a billion-dollar deal to sell missiles and other weapons to Iran? There are over one thousand Iranian nuclear scientists that have been trained in Russia by Russian scientists. A recent news article quotes the Russian deputy foreign minister as saying, "Russia is determined to boost its military-technical ties with Iran."[86]

It may be in today's headline, but it was all prophesied in the Bible thousands of years ago.

The current president of Iran, Mahmoud Ahmadinejad, has threatened repeatedly to wipe Israel off the face of the map.[87] At a speech he gave awhile back, he said, "Is it possible for us to witness a world without America and Zionism [referring to Israel]? But you had best know that slogan and goal are altogether attainable and surely can be achieved. . . .The regime that is occupying Jerusalem must be eliminated from the pages of history."[88]

Why these threats and animosity toward Israel? Ahmadinejad is a disciple of the Ayatollah Khomeini. Khomeini was the one who launched the successful 1979 revolution, driving out the Shah of Iran and turning Iran into a strict Muslim state. In 2005

Ahmadinejad was called before the U.N. Security Council to explain his continued determination to develop nuclear weapons.

He began his speech by declaring, "In the name of the god of mercy, compassion, peace, freedom, and justice…. " He ended his speech with a prayer to Allah, and I want you to note his words very carefully. He says, speaking to Allah, "I pray for you to hasten the emergence of your last repository, the promised one, the pure and perfect human being, the one who will fill this world with justice and peace."[89]

Of whom was Ahmadinejad speaking? In this particular branch of Islam, "the promised one" refers to the "Twelfth Imam"—an Islamic messiah. And it is believed that this messiah cannot appear until there is a period of great chaos. So Ahmadinejad feels that by stirring up trouble threatening Israel and even the United States, his nation can bring about the chaos that would bring this Twelfth Iman, this Islamic messiah, onto the scene.

Just recently a top official with Iran's revolutionary force warned that Iran will blow up the heart of Israel if the United States or the Jewish state attacks it first. He said, "Should a single American or Zionist missile land in our country, before the dust settles Iranian missiles will blow up the heart of Israel."[90]

No. Actually they won't.

That's not the way events will play out. It will play out in the way that God has said it will.

I had the opportunity to attend a briefing by a top-ranking general with the Israeli military and a close confidant of President Benjamin Netanyahu.

How does Israel view these threats from Iran?

"We take these threats very seriously," he said. "We don't think they are empty threats. And we will respond appropriately."[91]

Israel is saying in so many words they will do what needs to be done, with or without the help of the United States, to stop this threat.

Could this explode and culminate in the scenario we read about in Ezekiel 38 and 39?

Yes, it could.

Will it?

That I don't know. Perhaps and perhaps not. We have to be very careful in interpreting the headlines today. But here is what we do know: A large force from the north, identified as Magog, will attack Israel. It will happen, but we don't know why or when at this point. There are many things taking place in our world, however, that make me realize that it could happen at any time.

And quickly.

When these events begin, they will occur in rapid succession, like falling dominoes.

But What Does This Mean to Me?

Consider this: When Magog and her allies attack Israel, God will intervene and decimate her army and the armies of the allies as well. And because of this, the Jewish people will give glory to God.

When you go to Israel today, you might be surprised to learn that most Israelis are not believers in God. Many of them are atheistic. Certainly you will find very few Jewish people who believe in Jesus as their Messiah. There are some, thank God, but not all that many.

But when the Holy Spirit is poured out upon Israel after He drives back the invading armies of Magog, there will be a revival in Israel and many, many, many Jewish people will come to believe *Yeshua Hamashiach*—Jesus is the Messiah.

This outpouring of the Spirit on Israel, however, can't happen until the full gathering of the Gentiles is accomplished. What does that mean? Most people who read these pages are Gentiles, not Jewish by birth. As Paul explains in Romans 11, we have been effectively grafted into the promises God originally offered to Israel. This is the time when God is working with the non-Jews, the Gentiles. But this time will come to a close, and then the Spirit will be poured out again on the land and people of Israel. But before that can happen, God needs to wrap things up with us.

In Romans, Paul says,

I want you to understand this mystery, dear brothers and sisters, so that you will not feel proud about yourselves. Some of the people of

Israel have hard hearts, but this will last only until the full number of Gentiles comes to Christ. (11:25, NLT)

The full number of Gentiles? In other words, as I said earlier, until the last Gentile person finally believes in Jesus. And then . . . we will be gone. Caught up. Raptured. In a microsecond. And we will meet the Lord in the air and be with Him forever.

So that means when we see these events in the world beginning to happen, we need to look up, for our redemption is drawing near.

"I Will Receive You . . ."

When we speak of the rapture of the church, there are some who will say, "The word *rapture* isn't even in the Bible."

Maybe not, but the event certainly is!

For the Lord Himself will descend from heaven with a shout, with the voice of an archangel, and with the trumpet of God. And the dead in Christ will rise first. Then we who are alive and remain shall be caught up together with them in the clouds to meet the Lord in the air. And thus we shall always be with the Lord. (1 Thessalonians 4:16-17)

In John 14:2-3, Jesus said,

In My Father's house are many mansions; if it were not so, I would have told you. I go to prepare a place for you. And if I go and prepare a place for you, I will come again and receive you to Myself; that where I am, there you may be also.

That phrase *receive you* means to take you by force.
And then in Matthew 24:40-42, Jesus says,

Two men will be in the field: one will be taken and the other left. Two women will be grinding at the mill: one will be taken and the other left. Watch therefore, for you do not know what hour your Lord is coming.

John addressed it as well in 1 John 3:2 (NLT), "Dear friends, we are already God's children, but he has not yet shown us what we will be like when Christ returns. But we do know that we will be like him, for we will see him as he really is."

Paul speaks of this same event in 1 Corinthians 15:51-52:

> Behold, I tell you a mystery: We shall not all sleep, but we shall all be changed—in a moment, in the twinkling of an eye, at the last trumpet. For the trumpet will sound, and the dead will be raised incorruptible, and we shall be changed.

Now imagine this for a moment: In an instant, all over the world, millions of believers are caught up to meet the Lord in the air.

When Paul made his statement about the Rapture to the believers of Thessalonica, there was some concern about their loved ones who had already gone on to heaven. Martyrdom was a far more common occurrence to first-century believers than perhaps it is to us today, at least in the United States. These people lived with the threat of imminent death of their friends and loved ones who were believers in Jesus. The church was persecuted, and thousands upon thousands of believers were martyred.

These believers in Thessalonica were left wondering, *What does it all mean? How does this work for our loved ones who are no longer with us?* So Paul gives them these words:

> But I do not want you to be ignorant, brethren, concerning those who have fallen asleep, lest you sorrow as others who have no hope. For if we believe that Jesus died and rose again, even so God will bring with Him those who sleep in Jesus.
>
> For this we say to you by the word of the Lord, that we who are alive and remain until the coming of the Lord will by no means precede those who are asleep. (1 Thessalonians 4:13-15)

It's interesting that the Bible doesn't speak of believers as being dead; it speaks of them as being asleep. No, the Bible is not in denial. It simply chooses a different word. You see, when you are a believer in Jesus, you never die. Jesus said, "I am the resurrection and the life.

He who believes in Me, though he may die, he shall live. And whoever lives and believes in Me shall never die. Do you believe this?" (John 11:25-26).

So death for the believer is compared to sleep. It's funny how you dread sleep so much when you're young and look forward to it when you're old. Our four-year-old granddaughter has to take a nap every day, and she doesn't like it one bit. She fights it.

But Stella's grandpa looks forward to his naps—even if it's only a ten-minute catnap where I put my feet up on my desk and slip into dreamland. Just a few minutes of sleep and I wake up refreshed.

Really, a nap is a beautiful picture and speaks of someone who is at peace.

The Bible isn't suggesting that when a believer dies he or she goes into some kind of "soul sleep." It is rather a picture used to describe a person who is at peace. The reality is that people in heaven are active—worshiping and serving the Lord.

So Paul is saying, "Listen. I don't want you guys to worry about this. Those who have fallen asleep, those who have gone before you, you're going to see them again. There will be a great reunion, and you'll all be together again."

Perhaps you've recently lost a loved one to death, and you're enduring a time of grief right now. Paul writes this passage in Thessalonians just for you. "Remember this," he is saying. "You could be going about your business one day, thinking about your departed loved one, and then suddenly, so quickly that it can't be measured with time, you will be seeing that person face-to-face. Mothers and fathers will be reunited with sons and daughters. Husbands will be reunited with wives and wives with husbands. Children with their parents. Brothers with brothers. Sisters with sisters. Friends with friends. Your sorrow will immediately vanish and be replaced by ecstatic joy."

Not only will you find yourself reunited with loved ones, you will open your eyes in the very presence of Love Himself, the Lord Jesus Christ. That is what will happen in the rapture.

I personally look forward to this so much, now that our oldest son

Christopher is with the Lord.

We grieve his loss deeply each and every day.

We miss his so very, very much.

We long to see him and speak with him.

That day is coming for us and for everyone who has had loved ones precede them to heaven.

So think about that, and let heaven fill your thoughts. What if it happened today? Is that escapism? If it is, then count me in. I'll accept that label. The rapture will be a great escape, and I don't mind admitting that I'm looking forward to it.

. . .

To summarize, let's just briefly consider some of the effects the Rapture will have on each of us.

1. The Rapture means no death

There is a generation that will not see death. They will go straight into the presence of God. Will we be that generation? Very possibly. We need to be ready.

2. The Rapture is instantaneous

First Corinthians 15:51-52 says, "I tell you a mystery: We shall not all sleep, but we shall all be changed—in a moment, in the twinkling of an eye."

It has been said that the twinkling of an eye is about one one-thousandth of a second. How fast is a second? And this is a thousandth of that? If we have the privilege of being raptured, there will no real sense of departure and arrival; we will simply be there, in the Lord's presence.

3. The Rapture is a transformation

In that moment, God will give you a brand-new resurrection body. Perhaps you struggle now with the effects of old age, disease, or some other physical difficulty or problem. All of that will be gone in an instant. Age melts away. Disability disappears. Sorrows are replaced by pure joy.

Philippians 3:20-21 gives us these glorious words:

> But we are citizens of heaven, where the Lord Jesus Christ lives. And we are eagerly waiting for him to return as our Savior. He will take our weak mortal bodies and change them into glorious bodies like his own, using the same power with which he will bring everything under his control. (NLT)

4. The Rapture will be a rescue operation

In 1 Thessalonians 1:9-10, Paul declares: "They tell how you turned to God from idols to serve the living and true God, and to wait for his Son from heaven, whom he raised from the dead—Jesus, who rescues us from the coming wrath" (NIV).

From what is He rescuing us? The wrath to come. What is that a reference to? The Tribulation period, inaugurated by the emergence of Antichrist and lasting for seven years. So God is sending his special ops team of Michael and His angels to evacuate the church—to get us out of here before the Tribulation begins.

Sometimes there is confusion about the Second Coming and the Rapture. Some people think it is one event. But the Bible is very clearly speaking of two distinct events.

- The Rapture will be a stealth event; the Second Coming a very public one.

- In the Rapture we meet the Lord in the air; in the Second Coming, He returns to the earth.

- In the Rapture He comes *for* His church; in the Second Coming, He returns *with* His church.

- In the Rapture He comes before judgment; in the Second Coming He comes with judgment.

So how should this affect us today? How should I respond to these truths? Very simply, I need to walk with God.

Walk with God

We have a great Old Testament prototype of walking with God in the life of a man named Enoch. Enoch had what we might describe as a solo rapture.

In Genesis 5:24 we read these intriguing words: "*And Enoch walked with God; and he was not, for God took him.*" That phrase *God took him* could be rendered "God *translated* him." In other words, God carried him over or carried him across. Enoch didn't have to die like everybody else. He just took a walk one day and didn't come home. Or maybe I should say he took a walk and went home! He started on one shore and ended up on another.

He walked with God.

Are you walking with God? Notice it doesn't say, "Enoch *sprinted* with God." He walked with God.

I was always pretty good as a short distance sprinter but never much good as a long distance runner. I would have this great, explosive burst of energy, but then I would quickly give out.

A number of years ago I did a bicycle trip with a bunch of people who ride all the time. So there I was on a nice road bike, full of vim and vigor, zooming by people, and feeling pretty good about myself. But then about halfway through the ride, all of that energy started to evaporate. By the time the trip was over, one of the guys had to push me on my bike because old Greg had run out of steam.

Many people are like that spiritually. They have a burst of energy and say, "I love the Lord so much. I'm really going to follow Him." But all too soon, they crash and burn. Then they get up again and they go for a while—only to crash and burn again.

Here's the thing: Just walk with God.

Don't be in a big hurry. Be regular, be consistent, and stay at it. Be disciplined enough to maintain that relationship. Walking implies steady effort and speaks of regularity—doing something over and over.

Remember when your kids first learned to walk? I remember when our granddaughter Stella took her first steps. I was over at Christopher and his wife Brittany's house, and they were talking in the kitchen with my wife, Cathe, while I was playing in the other room with Stella. She was standing up, hanging on to a chair or the couch or something, and she put out one foot and took a step.

"That looked like a step to me," I said.

Then she did another, and I was getting excited. "That's a second step!" Then she did a third and fell down. I yelled from the living room, "Stella just walked!"

They came running in. "No, not really!"

"Yes," I said triumphantly. "And I saw it first!" Then she did it again for all of us, and that made it an exciting day.

We're like that as we start out in our relationship with Christ. We take our first steps, and then we trip and fall and hit our head on the table. Get up again. Fall down again. Get up again . . . and gradually gain balance and get strong. Kids learning to walk never give up, and neither should we.

That's walking with God. You just stay with it, day by day, hour by hour, step by step, and seek to be consistent in your relationship with Jesus Christ.

> "As you therefore have received Christ Jesus the Lord, so walk in Him." (Colossians 2:6)

> "Walk in the Spirit, and you shall not fulfill the lust of the flesh." (Galatians 5:16)

> "Walk in love, as Christ also has loved us and given Himself for us." (Ephesians 5:2)

> "If we walk in the light as He is in the light, we have fellowship with one another, and the blood of Jesus Christ His Son cleanses us from all sin." (1 John 1:7)

Jesus Christ is coming back, and it could happen at any time. This year. This month. This week. Today.

And when He comes, I want Him to find me walking with Him. Isn't that a great thought? You could take one step on earth and then find that your next step is into His presence.

Come soon, Lord. Come soon.

chapter

18

Antichrist, America, and Armageddon

The Antichrist generates a lot of interest among Christians and non-Christians alike. Hollywood has featured him in a number of movies, including *Rosemary's Baby, The Devil's Advocate, The Omen*, and another recently released film simply called *The Antichrist*. Singer Marilyn Manson dedicated an entire album to him, calling it *Antichrist Superstar*. Search for "antichrist" on Google and you will generate over 30 million results.

Many people are fascinated by this mysterious figure whose emergence on the modern scene was prophesied thousands of years ago.

His aliases include: the Man of Sin, the Son of Perdition, the Little Horn, the Wicked One, and the prince who is to come.

Who is this man? What will he be like?

Personally, I don't think he'll be anything like what we expect. He won't be dressed in all black, with glowing red eyes and steam rising from his back. He won't stride onto the world scene with the

Darth Vader theme playing in the background.

I think this man will be suave, intelligent, well-read, engaging, magnetic, and charismatic. He will probably be well-dressed, and he might very well grace the cover of *Time* magazine, as well as *GQ*.

Yet no matter what he looks like or how he comes across, the Antichrist will be the most wicked individual who has ever walked the face of the earth. If Satan ever had a son, it would be this person that we call the Antichrist.

And by the way, most Americans believe such a man is coming. In a *US News and World Report* article some years ago, a poll stated that 49 percent of Americans believe there will be an Antichrist sometime in the future.[92] In a *Newsweek* poll, 19 percent of Americans said they believe the Antichrist is on earth right now.[93]

You might be surprised to know that the Bible has quite a lot to say about this individual. There are at least a hundred passages of Scripture describing the origin, nationality, character, career, kingdom, and final doom of the Antichrist.

From what I can surmise from my study of Scripture and how those truths correlate with today's events, I believe we are close to seeing the events of the end times unfold right before our eyes.

Some will say, "Oh come off it, Greg. I've heard that kind of talk for years." Yes, and so have I. Be that as it may, there has never been such a unique alignment of events—along with the latest breakthroughs in technology—that could actually produce the scenario we'll be considering in the remaining pages of this chapter.

And bear in mind that it isn't only Bible-believing evangelicals who see this pattern taking shape. In fact, there is a group of scientists—including eighteen Nobel Laureates—who get together and vote periodically on how close they believe we are to the end of the world.

The so-called Doomsday Clock is a symbolic clock face, maintained since 1947 by the board of directors of the *Bulletin of the Atomic Scientists* at the University of Chicago. The closer the clock is to midnight, the closer the world is estimated to be to global disaster. Since its creation, the time on the clock has changed nineteen times. As of January 14, 2010, the Doomsday Clock now stands at six minutes to midnight.[94]

Why do they believe this? Because they are aware of the fact there are 27,000 nuclear weapons on the face of the earth today—and not all of them are possessed by the so-called super powers. Nuclear weapons are now within the grasp of rogue nations like North Korea and Iran who threaten on a regular basis to actually *use* these weapons of mass destruction to further their evil aims.

Add the possibility of one of these nukes ending up in the hands of a terrorist group—who no doubt would use them—and you have a frightening scenario indeed.

So What Will Happen Next?

As I mentioned earlier, I believe the next event on the prophetic calendar will be the rapture of the church. In fact, some of the events we will read about in the next few pages could not even unfold until after the rapture has taken place. I don't believe the Antichrist will emerge onto the world scene until the church is removed.

Why do I say this? One big reason is because of what I read in 2 Thessalonians 2:7-8:

> For the mystery of lawlessness is already at work; only He who now restrains will do so until He is taken out of the way. And then the lawless one will be revealed, whom the Lord will consume with the breath of His mouth and destroy with the brightness of His coming.

I believe "the lawless one" refers to the Antichrist, and "He who restrains" refers to the work of the Holy Spirit through the church. In other words, godly, Christ-loving men and women are part of that restraining force in these days in which we live—people who speak out against what is wrong and fearlessly declare what is right. But once we are removed from this planet through the Rapture, then this wicked one—the beast, the Antichrist—can quickly be revealed and will step out onto the world stage.

There is no point in trying to figure out who this Antichrist might be. You won't be able to. No one will. The fact is, the Bible doesn't tell us to be watching for the Antichrist, but to be looking for *Jesus Christ*

Himself! Our focus and our attention in these turbulent times needs to be totally on Him. Hebrews 9:28 tells us, "Christ was sacrificed once to take away the sins of many; and he will appear a second time, not to bear sin, but to bring salvation to those who are waiting for him" (NIV).

Jesus said, "Now when these things begin to happen, look up and lift up your heads, because your redemption draws near" (Luke 21:28).

That doesn't mean we're all supposed to stand out on street corners and stare up into the sky like a bunch of idiots. To "look up" means to live with a sense of anticipation and in a state of readiness. We need to be ready to go at any time, because the Lord will come for His own and snatch us away in the twinkling of an eye.

Nevertheless, Antichrist is close.

And if he is close, then the coming of Jesus is even closer.

Kept from the Hour of Trial

I do not believe that the church, those who belong to Jesus Christ, will be left to go through the horrendous period of time known in Scripture as the Great Tribulation. In Revelation 3:10 (NIV), the Lord says to the church, "Since you have kept my command to endure patiently, I will also keep you from the hour of trial that is going to come on the whole world to test on the inhabitants of the earth."

In other words, the Lord is saying, "Because you have persevered, because you have stayed close to me, I'm going to keep you from this hour of trial, this hour of tribulation."

Now, some might say, "Wait a second. Doesn't the Bible say, 'In this world you will have tribulation'?" Yes it does. But there is a big difference between personal troubles and trial and what the Bible describes as the Great Tribulation period. Obviously, we all go through deep waters and have to endure hardships, disappointments, and tragedies in our lives. But these heartaches and trials can't really be compared to that seven-year period of human history when God's white-hot wrath will be poured out on a world that has rejected His Son.

Why do I believe the church won't go through this specific period of wrath and judgment? Because you won't find any precedent for such a thing in Scripture.

I think the apostle Peter himself makes one of the greatest defenses for a pre-tribulation Rapture when he points out in his second letter that God spared Noah and his family, getting them safely into the ark before the flood came. He also cites the example of Lot, who was delivered from Sodom and Gomorrah before the judgment came upon those evil cities. And then Peter concludes in 2 Peter 2:9, "The Lord knows how to deliver the godly out of temptations and to reserve the unjust under punishment for the day of judgment."

We are also told in 1 Thessalonians 5:9, "For God did not appoint us to suffer wrath but to receive salvation through our Lord Jesus Christ" (NIV).

For these reasons and more, I don't believe the great tribulation can begin until after the church has been removed from the scene.

After the church is raptured, then, after we are caught up in the twinkling of an eye to meet the Lord in the air and we are reunited with our loved ones . . . then what?

Then the Antichrist emerges.

Let's take a closer look at the description of him that we are given in the sixth chapter of the book of Revelation.

The Unveiling

Revelation 6 is an *unveiling*—which is literally what the word *revelation* means. In the pages of this last book of the Bible, we have the unveiling of human history. Chapter 6 gives us a bird's eye view of those events—especially the Great Tribulation—as illustrated by the four horsemen of the apocalypse.

Now I saw when the Lamb opened one of the seals; and I heard one of the four living creatures saying with a voice like thunder, "Come and see." And I looked, and behold, a white horse. He who sat on it had a bow; and a crown was given to him, and he went out conquering and to conquer.

When He opened the second seal, I heard the second living creature saying, "Come and see." Another horse, fiery red, went out. And it was granted to the one who sat on it to take peace from the earth, and that people should kill one another; and there was given to him a great sword.

When He opened the third seal, I heard the third living creature say, "Come and see." So I looked, and behold, a black horse, and he who sat on it had a pair of scales in his hand. And I heard a voice in the midst of the four living creatures saying, "A quart of wheat for a denarius, and three quarts of barley for a denarius; and do not harm the oil and the wine."

When He opened the fourth seal, I heard the voice of the fourth living creature saying, "Come and see." So I looked, and behold, a pale horse. And the name of him who sat on it was Death, and Hades followed with him. And power was given to them over a fourth of the earth, to kill with sword, with hunger, with death, and by the beasts of the earth.

When He opened the fifth seal, I saw under the altar the souls of those who had been slain for the word of God and for the testimony which they held. And they cried with a loud voice, saying, "How long, O Lord, holy and true, until You judge and avenge our blood on those who dwell on the earth?" Then a white robe was given to each of them; and it was said to them that they should rest a little while longer, until both the number of their fellow servants and their brethren, who would be killed as they were, was completed. (Revelation 6:1-11)

The First Horseman

The Tribulation period begins with the emergence of the white horse, or the Antichrist. Some have mistakenly thought that the rider of the white horse, the first of the four horsemen portrayed here in Revelation 6, is a reference to Christ Himself. But it isn't. This is the Antichrist. Why does the description sound similar to a description of Jesus? Because that's the Antichrist's method of operation.

He is an *imitator*. A pale version of the real thing. He seeks to appear to be like Christ, and quite frankly, some will think he is the Christ. In a parallel passage in Matthew 24 that closely resembles Revelation 6, Jesus declared, "Many will come in My name, saying, 'I am Christ.' "[95]

The Antichrist will deceive many because he will be a "man of peace." He'll be a charismatic leader, a gifted orator, and an individual who will persuade old enemies and warring parties to finally lay down their suspicions and their arms and sign agreements. He will even get Israel and the Arab nations to sign a peace treaty, paving the way for the long-awaited third temple. No diplomat, president, king, or prime minister has ever been able to pull this off before, but the Antichrist will break new ground, and many will be awed and amazed by his abilities.

There have certainly been any number of signed agreements in the Middle East, but none of them ever last. The parties may sign a peace treaty in the morning, but they'll be fighting before lunch. *But where others have failed, the Antichrist will succeed.* In fact, his accomplishments will be so spectacular in the eyes of some—so far-reaching and unprecedented—that many will hail him as the very messiah. The Christ.

I was speaking with an Israeli man awhile back, and we were talking about Messiah. Like most Israelis, he didn't believe that Jesus is the Messiah, as Christians do.

"Well," I asked him, "who do you believe the Messiah will be?"

"I believe the messiah will be a man of peace," he replied. "And when he comes, he'll help us rebuild our temple, and he will bring a peace agreement."

"Sir," I replied, "you just described the Antichrist."

"Call him what you like," he said. "*He* will be our messiah."

It's perfectly understandable how the Jewish people living in their homeland long for peace. They've had war for generations, and they don't want any more. They're just trying to defend their borders and live normal lives, without the shadow of threats, terrorism, and attacks on innocent civilians.

So can you imagine how many Israelis will respond when a man comes along who seems able to actually get that done—to obtain a Middle East peace agreement where so many have failed before. That's why he'll be thought of as the messiah.

The Bible, however, tells us who he really is.

Scriptures describes him in a number of different ways. One of those descriptions is "the man of sin." In 2 Thessalonians 2:3-4 (NIV), Paul writes,

> Don't let anyone deceive you in any way, for that day will not come until the rebellion occurs and the man of lawlessness is revealed, the man doomed to destruction. He will oppose and will exalt himself over everything that is called God or is worshiped, so that he sets himself up in God's temple, proclaiming himself to be God.

The Antichrist will be history's vilest embodiment of sin and rebellion. He is also called "the man of lawlessness."

> Then the man of lawless one will be revealed, whom the Lord will consume with the breath of his mouth and destroy by the brightness of his coming. (2 Thessalonians 2:8)

He will oppose every law of God. He will not only be against Christ, but he will also come offering himself in the place of Christ. And as he becomes entrenched in power, he will show himself to be a bloodthirsty world dictator that would make Mao Tse-Tung, Adolf Hitler, Joseph Stalin, Saddam Hussein, and Osama bin Laden look like lightweights in comparison.

But that's not how he'll begin.

He'll effectively come onto the world scene singing, "All we are saying is give peace a chance." Swept off their feet by his power and charm and astounding abilities, the people of the world will happily join his parade.

It reminds me a little of how Rome conquered much of the world, making seemingly benevolent gestures—only to suppress people and demand they worship Caesar or face execution later on. For many, the *pax Romana*, or "peace of Rome," became a terrible nightmare of persecution and violence.

It was Malcolm Muggeridge who said, "All new news is old news happening to new people."[96]

So the Antichrist will come at first with gestures of peace and brotherhood, and people will embrace him.

Antichrist and Hitler: A Comparison

Looking back in history, Adolf Hitler did much the same thing. Hitler initially rallied the support of the German people through an interesting turn of events. When Hitler emerged on the scene, Germany was in desperate financial straits. The nation was being ravaged by chaos, with many people literally starving and Communists rioting in the streets.

When Hitler came along, he seemed to be a voice of authority in the midst of this upheaval and turmoil. He spoke to the German people about being a people of destiny, and he promised glories to come. He told them that Germany would rule the world; he said the Roman Empire would be revived, and Hitler would be its head, leading them out of their morass into unimagined heights.

His prophecies seemed to be coming true before the eyes of all, as in the next five years he led the German economy out of shambles, built roads and schools, and managed to bring a sense of pride back to Germany again after its devastating defeat in World War I.

And after some initial reluctance, he won the churches over too.

On one occasion he gathered many of the clergy together, assuring them that all would be well under his rule. One brave minister spoke up and said, "Well, Herr Fuhrer, we know the church will be fine because Jesus said the gates of hell will not prevail against her. But our concern is for the soul of Germany."

And Hitler responded, "Oh, the soul of Germany. You just leave that to me." And they did. The rest, of course, is history.

As Hitler began to show his true colors, however, he persecuted Christians as well as Jews. Sometimes people say, "The church cooperated with Hitler." Yes, some did, not knowing what they were getting themselves into. But their eyes were undoubtedly opened when his followers went into houses of worship, removed the crosses, and put up the swastikas in their place. The fact is, many courageous believers and Christians–like Dietrich Bonhoeffer–were executed under Hitler, along with the Jewish people.

In this sense, Hitler was a prototype of the Antichrist.

In his book *Hitler's Cross*, author Erwin Lutzer writes the following about the enigma of Adolf Hitler.

> Privately Hitler prepared for war. Publicly he gave speeches about his desire for peace. Privately he enjoyed pornography. Publicly he insisted on right conduct. No swearing. No off-colored jokes in his presence. At times he could be charming and forgiving. Many other times he was monstrously cruel. He prided himself on his honesty yet he reveled in his ability to deceive. The German people must be misled if the support of the masses is required, he mused. Hitler was a cauldron of contradictions. He could weep with tenderness when talking with children and rejoice over the completion of another concentration camp.[97]

That is what the Antichrist will be like. Initially he will come as a man of peace, even helping the Jews to rebuild their temple. But three-and-a-half years into the Tribulation period, he will show his true colors. It will be at that point that the Antichrist will commit what the Bible describes as the "abomination of desolation," spoken of by Daniel the prophet and referred to by Jesus in Matthew 24. In his second letter to the Thessalonians, Paul sets the scene like this:

> Don't be so easily shaken or alarmed by those who say that the day of the Lord has already begun. . . . Don't be fooled by what they say. For that day will not come until there is a great rebellion against God and the man of lawlessness is revealed—the one who brings destruction. He will exalt himself and defy everything that people call god and every object of worship. He will even sit in the temple of God, claiming that he himself is God. (2 Thessalonians 2:2-4, NLT)

The abomination takes place when the Antichrist, standing in the temple of God, commands people to worship him. War, pestilence, and famine follow in his wake as represented by the red horse, the black horse, and the pale horse that we have read about in Revelation 6.

At that time, the Antichrist will have someone called "the false prophet" in cahoots with him, serving as his religious/spiritual leader.

Revelation 19:20 (NIV) says,

> But the beast was captured, and with it the false prophet who had per-
> formed the signs on its behalf. With these signs he had deluded those
> who had received the mark of the beast and worshiped its image. The
> two of them were thrown alive into the fiery lake of burning sulfur.

The First Church of the Antichrist

Together, the beast and the false prophet will develop some kind of
all-embracing religious system that will be accepted by believer and
nonbeliever alike. I would imagine it to be some sort of brew of New
Age mysticism with some occultism thrown in. And those who don't
know any better will buy into it.

We already see this kind of thinking becoming more prevalent
in our culture today as more and more people seek to make God in
their own image. When push comes to shove, there really aren't that
many aggressive atheists in our country; most Americans believe in
God. The problem, however, is they often believe in a god who isn't
real—a god of their own making. They may borrow a little bit from
here and a little bit from there and make up a few things on their
own, and that becomes their belief system.

That's very convenient isn't it? In your own personal belief system, you can keep the things you like—such as love, forgiveness, and
heaven. You can take out the parts you don't like—such as hell, judgment, and righteousness. Just highlight them and hit the "delete" key.
The glaring problem with all of this self-made theology is that it's really
just the worship of ourselves, and that god will never save us.

We will see a similar type of self-made theology in this last days
scenario that the false prophet will be promoting and the Antichrist
will be pushing. It will be a mixture of old and new beliefs, shot
through with occultism, and it will swallow up the hearts and minds
of those who are unprepared to resist.

In addition to a new one-world religion, the Antichrist will also
change economics as we know them today. He will bring solutions
to the global economic woes of the world through his sophisticated
international ID system. The book of Revelation tells us,

He required everyone—small and great, rich and poor, free and
slave—to be given a mark on the right hand or on the forehead.
And no one could buy or sell anything without that mark, which
was either the name of the beast or the number representing his
name. Wisdom is needed here. Let the one with understanding
solve the meaning of the number of the beast, for it is the number of
a man. His number is 666. (Revelation 13:16-18, NLT)

The New ID System

Let's consider this for a moment. We have seen the Bible predicting
the collapse of the economies of the world and a new numbering system where people with some special mark can buy or sell. This would
have been hard to image a hundred years ago. But not anymore.
With all of our computer technology and with what is happening
in the economy today, we can now see how something like this could
become a reality by tomorrow morning!

One expert said,

> Amidst the global economic crisis in which upwards of 45 percent
> of the world's wealth has been lost in the last 18 months, talk of
> radically restructuring the global economic system is growing. In
> recent weeks leaders in Europe, Africa, and the Middle East have
> proposed scrapping the current economic order and going to a
> single common currency.[98]

Right now, the problem is that these economic planners can't
decide which currency to go to. The dollar? It has never been
weaker. The euro? No, that's not strong, either.

A number of prominent economists are now promoting the idea
of a cashless society. In fact, we're already moving rapidly in that
direction with all our technology. We have our debit cards, fast-
pass MasterCards, and bar scans on almost every product. At the
same time, we have developed keyless car ignitions, OnStar satellite
vehicle systems, and GPS units in our little phones, iPhones, and
even watches! Not to mention the fact that people have been putting
microchips in dogs and cats for years now. All of this global positioning technology is handy for determining where you are and getting

to where you want to go. But it would also be handy for those who wanted to track your movements for reasons of their own.

There is even a device out now called the VeriChip—a chip that stores all of an individual's personal identification data—that some people have already had implanted in their bodies.

It makes sense, doesn't it? Who wants to pack around a massive purse or a wallet so big it can dislocate your hip? Wouldn't it be handier to have all your personal information in a tiny microchip stored just under your skin? Perhaps in the back of my hand, where you could wave it in front of a scanner?

Some people seem to think so.

Contemporary historian Arnold Toynbee wrote,

> By forcing on mankind more and more lethal weapons and at the same time making the world more and more interdependent economically, technology has brought mankind to such a degree of distress that we are ripe for the deifying of any new Caesar who might succeed in giving the world unity and peace.[99]

Yes, that's exactly right, and we can count on the fact that such a new Caesar will come. And his name will be Antichrist.

He will be the devil's son, and he is coming.

This will all culminate in a final battle called the Battle of Armageddon. Out on the plains of Megiddo, the Antichrist will have ten confederated forces behind him, and he will face off with an army identified in the Bible as the kings of the east.

But that final battle will be interrupted by the greatest event of all: the second coming of Jesus Christ, in all His power and glory.

So Where Is America?

In its many prophetic passages, the Bible speaks of specific nations—and some with recognizable names. Israel is clearly identified, as is Iran (Persia) and Libya. Most likely, we can also identify Sudan, Russia, China, and perhaps even Europe. But there is no passage that one can point to that clearly would represent the reigning superpower on the face of the earth today: the United States of America.

Our absence is conspicuous. Where are we? We can only guess. But I think it is safe to say that our nation will not play a major role in the end times events. Why is that? Here are just a few possibilities.

Possibility 1: The U.S. will be decimated

It is possible that the United States is not mentioned in Bible prophecy because our country will have been all but wiped out in a nuclear attack. We can't rule this out, because it *could* happen. I mentioned earlier that there are 27,000 nuclear weapons on the planet, and some of those weapons are in the hands of rogue nations who have already threatened to use them. Would it be impossible to imagine that some terrorist group could lay hands on such weapons someday?

It's a terrible thought, and one that I hope never comes to pass. But neither can we rule it out.

Possibility 2: The U.S. simply declines as a world power

As we all know, nations rise and nations fall. As Mark Hitchcock pointed out in his book *Is America in Bible Prophecy?*, the might of Babylon lasted only 86 years. The powerful Persian Empire did better, hanging around for 208 years. The glory of Greece was eclipsed after 268 years. Mighty Rome lasted for eight centuries. The British Empire endured for almost 250 years. And now, as of this writing, the United States of America is 233 years old and counting.[100]

Every nation's days are numbered. And as our dollar gets weaker and the euro and other currencies stronger, as China and others nations become economic powerhouses, you see how this could happen. We could just simply diminish as a world power. To use the terminology of the poet T. S. Eliot, America might end, "not with a bang, but a whimper."[101]

Possibility 3: Many in America will be raptured

This is my favorite option by far! America may not be mentioned in Bible prophecy because a great revival sweeps our nation and millions become believers in Jesus Christ.

How would that remove us from the world stage?

If the Lord graciously sent a spiritual awakening to our country so that many came to faith in Christ, the rapture of the church would radically change our nation overnight.

If you polled Americans today—all 308 million of them—approximately half of them would claim to be "born again." So at least 150 million Americans would say right now, "I am a Christian." Are they? God only knows, but I tend to doubt that. So let's cut that number in half. What if there were 75 million Christians in our country? Let's make it even smaller. Let's say for the sake of a point that 50 million of us are genuine followers of Jesus.

Can you imagine what would happen if 50 million Americans suddenly disappeared? Can you begin to calculate the effect that would have on industry, government, the military, business, agriculture, education, and medicine? It could cut us down overnight.

After a scenario like that, it's easy to imagine how the Antichrist could emerge on the scene with a calm voice and an aura of great competence and authority, bringing startling economic solutions to the world's woes, and a strong global worldview. The America left after the rapture of the church might easily fall in line and become just another one of the nations confederated behind him.

How Should We Respond?

So what are we supposed to do in light of all this? I think that we as the church ought to do what we do best: We need to pray for our country like never before. And we need to reach out to a lost world with the gospel like never before.

The answer for America's problems is not a military one but a spiritual one. We need more people hearing about who Jesus is and what He promises, not some vague, inclusive, whatever-you-believe-god-to-be spirituality.

We need to get back to the true God of the Bible. The God of Abraham, Isaac, and Jacob. The God who sent His Son Jesus Christ to be born in the manger, to die on the cross, and to rise again from the dead three days later. If we turn to back to God—to that God—He promises He will bless us.

Have we been doing that as a nation?

No, we haven't. In fact, we've been drifting further and further from Him. It seems like every time you turn around a new law is being passed to restrict the practice of one's faith, and it seems like those laws are always aimed against Christians. America seemingly will tolerate anything and anyone as long as he or she isn't proclaiming Christ or the Bible as the Word of God.

But here is the promise of God in Scripture to any nation, including ours. In 2 Chronicles 7:14, God says, "If My people who are called by My name will humble themselves, and pray and seek My face, and turn from their wicked ways, then I will hear from heaven, and will forgive their sin and heal their land."

I want you to notice where God directs His remarks. He doesn't say, "If Congress will turn from its wicked ways." (Though it should.) He didn't say, "If Hollywood would turn from its wicked ways." (Though it ought to.) Or, "If the President would turn from his wicked ways."

No, God doesn't point His finger at the White House. He points His finger at *God's* house. He points His finger at you and me. He says, *"If My people who are called by My name . . ."*

It's so easy for us to say, "If only those Democrats would change," or "If only those Republicans would see the light." Or maybe, "If only the mainstream media would get its act together." No doubt there are plenty of problems to go around in a nation such as ours.

But God is speaking to His own people in this passage.

He says, My people need to live as they ought to live. My people need to humble themselves and pray. My people need to turn from evil habits and preoccupations and distractions. And when that happens, God says that He will hear from heaven, forgive our sins, and heal our land.

That, my friend, is called revival.

And it's the best hope this nation—or any other nation—has for protection and prosperity in turbulent times such as these.

It may indeed be America's only hope.

chapter

19

The Second Coming of Jesus to Earth

Newspapers have a certain kind of headline type that they reserve only for mega events. They call it "second coming type."

It's the kind of type that was used when Pearl Harbor was attacked, when President Kennedy was assassinated in Dallas, and when the terrorists attacked the World Trade Center. It's the kind of type that leaps off the page and says *read me*.

Why do they call it "second coming type"? I think it's an implicit recognition that the greatest news event of human history will be the second coming of Jesus Christ.

Did you know that many people believe Christ is coming back? It's true—even among people who don't claim to be Christians. A Gallup poll found that 66 percent of Americans believe Jesus Christ is coming back to this earth sometime in the near future. And by the way, that was 25 percent *more* than those who claim to be born again.[102]

As they look at the way the world is going, there

is a sense even among nonbelievers that Christ will come back again
to set things right. The Bible speaks of this event frequently. In fact,
one verse out of every twenty-five makes some mention of the Lord's
return. Jesus Himself talked about it in what we call the Olivet Dis-
course in Matthew 24:

> "Immediately after the distress of those days 'the sun will be dark-
> ened, and the moon will not give its light; the stars will fall from the
> sky, and the heavenly bodies will be shaken.'
>
> "Then will appear the sign of the Son of Man in heaven. And
> all the peoples of the earth will mourn when they see the Son of
> Man coming on the clouds of heaven, with power and great glory."
> (verses 29-30, NIV)

Everyone who has put his or her faith in Christ will have the privilege of being there on that greatest of days.

Before Christ returns to the earth, however, another event must
first transpire.

Armageddon

That very word sounds ominous, threatening, and very final. It's
true—Armageddon will be the final conflict of mankind.

Many today invoke the term when seeking to make a point. Dr.
David Jeremiah tells the story of General Douglas MacArthur,
standing on the deck of the USS Missouri in Tokyo Harbor, when he
was signing a peace agreement with the Japanese, effectively bringing World War II to a close. The general made this statement: "We
have had our last chance. If we do not now devise some more greater
and more equitable system, Armageddon will be at our door."[103]

Soon after taking office as the fortieth President of the United
States, Ronald Reagan was astounded by the complexities of the
Middle East. On Friday, May 15, 1981, President Reagan wrote
these words in his diary: "Sometimes I wonder if we are destined
to witness Armageddon."

Three weeks later on Sunday, June 7, President Reagan heard that

Israel had bombed the Iraqi nuclear reactor. And later in that day he wrote again in his diary: "I swear I believe Armageddon is near."[104]

I wonder what General MacArthur and President Reagan would think of events that have happened in recent days in our country. The destruction of the World Trade Center and the attack on the Pentagon by Islamic terrorists . . . the arming of Iraq and of North Korea with nuclear weapons . . . the repeated threats by Iran to use nuclear weapons to wipe Israel off the face of the map . . . the current conflict in the Middle East.

Yes, we are going to face Armageddon.

The word *Armageddon* comes from a word that means "valley of Megiddo." When we talk about Armageddon, we are talking about the final conflict in this valley.

That valley lies within the borders of Israel today, and you can go and visit it. I've been there numerous times on our tours of the Holy Land. Many battles have already been fought in this vast plain. Deborah and Barak defeated the Canaanites there, and Gideon defeated the Midianites. We know that King Saul was killed by the Philistines on this battlefield of Megiddo.

Why should this particular valley be the scene for the final battle of mankind? Napoleon himself gave an answer to that. In 1799, Napoleon stood at Megiddo and said, "All the armies of the world could maneuver their forces on this vast plain. There is no place in the world more suited for war than this. It is the most natural battle-ground on the whole earth."[105]

The Kings of the East

After World War I ended, it was hoped that would be "the war to end all wars," because 10 million people lost their lives in that horrific conflict. But it took only 20 years for an even more terrible war to break out across our planet. In World War II, 50 million people died around the world.

It would be nice to say that we could reach the place in our world where there would be no more war. But friends, war is still going to happen. Jesus said so.

He told us that one of the signs of the end times would be wars and rumors of wars, which will eventually culminate in the great Battle of Armageddon.

As far as we can see in Scripture (and as I've mentioned), the United States of America doesn't seem to be a major player in that final conflict. In fact, the major players of the end times events will be the Antichrist, the ten nations confederated under him, and the kings of the east. These are the opposing forces that will come together in the valley of Megiddo, for humanity's last war, as described in Revelation 16:14: "For they are spirits of demons, performing signs, which go out to the kings of the earth and of the whole world, to gather them to the battle of that great day of God Almighty."

Who are the kings of the east? We're given a clue in Revelation 9:16, where we're told that they can field an army of 200 million men. Who on earth could field an army that large? Really only one nation qualifies, and that would be China. Are the "kings of the east" China? No one can say with complete certainty, but there are some interesting reasons why we might think that is a possibility.

Newsweek featured a cover story called "China's Century," where the writers made the case that "the future belongs to China."

The article says of China:

> They are already the world's fastest growing large economy, the second largest holder of foreign exchange reserves, mainly dollars, and they have the world's largest army. They have the fourth largest defense budget, which is rising annually by more than 10 percent. And they are the most powerful force on the global scene.
>
> For centuries, the rest of the world was a stage for the ambitions and interests of the West's great powers, but China's rise, along with that of India and the continuing weight of Japan, represents the third shift in global power. The rise of Asia.[106]

China is currently the largest nation on the face of the earth, with a population of 1 billion 300 million people. The rapid buildup of their military has caused our own military experts great concern in recent days.

In 1997 China announced that they could raise an army of 352 million soldiers. That means they could send 200 million to invade the Middle East and still have 152 million soldiers to defend their homeland.

Here's what I find so interesting: When John wrote these words about the kings of the east coming through the dried-up river Euphrates and marching on the valley of Megiddo, there weren't even 200 million people on the face of the earth. But today, this prophecy could happen before our very eyes.

We don't know with certainty who the kings of the east are, but this much we know: This massive army meets up with the forces of the Antichrist in mankind's final conflagration.

Bright Lights in Deepest Darkness

The Great Tribulation will be an intensely dark time in our world, when wickedness will reign freely. After he shows his true colors, the Antichrist will begin to hunt down and martyr Jewish people as well as Christians. Bottom line: if you don't have the mark of the beast on your body, you are put to death.

Despite this dark backdrop and bleak scenario, however, God will still get His Word out. In fact, the world will experience one of the greatest revivals in human history during the Tribulation period.

We as Christians won't be there for it. We will be in heaven at that point, because the Rapture will happen before the tribulation begins. But God's Word assures us that He will do a great work, even in Earth's deepest hour of darkness.

Sometimes people will ask me, "Won't the Holy Spirit be out of the world at this point? Isn't He going to be removed?"

The Bible doesn't say that, but here is what it does say:

For the mystery of lawlessness is already at work; only He who now restrains will do so until He is taken out of the way. And then the lawless one will be revealed, whom the Lord will consume with the breath of His mouth and destroy with the brightness of His coming. (2 Thessalonians 2:7-8)

Yes, once we have completed our work on earth and we are caught up to meet Him in heaven, wickedness will indeed break loose. But doesn't mean the Holy Spirit will be removed. It just means that *the church* will be removed. Otherwise, how could people come to Christ without the work of the Holy Spirit? They couldn't. The Holy Spirit will not be removed.

The Lord will be raising up His faithful witnesses during the Tribulation. First of all, many people will come to faith after the Rapture. They'll show up for church on a Sunday, and (hopefully) it will be empty. Many will say to themselves, *"It was all true."* They'll try to call their Christian friends on their cell phones, and there won't be any answer. At that point, they will realize what has taken place and that they have been left behind to face the Tribulation period. I have no doubt that many will come to faith at that time, responding to the Holy Spirit the same as they would now.

The Bible also tells us that God will raise up 144,000 Jews who will receive Jesus as their Messiah. This vast group of evangelists will have divine protection on them as they travel around the world preaching the gospel. And they will do a great job in reaching many.

If those things weren't enough, there will also be what we might describe as an angelic mop-up operation taking place as well. Sometimes people will say, "Christ can't come back until the gospel is preached to the whole world." And they base that on the statement of Jesus when He said in Matthew 24:14, "This gospel of the kingdom will be preached in all the world as a witness to all the nations, and then will the end come."

That statement, however, isn't making reference to something that must happen before the Rapture, but rather what must happen before the Second Coming. So here's my point: Even if the 144,000 and others miss evangelizing certain people, there will still be one final opportunity. Looking through the years into the future, the apostle John saw an amazing sight:

> Then I saw another angel flying in the midst of heaven, having the
> everlasting gospel to preach to those who dwell on the earth—to
> every nation, tribe, tongue, and people—saying with a loud voice,

"Fear God and give glory to Him, for the hour of His judgment has come; and worship Him who made heaven and earth, the sea and springs of water." (Revelation 14:6-7)

Perhaps the most intriguing witnesses that God will raise up in the tribulation period, however, will be the two witnesses. These are two men whom God will put in place and who will have a powerful impact on people during those stressful days. They will have a powerful miracle ministry, including the ability to call fire down from heaven and to stop the rain and turn water to blood. Who will these two witnesses be?

I would suggest they will probably be Moses and Elijah. You'll remember from the book of Exodus that Moses was given the ability to turn water into blood, and in 1 Kings God enabled Elijah to call down fire from heaven.

Also, it was Moses and Elijah who appeared with Jesus on the Mount of Transfiguration, so heaven has already used these two as special agents! Whatever their identity, however, these men will have a powerful ministry.

In fact, they will so outrage the Antichrist that he will have them executed. The Bible tells us that their bodies will lie where they have fallen, in the streets of Jerusalem, and that all the world will see it.

How could that last part—about the whole world's witnessing these events—have even been possible until fairly recently? Today, through satellite technology and the Internet, nobody even thinks twice about it. The residents of the world could watch it all play out on their TVs, laptops, or cell phones.

As they are watching, however, they will see something that will shock the whole world:

Now after the three-and-a-half days the breath of life from God entered them, and they stood on their feet, and great fear fell on those who saw them. And they heard a loud voice from heaven saying to them, "Come up here." And they ascended to heaven in a cloud, and their enemies saw them. (Revelation 11:11-12)

Wow, talk about must-see TV!

God always has the last word, doesn't He?

But an even greater event follows this. In Revelation 19, we see the return of Christ, which brings the tribulation period to a close.

> Now I saw heaven opened, and behold, a white horse. And He who sat on him was called Faithful and True, and in righteousness He judges and makes war. His eyes were like a flame of fire, and on His head were many crowns. He had a name written that no one knew except Himself. He was clothed with a robe dipped in blood, and His name is called The Word of God. And the armies in heaven, clothed in fine linen, white and clean, followed Him on white horses. (19:11-14)

It is the second coming of Jesus Christ, and here are a few aspects of that occasion we can immediately notice.

1. The second coming of Jesus Christ will be public, and seen by all

There will be no question in the minds of those witnessing this climactic event. No one will say, "Oh, it's just a bad storm or some kind of atmospheric disturbance." Jesus said, "For the Son of Man in his day will be like the lightning, which flashes and lights up the sky from one end to the other" (Luke 17:24, NIV).

The newspapers won't need to employ their "second coming" type. Everyone will see this, and everyone will realize, "This is it."

2. The second coming will be accompanied by sadness and weeping

The nation of Israel will mourn as they realize that Jesus indeed was and is their Messiah. In Zechariah 12:10 (NLT), God says,

> Then I will pour out a spirit of grace and prayer on the family of David and on the people of Jerusalem. They will look on me whom they have pierced and mourn for him as for an only son. They will grieve bitterly for him as for a firstborn son who has died.

This event, the second coming of Jesus, will finally bring an end to the senseless wars of mankind. Humanity will never be able to wipe out terrorism and violence with military or political solutions. This will only happen when Christ returns and establishes His kingdom.

Now again, let's understand the difference between the Rapture and the Second Coming. At this point, the Rapture will have already happened. In fact, it will have happened before the appearance of the Antichrist and before the beginning of the Tribulation.

Notice that it says He comes on a white horse. As we've already noted, His imitator Antichrist does the same. But this will be the real deal; this will be *Air Horse One!* This will not be the Antichrist wearing a crown, this will be the King of Kings and Lord of Lords wearing many crowns.

People often wonder what Jesus looked like in His days on earth. In the Second Coming, we know what He will look like. Revelation 19:12 says that His eyes will be like a flame of fire, on His head will be many crowns, and He will have a name written that no one will know except Himself.

Three things stand out in the description of Jesus as He returns in power and glory.

His eyes are like a flame of fire. (verse 12)

When you meet someone for the first time, you look them in the eyes and say, "Hello. It's nice to meet you." I am always suspicious of people who won't make eye contact—who look down or look away. It will be extremely difficult to make eye contact with Jesus at this point, because there will be fire coming out of His eyes. This speaks of His power, His glory, His holiness, and His wrath at this point.

On His head are many crowns. (verse 12)

Why? Because He is Lord over all the universe.

His robe will be dipped in blood. (verse 13)

A better translation might be that His robe will be spattered with blood, reminding us of His death when He came the first time.

It's interesting to contrast the first and second comings of Jesus. In his first coming, when He arrived in that manger in Bethlehem, He was wrapped in swaddling cloths. In His second coming, He will be clothed royally, in a robe spattered in blood. In His first coming He was surrounded by animals and shepherds. In His second coming He will be accompanied by saints and angels. At His first coming the door of the inn was closed to Him. But in His second coming the door of the heavens is opened to Him. The first time He came He was the Lamb of God, dying for the sin of the world. At His second coming He is the ferocious Lion of the Tribe of Judah, bringing judgment.

And notice this: When He returns, Jesus will not be alone.

Verse 14 speaks of "the armies in heaven, clothed in fine linen, white and clean" who follow Him on white horses. Who are these armies? They are also mentioned in Jude 14 as the Lord coming with ten thousands of His saints.

Who are these saints who will return with Jesus when He comes to the earth? Colossians 3:4 (NIV) gives us the answer when it says, "When Christ, who is your life, appears, then you also will appear with him in glory."

He will return with His saints, and that is what you are if have received Jesus as your Savior.

Some would say, "Me? Greg, I'm no saint."

You might say such a thing only because we have misunderstood and misused this biblical term through the years. The term has been attributed to someone who performs a miracle—or lived an especially holy life and has been canonized by the church.

That may be a church tradition, but it's not what the Bible teaches.

Scripture tells us that if you are a believer, then *you* are a saint. It's just another word for believer. Because of Christ's death on the cross, God has placed the very righteousness of Jesus Christ into my spiritual bank account, and now He regards me as a saint—not because of what I have done or accomplished, but because of what He accomplished for me in His love and grace.

And on the day that He returns to earth as King of Kings, I will return with Him. And so will you, if you belong to Him.

Now how should this affect me? How should I live? What should I be doing in light of the fact that Christ could come for me at any time, and one day I will return with Him to this earth when He establishes His kingdom? To find the answer to those questions we have to shift gears and consider an eye-opening passage in the book of Luke.

"When You Do Not Expect Him ..."

These are the words of Jesus to His people on how we are to live in recognition of the fact that He could come back at any moment.

> "Be dressed ready for service and keep your lamps burning, like servants waiting for their master to return from a wedding banquet, so that when he comes and knocks they can immediately open the door for him. It will be good for those servants whose master finds them watching when he comes. Truly I tell you, he will dress himself to serve, will have them recline at the table and will come and wait on them. It will be good for those servants whose master finds them ready, even if he comes in the middle of the night or toward daybreak. But understand this: If the owner of the house had known at what hour the thief was coming, he would not have let his house be broken into. You also must be ready, because the Son of Man will come at an hour when you do not expect him."
>
> Peter asked, "Lord, are you telling this parable to us, or to everyone?"
>
> The Lord answered, "Who then is the faithful and wise manager, whom the master puts in charge of his servants to give them their food allowance at the proper time? It will be good for that servant whom the master finds doing so when he returns. Truly I tell you, he will put him in charge of all his possessions. But suppose the servant says to himself, 'My master is taking a long time in coming,' and he then begins to beat the other servants, both men and women, and to eat and drink and get drunk. The master of that servant will come on a day when he does not expect him and at an hour he is not aware of. He will cut him to pieces and assign him a place with the unbeliev-ers." (Luke 12:35-46, NIV)

While this illustration would have been readily understood by people of the first century, it may be a little perplexing to us. Jesus is describing a first-century wedding that wasn't anything like our weddings of today.

Today's weddings usually last no longer than an hour or ninety minutes, followed by a reception. But the Jewish weddings of Jesus' time were quite different and could last for days. One of the elements of those weddings is that no one really knew when the bridegroom would arrive. As a result, everyone would be dressed and ready for his coming. And once the bridegroom showed up, the announcement would be given, "The bridegroom is here," and the wedding would start.

It could happen at 2:00 in the afternoon or 2:00 in the morning. The point was, you needed to be ready because he could come at any moment.

So with this backdrop in mind, everybody understood what Jesus was saying. Jesus says in verse 35, "Let your waist be girded and your lamps burning." Now what on earth does it mean to gird your waist? As you know, people wore long, flowing robes in those days. And to gird your waist simply meant that you pulled your robe up above your knees and cinched in your belt, giving you freedom of movement.

Another way we could translate this might be, "Just have your comfortable pants on—or your workout clothes!—and be ready to move." You get the idea. Jesus was simply saying, "Be ready to go at a moment's notice."

And to "have your lamp burning" meant that you would have oil in your lamp. We might say, "Check to make sure you have fresh batteries for your flashlight." I don't know if you're like me, but I have a number of flashlights around the house that are basically useless to me because they don't have good batteries in them. That's not wise, because if you need a flashlight, you really need a flashlight, and you want to make sure it's ready to go when the need arises.

Jesus is essentially saying the same thing when he says, "Have your lamps burning." In other words, always be prepared.

In verse 38, the Lord says, "And if he should come in the second watch, or come in the third watch, and find them so [watching for their master], blessed are those servants."

Back in those days the night was divided into four watches, or shifts. The first watch was from 6:00 to 9:00, the second from 9:00 to 12:00, and the third from 12:00 to 3:00. And the fourth watch of the night was that time right before dawn. So Jesus was effectively saying, "Even if I come later than you originally expected, be ready."

It may seem to us at times that the Lord is delaying His coming, and we wonder why He hasn't come sooner. But the fact is, the Lord is not late. He's right on schedule. He is paying close attention to what is going on in the world today, and there is a day and an hour when He will return.

No one knows that day or the hour. When someone comes along and tells you, "I've got it all figured out! I know the day when He will return," don't believe them.

Bottom line? Don't get into date-setting. It's pointless and really quite silly. Just be ready.

The Lord is not late. He is waiting for people to believe. The apostle Peter said, "The Lord isn't really being slow about his promise, as some people think. No, he is being patient for your sake. He does not want anyone to be destroyed, but wants everyone to repent" (2 Peter 3:9, NLT).

If He comes in the second watch, the third watch, or even the fourth watch, be ready, because we know this much: He *is* coming. We have never been closer to the Lord's return than we are at this very moment.

So what are we to do until then? I'd like to bring a few things to your attention:

1. We are to be watching for Him

Luke 12: 37 says, "Blessed are those servants whom the master, when he comes, will find watching."

That doesn't mean that we are standing around staring up into the sky. But what it does mean is that we hold on to the awareness that Christ could return at any time. And when we see the signs of His coming, we're to take note of those things.

When you open up your newspaper or go to your favorite news site on the Web and hear about another killer quake or a global currency or threats to wipe Israel off the face of the earth or new conflicts breaking out in the Middle East, these are signs of the times. And they should serve as prods or a wake-up call to pay attention. We're to be actively waiting and watching for His return.

2. We are to be ready to go

When I leave on a trip, I always pack my bag the night before so I can be ready. That's the idea here. We, in a sense, should have our bags packed and sitting close to the door within easy reach. Why? Because we could leave this world at any moment.

So here is a question I ought to ask myself periodically.

When I am about to go to a certain place or do a certain thing, would I be embarrassed if Jesus came back when I was right in the middle of it? If the answer to that question is yes, then it would be best for me to refrain from doing that activity or going to that place.

The truth is, we can study Bible prophecy all day long and can get excited about it, but if it isn't impacting us *in the way that we live*, then we're simply missing the point. In 1 John 3, we read:

> Dear friends, we are already God's children, but he has not yet shown us what we will be like when Christ appears. But we do know that we will be like him, for we will see him as he really is. And all who have this eager expectation will keep themselves pure, just as he is pure. (verses 2-3, NLT)

Stay ready. Stay steady. Living in the light of Christ's imminent return should make a difference in our behavior. The apostle John adds these words:

> So now we can tell who are children of God and who are children of the devil. Anyone who does not live righteously and does not love other believers does not belong to God.
>
> This is the message you have heard from the beginning: We should love one another. We must not be like Cain, who belonged to the evil one and killed his brother. And why did he kill him? Because Cain had been doing what was evil, and his brother had been doing what was righteous. So don't be surprised, dear brothers and sisters, if the world hates you.
>
> If we love our Christian brothers and sisters, it proves that we have passed from death to life. But a person who has no love is still dead. (verses 10-14, NLT)

3. We should not only be ready, but we should be anxiously awaiting His return

Anxiously awaiting . . . not dreading it. I used to have a dog that would sleep outside of my door at night, actually resting his weight against the door. In fact, there were times I would hear knocking in the middle of the night and think somebody was at the door. But it was only the dog, scratching.

I would know that he had been leaning against the door all night because when I opened it in the morning, he would sort of roll into the room. He would look at me, all excited, as if to say, "Oh, you're up! Good!" He would start going around in circles, singing in his dog mind, "Happy days are here again. The sky is blue! Oh, we are going on a walk. It's so thrilling. Life is good." That's the way he greeted me in the mornings.

It reminds me of that bumper sticker that says, "Lord, help me be the person my dog thinks I am." Dogs have so much love and admiration for their masters. Cats? They couldn't care less. With them it's more, "What? You again? I'm leaving for two weeks. See ya."

To shift this out of the animal realm, imagine you were anxiously awaiting the arrival of a close friend whom you hadn't seen for years. You've experienced that, haven't you? You get up every couple of minutes to look out the window. Finally, you see their car pull up and they come walking up to your front door. You open the door before they can even knock, practically pulling them inside.

That is how we should be waiting for the Lord's return. Not with dread, but with joyful, anxious anticipation and excitement. Is that how you feel?

Jesus says, "Behold I come quickly." And we, along with the apostle John, should be able to say in response, "Even so, come quickly, Lord Jesus." Anything in our lives that would cast a shadow over that answer is out of place.

That brings us to this statement Jesus made about His return:

> But if that servant says in his heart, "My master is delaying his coming," and begins to beat the male and female servants, and to eat and drink and be drunk, the master of that servant will come

on a day when he is not looking for him, and at an hour when he is not aware, and will cut him in two and appoint him his portion with the unbelievers. (Luke 12:45-46)

Now this is interesting, because it says, "The *servant* says in his heart, 'My master is delaying his coming.'" I think this may be speaking about an individual who appears to be a Christian, but in fact really isn't. In other words, he or she isn't a pagan or a person outside of the church, but an individual who is involved in things of the Lord, to one degree or another.

"My master is delaying his coming ..."

The idea here is that he is not a real servant, and the master is not his real master but only appears to be.

As I read these words, my concern would be for people in church—even people who seem to be active and involved in church—who are in reality not right with God.

If you come to church with a heart open to God and a desire to worship and to pray and to hear God's Word and apply it, if you come to church and want to be a part of the body and want to serve the Lord and give to the Lord, then your church will be an oasis for you, a place of refreshment and blessing.

If, on the other hand, you come to church with a chip on your shoulder and a hardened heart full of bitterness and criticism, watch out! As it has often been noted, the same sun that softens the wax hardens the clay. And that is where church can be dangerous. If you come with a heart that is hard, it can actually become *harder* in the church than perhaps any other place.

• • •

Are you ready for the return of Jesus Christ?

Are you prepared for His coming, carefully watching the signs of the times and longing to see Him?

Jesus says, "Blessed [happy, and to be envied] is that servant whom his master finds so doing when he arrives. Truly I tell you, he will set him in charge over all his possessions."[107] I don't know about you, but that's more than enough motivation for me.

20 Heaven on Earth

Have you ever had one of those great days where everything just seemed to go perfectly?

Maybe you were gathered with friends or family, the weather was just right, and everything went according to plan—or even better than you'd planned.

And you said, "Oh, man, it's just like heaven on earth."

That's an interesting expression. Did you know a day is coming when heaven will *literally* come to earth?

We tend to think of heaven as some faraway, celestial place and earth as a familiar home that we will one day say good-bye to, never to return. Sometimes people will even say, "Someday I will leave this world and go to heaven forever."

But not so fast.

Technically, that statement isn't true. According to the Scripture, a day is coming when heaven and earth will become one. God won't abandon His creation, He will *restore* it. His perfect plan, according to Ephesians 1:10, is to bring all things in heaven *and on earth* together under one head, the Lord Jesus Christ.

In his excellent book, *Heaven*, Randy Alcorn writes,

> We won't go to Heaven and leave Earth behind. Rather, God will bring Heaven and Earth together into the same dimension, with no wall of separation, no armed angels to guard Heaven's perfection from sinful mankind.[108]

You see, our God is into restoration. Restoration of lives. Restoration of bodies. Restoration of His planet. He likes to restore something to its original condition. (And make it even better.)

Isn't it cool when you see an old classic car that has been lovingly restored? I have a friend here in Southern California who did a perfect restoration job of an old Woodie. (For those of you from another planet, a Woodie is a station wagon with the side panels constructed of wooden panels—or some facsimile thereof. They were especially popular in the 1940s and '50s—and especially with California surfers.)

My friend got the color exactly right, and he even put an old surfboard on top. What he didn't know was what kind of original surf stickers would have been placed on the windows in the 1960s, during the height of the California surfing culture.

Sadly, I knew about those stickers down to the last detail. I knew what surfboard companies were making what. And so I went to this surf store that actually had reproductions of these old stickers and picked the right ones out for him, so that he had proper sticker placement on his restored Woodie. And now? Ah, it's truly a thing of beauty to behold.

A perfectly restored Woodie is one thing. But can you imagine a perfectly restored Planet Earth? Can you imagine our world reinstated to its former glory, just as it was when the Creator spoke it into existence? A day is coming when God will make earth into heaven and heaven into earth. It will literally be heaven on earth.

A Quick Review

We've been considering the end-times events in the last few chapters of this book on essentials.

First we talked about the Rapture, when the Lord will come for all true believers, and in the twinkling of an eye, we will be caught up to meet the Lord in the air and return with Him to heaven.

And what then?

As it happens, we will be just a little bit busy. The Bible says that we will all appear before the judgment seat of Christ, and we will also experience what has been called the Wedding Supper of the Lamb.

Meanwhile, back on Planet Earth, things won't be going so well. The seven-year Tribulation period will begin with a promise of peace and progress, but the promises of the world ruler at that time, the Antichrist, will prove false.

The Antichrist will emerge on the scene as "a man of peace." The Bible says, "When people are saying, 'Everything is peaceful and secure,' then disaster will fall on them as suddenly as a pregnant woman's labor pains begin. And there will be no escape" (1 Thessalonians 5:3, NLT).

At the three-and-a-half year point, the Antichrist, or beast, this coming world leader, shows his true colors and performs what is called the "abomination of desolation." This is where he deliberately desecrates the rebuilt Jewish temple in Jerusalem, erecting an image of himself and commanding people to worship it. Then as the Tribulation rages on, with war and conflict and bloodshed, it culminates with the Battle of Armageddon, and Jesus Christ returns at what we call the Second Coming.

Then the Millennium begins.

The Millennium

You won't find the word *millennium* in your Bible, but you will find the time of the Millennium described many times over. Revelation 20 is one of the more notable Bible passages that speaks of this time.

Millennium is just simply a word that means "one thousand." So we are looking at the thousand-year reign of Jesus Christ on Planet Earth.

Finally, we are going to have peace on earth. It will be the ultimate fulfillment of what the angels declared at the birth of Jesus: "Glory to God in the highest, and on earth peace, good will toward men!"

Everyone longs for peace. Have you noticed the so-called "peace symbol" has made a big comeback recently? I used to wear it the first time around, back in the '60s. But it seems like a fashion icon now. You can see it pretty much everywhere you go—even on children's clothing.

People long for peace, and throughout the years we have marched for peace, joined peace movements, and given prizes for peace. We have even gone to war for peace. And when you read in the newspaper about somebody "disturbing the peace," you wonder where they found any to disturb! You might even have a person cut you off on the freeway, and then you notice they have a sticker on the back of their car that says, "Visualize world peace."

The simple fact is, we're not going to have real world peace until Christ comes back to this planet and hangs a new sign over it that says, "Under New Management."

New Management

Then I saw an angel coming down from heaven, having the key to the bottomless pit and a great chain in his hand. He laid hold of the dragon, that serpent of old, who is the Devil and Satan, and bound him for a thousand years; and he cast him into the bottomless pit, and shut him up, and set a seal on him, so that he should deceive the nations no more till the thousand years were finished. But after these things he must be released for a little while.

And I saw thrones, and they sat on them, and judgment was committed to them. Then I saw the souls of those who had been beheaded for their witness to Jesus and for the word of God, who had not worshiped the beast or his image, and had not received his mark on their foreheads or on their hands. And they lived and reigned with Christ for a thousand years. But the rest of the dead did not live again until the thousand years were finished. This is the first resurrection. Blessed and holy is he who has part in the first resurrection. Over such the second death has no power, but they shall be priests of God and of Christ, and shall reign with Him a thousand years. (Revelation 20:1-6)

As Jesus establishes His kingdom, the first thing He does is to chain up Satan. This is the devil's day of humbling. You will remember that Satan had said back in Isaiah 14,

"I will ascend into heaven, I will exalt my throne above the stars of God; I will also sit on the mount of the congregation on the farthest sides of the north; I will ascend above the heights of the clouds, I will be like the Most High." (verses 13-14)

And the Lord said in response, "You shall be brought down to Sheol, to the lowest depths of the Pit" (verse 15).

This humbling of Satan in Revelation 20:1-3 is not his final destruction. That comes at the end of the Millennium. But for a thousand years, Satan is chained and restricted from doing his dirty work.

Now some people actually suggest that we are already in the Millennium.

Really?

I have to admit to you, if this is the Millennium, I am *really* disappointed. If we are living today in the millennial reign of Christ . . . my, Satan has a long chain, doesn't he?

No. This is not the Millennium, and Christ has not yet established His rule and reign over our poor, troubled planet.

It's not yet time.

But when that time does come and Satan is locked away, we will experience a time of matchless peace on earth.

What Will Earth Be Like in the Millennium?

What will it be like when Christ is ruling and reigning on Planet Earth?

1. There will be world peace

No more war. No more terrorism. No more nukes. No more crime. No more abortions. Isaiah 2:4 (NIV) says that the Lord

> . . . will judge between the nations and will settle disputes for many peoples. They will beat their swords into plowshares and their spears into pruning hooks. Nation will not take up sword against nation, nor will they train for war anymore.

The Lord Himself will settle international disputes. All wars will stop and military training will come to an end.

2. There will be joy, peace, happiness and no more disabilities

As C. S. Lewis once said, "Joy is the serious business of heaven."[109] And joy will also be the serious business of heaven on earth. There will be no more human disabilities. Isaiah 35:5-6 (NIV) says, "Then will the eyes of the blind be opened and the ears of the deaf unstopped. Then will the lame leap like a deer, and the mute tongue shout for joy."

Another unique trait of the millennial reign of Christ will be the subduing of the animal kingdom. In Isaiah 11 we read,

> In that day the wolf and the lamb will live together; the leopard will lie down with the baby goat. The calf and the yearling will be safe with the lion, and a little child will lead them all. The cow will graze near the bear. The cub and the calf will lie down together. The lion will eat hay like a cow. The baby will play safely near the hole of a cobra. Yes, a little child will put its hand in a nest of deadly snakes without harm. Nothing will hurt or destroy in all my holy mountain. (verses 6-9, NLT)

Animals will be completely tame and docile during Christ's millennial reign. We won't need zoos or wild animal parks any longer. A little child will say, "Mom, I'm going to take the lions and gators for a walk. See you later." And she won't have to worry! What a glorious day that will be.

Not only that, but during the millennial reign of Christ the curse that has been upon the world will finally be lifted. Romans 8:19-21 (NLT) says,

> For all creation is waiting eagerly for that future day when God will reveal who his children really are. Against its will, all creation was subjected to God's curse. But with eager hope, the creation looks forward to the day when it will join God's children in glorious freedom from death and decay.

3. There will be universal justice and righteousness

No more corrupt lawyers and judges. No more cynical jury verdicts. No more injustice or frivolous lawsuits. Psalm 72 says,

> He will judge Your people with righteousness, and Your poor with justice. . . . He will bring justice to the poor of the people; He will save the children of the needy, and will break in pieces the oppressor. . . . In His days the righteous shall flourish, and abundance of peace, until the moon is no more. He shall have dominion also from sea to sea. (verses 2, 4, 7-8)

The Bible also says that you and I will have a special role that we will play in the Millennium. In fact, we are going to rule and reign with Christ for a thousand years. Revelation 20:4 says, "And I saw thrones, and they sat on them, and judgment was committed to them."

Over whom will we be ruling? There will be survivors of the Tribulation period who will still be in their physical bodies. (We, however, will be in our new, glorified bodies at this stage, no longer vulnerable to the enticements of sin.) We will rule and reign with Christ, then, over the Tribulation survivors and their descendants.

And the good news is that everyone everywhere will know of the Lord. Isaiah 11:9 (TLB) says, "Nothing will hurt or destroy in all my holy mountain, for as the waters fill the sea, so shall the earth be full of the knowledge of the Lord."

But here's the strange thing.

Even though there will a righteous Ruler, peace on earth, and a government with zero scandals, mistakes, or corruption, there will still be a rebellion at the end of those thousand years. Here is how it all turns out:

> When the thousand years are over, Satan will be released from his prison and will go out to deceive the nations in the four corners of the earth—Gog and Magog—and to gather them for battle. In number they are like the sand on the seashore. They marched across the breadth of the earth and surrounded the camp of God's people, the city he loves. But fire came down from heaven and devoured them. And the devil, who deceived them, was thrown into the lake of burning sulfur, where the beast and the false prophet had been thrown. They will be tormented day and night for ever and ever. (Revelation 20:7-10, NIV)

Following these events, we read of the Great White Throne judgment, which will be for nonbelievers only. Revelation 20 goes on to say,

> I saw the dead, great and small, standing before the throne, and books were opened. Another book was opened, which is the book of life. The dead were judged according to what they had done as recorded in the books. The sea gave up the dead that were in it, and death and Hades gave up the dead that were in them, and each person was judged according to what they had done. Then death and Hades were thrown into the lake of fire. The lake of fire is the second death. Anyone whose name was not found written in the book of life was thrown into the lake of fire. (verses 12-15, NIV)

That will be the terrible, final judgment, which will be followed by the grand finale.

The Grand Finale

If you want your heart to be encouraged, don't miss this amazing wrap-up to the story, where heaven literally comes to earth.

> Now I saw a new heaven and a new earth, for the first heaven and the first earth had passed away. Also there was no more sea. Then

I, John, saw the holy city, New Jerusalem, coming down out of heaven from God, prepared as a bride adorned for her husband. And I heard a loud voice from heaven saying, 'Behold, the tabernacle of God is with men, and He will dwell with them, and they shall be His people. God Himself will be with them and be their God. And God will wipe away every tear from their eyes; there shall be no more death, nor sorrow, nor crying. There shall be no more pain, for the former things have passed away.

Then He who sat on the throne said, "Behold, I make all things new." And He said to me, "Write, for these words are true and faithful." (Revelation 21:1-5)

This is the culmination of all things. The grandest of all grand finales. Heaven and earth coming together. At this moment we will pass from the realm of time into eternity. In the immortal words of that great theologian Buzz Lightyear, it is to infinity—or rather, eternity—and beyond.

Heaven and earth effectively become one in that moment. The last marking of time is back in Revelation 20. But as we come out of the millennial reign of Christ when the New Jerusalem comes to Planet Earth, we enter into eternal timelessness.

Everything is now forever.

Have you ever been on vacation and entered into such a relaxed state that you actually forgot what day it was? When we are at last in God's presence, reunited with loved ones, doing the work of God, serving Him, and reigning with Him, we won't care what day it is because every day will be the Lord's day.

The hymn "Amazing Grace" says it like this:

When we've been there ten thousand years,
bright shining as the sun,
we've no less days to sing God's praise
than when we first begun.

But don't imagine we'll be sitting around idly. No, we will be busy doing the Lord's work, engaging in tasks and experiencing accomplishments that right now are beyond our finite imagination. Remember, Revelation 7:15 tells us that we will be serving God in heaven. Then Revelation 22:3 adds, "And His servants shall serve Him."

Because we are so accustomed to thinking in terms of time limitations and our finite humanity, we tend to think that everything that must be done can only be accomplished during this short span of time called life on earth. Of course, it's vitally important that we live our lives well and spend our time wisely. The Bible teaches us to pray, "Teach us to number our days and recognize how few they are; help us to spend them as we should" (Psalm 90:12, TLB).

But what about the life that is cut short? What about when an infant or child dies? Or a young man or a young woman? What about when a person has to live with a severely limiting disability? Are those people just the losers of life, with no hope for accomplishing anything significant for their Creator?

Not at all. There is a future for the believer. Because we need to remember this: *Death for the believer is not the end of life, but rather the continuation of it in another place.* God has other places and times when those purposes of His heart for each one of us may be fulfilled. Heaven on earth will be the restoration of earth's lost privileges.

He will restore what you have lost. Not just compensate. He will restore it.

We know God loves us, we know He is in control of our lives, and we know that "Eye hath not seen, nor ear heard, neither have entered into the heart of man, the things which God hath prepared for them that love him" (1 Corinthians 2:9, KJV).

Here, then, is what we need to do. We need to live our lives in a purposeful way as we await the moment when we enter into eternity. And we need to remember that *at any moment* we could be caught up to meet the Lord in the air.

Not long ago, a pastor friend and I were talking about end times events. I said to him, "I've been teaching Bible prophesy for 35 years, and I have never believed it as much as I believe it today."

It's not that I didn't believe it before, because I have always believed everything that I preached. But as I look at what is happening all around us right now, and as I observe the events that are transpiring on the world stage, I can see the events described in the Bible playing out right before my eyes, in real time and in rapid succession.

If the Antichrist is close, then the coming of Jesus for His church is even closer!

It's good news.

If you are ready.

How, then, shall I live this life God has given me in such a time as this?

Everybody Lives for Something

The fact is, everybody needs something to live for. Everyone needs a driving passion, something that gets him or her out of bed in the morning.

I recently read a *Wall Street Journal* article about a man whose driving passion is to visit every single Starbucks store on the face of the earth. (I'm not making this up.) This 37-year-old software programmer, Winter, still lives with his parents and admits to a "mild addiction" to coffee. At the time the article was written, he had been to 9,000 Starbucks stores in the United States, Japan, Lebanon, Turkey, and 13 other countries in the course of a dozen years.

When Winter learned that a Starbucks in Prince George, British Columbia, was closing the next day, he spent $1,400 to jet there for a cup of coffee and a photograph. Afterwards, he made this statement: "If this store closed before I visited, I would lose another piece of my soul."

Hmmm …

Winter describes himself as a man in a race against time. "People should be out doing something rather than just existing or surviving," he told the interviewer. "Even if you think what I am doing is meaningless, it is a purpose at least."[110]

Yes it is. And I sincerely hope you have a better purpose than that.

What is your purpose? What are you focused on? What are you doing with your life? What are you doing *for heaven's sake*? Because if you don't have a purpose in life, you'll end up simply throwing it away. As the old saying goes, "If you aim at nothing, you're bound to hit it."

In a poll taken on *The Oprah Winfrey Show* awhile back, the hostess asked her audience, "What is your life's passion?"

About seventy percent had no idea at all.

The parable Jesus told in Luke 19 might help every one of us to think that through.

A nobleman was called away to a distant empire to be crowned king and then return. Before he left, he called together ten of his servants and divided among them ten pounds of silver, saying, "Invest this for me while I am gone." But his people hated him and sent a delegation after him to say, "We do not want him to be our king."

After he was crowned king, he returned and called in the servants to whom he had given the money. He wanted to find out what their profits were. The first servant reported, "Master, I invested your money and made ten times the original amount!"

"Well done!" the king exclaimed. "You are a good servant. You have been faithful with the little I entrusted to you, so you will be governor of ten cities as your reward."

The next servant reported, "Master, I invested your money and made five times the original amount."

"Well done!" the king said. "You will be governor over five cities."

But the third servant brought back only the original amount of money and said, "Master, I hid your money and kept it safe. I was afraid because you are a hard man to deal with, taking what isn't yours and harvesting crops you didn't plant."

"You wicked servant!" the king roared. "Your own words condemn you. If you knew that I'm a hard man who takes what isn't mine and harvests crops I didn't plant, why didn't you deposit my money in the bank? At least I could have gotten some interest on it."

Then, turning to the others standing nearby, the king ordered, "Take the money from this servant, and give it to the one who has ten pounds."

"But, master," they said, "he already has ten pounds!"

"Yes," the king replied, "and to those who use well what they are given, even more will be given. But from those who do nothing, even what little they have will be taken away." (Luke 19:12-26, NLT)

Now let's understand the meaning of this parable. At this point in His ministry, Jesus was making His final ascent into Jerusalem. Messianic expectation had reached a fever pitch—so much so that people thought Jesus would establish His kingdom right then and there. In fact, we read in Luke 19:11, "As they heard these things, He spoke another parable, because He was near Jerusalem and because they thought the kingdom of God would appear immediately."

So Jesus tells a story, essentially explaining that He was a King who would first have to leave and would then come back. What He was trying to say to them was, "Look, I'm not coming to receive a crown of gold (this time). Very soon I will receive a crown of thorns, and I will die for the sin of the world. But I will return again at a future time to establish My kingdom."

That is the time we are living in now. Christ has come. He has died, risen, and now we await His return to our poor, troubled planet. We are the servants that He speaks of in this parable. Every one of us will fit into one of those three categories that Jesus portrayed in His story.

What are those categories? I would list them as the superfaithful, the less faithful, and the unfaithful.

The Superfaithful and the Less Faithful

Each of the servants received an amount of money identified as a "pound." A pound was simply 100 days' wages for a laborer of that time—essentially three months' salary. How did the first servant make ten times as much for his master? We're not told, but this guy seemed to have no limitations whatsoever. He just went for it and he achieved.

The second servant went for it too, but more conservatively. And he, too, was commended.

We can see servants of the Lord like these in our own churches. There are some who plunge right in and take risks and chances for the kingdom of God, and they often accomplish great things for the Lord. There are others who are more conservative, cautious, and reticent. (Some people are setting the world on fire, while others are still looking for a match!)

I appreciate anyone who does anything for the kingdom of God, whether their approach is all-out and gung-ho or more quietly and behind-the-scenes.

But none of us want to be like the pathetic third servant. Not only was he unproductive, but he had the audacity to impugn his master.

The Unfaithful

In verses 20 and 21 he says to the master, "I hid your money and kept it safe. I was afraid because you are a hard man to deal with, taking what isn't yours and harvesting crops you didn't plant" (NLT).

In essence, he was blaming his boss for his own shortcomings and timidity when he should have just gone out there and worked harder. He had a faulty concept of who his master was. And there are some people today who have a faulty concept of who God is. They think He is unfair and demanding, and they are motivated to serve Him by fear, rather than in love. They simply don't understand God as He is presented in Scripture.

Our primary motive for serving the Lord should be love. As Paul said, "The love of Christ constrains me, or motivates me."[111]

Let's try to bring this story into a more modern vernacular. Let's say there was a guy who owned a fleet of cars, and he gave one of those cars to each of ten people. The man in charge says, "Sell my car and make the most money you possibly can." So he leaves for a time and comes back later to settle up accounts.

Let's further imagine that one out of the ten people approaches the boss and says, "Well, sir, I actually didn't sell your car. I drove your car and I put a lot of miles on it, and it's now due for a tune-up, oil change, and new tires. Oh, and by the way, I also got into a couple of fender-benders."

Would you promote that person in your company?

Then another guy says, "Yes, sir, I sold your car and made a profit. With the money I made, I bought a couple of other cars, then sold them too, making even more profit. Here's a check for the full amount."

Now that is the kind of guy you would want to advance in your corporation.

But what about the guy who sold your car, bought another car, sold that car, bought five more, sold those, bought 10 more, sold those, bought 20 more, and eventually set up a dealership with your name on it when you returned? How fast would you promote an employee like that? You'd probably want him for your vice president—or at least the sales manager!

Only One Life to Invest

"Thanks, Greg," you say, "that's interesting. But what does this mean to me?"

The fact is, each one of us has been given the same thing.

A life.

Your life. My life.

We have all been given one life to use for the glory of God during our lifespan on earth, be it long or short. While most of us know the date of our birth, very few of us know the date of our death. And in between birth and death we have that little dash in the middle.

That line, that dash, is our lifetime, our one opportunity to invest for the glory of our Creator and our God.

The Scripture says, "Teach us to number our days, that we may gain a heart of wisdom" (Psalm 90:12, NIV). And again, "There is a time for everything . . . a time to be born and a time to die" (Ecclesiastes 3:1, 2, NIV).

We don't know when that time will come for us. So we want to live our lives wisely in the interim.

How, then, should we be living? Why am I alive and living on earth? According to Scripture, I am here to glorify God. I exist—each of us exists—to bring glory to the One who made us. In fact, according to Revelation 4:11, one of the songs we'll be singing in heaven will be, "For you created all things, and by Your will they exist and were created."

We exist for the pleasure of God. We exist to bring Him glory. And we also exist to bring forth spiritual fruit. Jesus said, "By this My Father is glorified, that you bear much fruit." He also said, "You did not choose Me, but I chose you and appointed you that you should go and bear fruit, and that your fruit should remain" (John 15:8, 16).

So I am here on earth to know God, glorify God, and bring forth fruit for God. And I need to "get after it," because Ephesians 5 tells me to be "making the very most of the time [buying up each opportunity] because the days are evil" (verse 16, AMP).

Another translation speaks of making "sacred and wise use of every opportunity." God has given you this special gift called life, and He wants you to make the most of it.

Secondly, God has given to all of us as Christians this sacred trust of delivering the gospel message. Our Lord's marching orders to every one of His followers is to go into all the world and preach the gospel.

Now, granted, not all of us are called to be evangelists. But all of us are called to *evangelize*. And it is a sacred trust delivered to us, as Paul told his young pastor friend in 1 Timothy 1:11.

Again, emphasizing this sacred trust of the gospel, Paul tells us that we are "approved by God to be entrusted with the gospel" (1 Thessalonians 2:4).

So here is what Jesus is essentially saying. "I am coming soon. Take this message that I have entrusted to you and get it out to others. Be about your Father's business until I return."

A Final Question

As this book on *Essentials* comes to a close, I want to ask you one last question.

Do you have the absolute confidence that you will go to heaven when you die?

Do you know this for certain?

It's possible to go to church, to hear the Word of God taught, and even to hear the gospel preached, and yet not be right with God. And I don't want to wrap up this book without extending an invitation to you, if you have not yet made that personal commitment to Jesus Christ.

How do you get to heaven? Simply by turning from your sin and believing in Jesus. Not by living a good life. Heaven is not for perfect people; it is for forgiven people. And if you have been *forgiven* by Jesus Christ, you can know with certainty that you will indeed go to heaven when you die.

Have you made that decision? Are you ready to meet God?

There can be no more essential question in life than that.

Endnotes

1   Barna Group website, April 10, 2009, "Most American Christians Do Not Believe That Satan or the Holy Spirit Exist" http://www.barna.org/barnaupdate/article/12-faithspirituality

2   C. S. Lewis, *Mere Christianity: A Revised and Amplified Edition* (New York, NY: HarperCollins, 1980), chapter 23.

3   A.W. Tozer, *The Root of the Righteous* as quoted in the newest *Banner of Truth Magazine* (issue 531; Dec. 2007), 13-16.

4   A.W. Tozer, *Born After Midnight* (Christian Publications, 1959), 58.

5   C. S. Lewis, *Letters to Malcolm: Chiefly on Prayer* (New York: Harcourt, Brace, Jovanovich, 1963), 75.

6   2 Timothy 2:13

7   G. K. Chesterton and George Bernard Shaw, *Christianity Today* (November 9, 1992), 37.

8   Charles Swindoll, "Lord, For What Purpose." *Insights* (May 2009), accessed at http://insight.domain7.com /node/89.

9   See Numbers 14:24.

10 Numbers 6:24-26.

11 Luke 23:4.

12 All quotes in this paragraph are taken from Jack Graham, *Life According to Jesus* (Wheaton, IL: Tyndale House Publishers, 2004), 150.

13 Rajmohan Gandhi, *Gandhi: The Man, His People and the Empire*, (Berkeley, CA: University of California Press, 2007), 538.

14 From an interview with Ravi Zacharias, referenced at http://www.rzim.org/resources/read/asliceofinfinity/todaysslice.aspx?aid=8996.

15 Gene Edward Veith, "Salty Dogma," *World Magazine* (August 06, 2005, Vol. 20, No. 30), accessed at http://www.worldmag.com/articles/10892.

16 C. S. Lewis, *Mere Christianity*, 40-41.

17 "Letter to the Finkenwalde Bretheren" in *Dietrich Bonhoeffer: Witness to Jesus Christ*, 209.

18 C. S. Lewis, *Mere Christianity*, 178.

19 Harry S. Stout, Editor. *The Works of Jonathan Edwards: Volume 21* (Yale Press, 2003), 134

20 Matthew 3:13-17

21 Acts 2:37

22 Marcus Tullius Cicero, *De Officiis*, trans. Walter Miller (Cambridge: Harvard University Press,1913). Accessed at http://www.constitution.org/rom/de _officiis.htm.

23 Pat Williams and John Denney. *How to Be Like Walt*. (HCI, 2004), 375.

24 From Augustine's *Confessions*, Volume 1, 1.

25 Ephesians 2:2

26 C. S. Lewis, *The Problem of Pain* (Clearwater, FL: Touchstone Books, 1996), 145.

27 E. M. Bounds, *A Place Called Heaven* (Whitaker House; updated edition, November 1, 2003), 130.

28 Warren Wiersbe, *Be Victorious* (David C. Cook: 1985), 186.

29 Randy Alcorn, *Heaven* (Wheaton, IL: Tyndale House Publishers, 2004), 165.

30 See Exodus 33:18-23.

31 Rosemarie Jarski, *Words from the Wise: Over 6,000 of the Smartest Things Ever Said* (Sky Horse Publishing, 2007), 18.

32 Randy Alcorn, *Heaven*, 18.

33 Luke 23:42-43

34 C. S. Lewis, *Letters to Malcolm*, 123.

35 See Matthew 5:27-28.

36 C. S. Lewis, *Mere Christianity*, 118.

37 Ecclesiastes 3:11

38 C. S. Lewis, *The Problem of Pain*, 134.

39 Joni Eareckson Tada, *Heaven: Your Real Home* (Grand Rapids, MI: Zondervan,1995), 34.

40 Billy Graham, *Hope for Each Day*, (Nashville, TN: Thomas Nelson, 2008), 20.

41 D. L. Moody, cited in Greg Laurie, *Why Believe?* (Wheaton, IL: Tyndale House Publishers, Inc., 2002), 77.

42 Randy Alcorn, *Heaven*, 336.

43 C. S. Lewis, *Mere Christianity*, 118.

44 John Pollock, *Billy Graham, Evangelist to the World*, (New York: Harper & Row, 1979), 300.

45 J. I. Packer, original source unknown, accessed at: http://johnsnotes.com/archives/end_times/03_05_04_Hell2.shtml

46 Martin Manser, *The Westminster Collection of Christian Quotations* (Louisville, KY: Westminster John Knox, 2001), 93.

47 Rosemarie Jarski,*Words from the Wise: Over 6,000 of the Smartest Things Ever Said* (New York, NY: Sky Horse Publishing, Inc., 2007), 162.

48 From an interview on *Inside the Actors Studio* (31 January 1999).

49 J. I. Packer, *Concise Theology* (Carol Stream, IL: Tyndale House Publishers, 2001), 262-263.

50 C. S. Lewis, *The Great Divorce* (New York: Harper Collins, 1946), chapter 9.

51 Timothy Keller, "The Importance of Hell." Accessed at http://www.redeemer .com/news_and_events/articles/the_importance_of_hell.html.

52 Nancy Gibbs; Sam Allis/Boston, Nancy Harbert/Angel Fire and Lisa H. Towle/ Raleigh, with other bureaus, "Angels Among Us," *Time* (December 27, 1993). Accessed at: http://www.time.com.

53 Billy Graham, *Angels: God's Secret Agents* (Nashville, TN: Thomas Nelson, 2007), 5.

54 C. S. Lewis, *The Screwtape Letters* (New York: Macmillan, 1982), Preface.

55 Luke 10:18

56 See Revelation 12:4.

57 See 1 Peter 5:8.

58 See 2 Corinthians 11:14.

59 See 2 Corinthians 10:5.

60 Hebrews 12:6

61 Romans 3:10

62 Accessed at http://blessedquietness.com/Journal/housechu/spurgeon.htm.

63 Quoted in Martyn Lloyd-Jones, *Authentic Christianity* (Crossway Books, 2000), 5.

64 Quoted in Bob Kelly, *Worth Repeating* (Grand Rapids: Kregel Publications, 2003), 171.

65 Janice Beck Stock (Nashville: Rutledge Hill Press, 2003), 134.

66 Charles H. Spurgeon, *The Metropolitan Tabernacle Pulpit* (London: Passmore & Alabaster, 1872), 598.

67 Joseph Sanderson, ed., *The Treasury* (New York: E.B. Treat, 1885), 713.

68 See Luke 22:41-43.

69 See Luke 23:34.

70 Matthew 28:46

71 John 11:41-43

72 Revelation 22:20

73 See Malachi 3:10.

74 Rita Mae Brown. Accessed at http://www.quotegarden.com/humorous.html

75 Richard Lederer, *Anguished English* (Random House, 1989), 140-141.

76 Luke 21:10-36

77 Daniel 8:17

78 Tim LaHaye, *The Rapture* (Eugene, OR: Harvest House Publishers, 2002), 88.

79 Hal Lindsey, *Apocalypse Code* (Palos Verdes, CA: Western Front Ltd., 1997), 296.

80 Wikipedia, http://en.wikipedia.org/wiki/History_of_Israel#The_State_of _Israel_declared.

81 C. H. Spurgeon, "Watching for Christ's Coming," (April 7, 1889), http://www
    .spurgeongems.org/vols37-39/chs2302.pdf.

82 See 1 Timothy 4:1.

83 See Luke 21:29-33.

84 John Walvoord, in Tim LaHaye, Jerry Jenkins, *Are We Living In The End Times?*
    (Wheaton, IL: Tyndale House Publishers, Inc., 1999), 47.

85 Address by Benjamin Netanyahu at ceremony marking 65 years since the libera-
    tion of the Auschwitz, January 27, 2010. Accessed at: http://www
    .worldjewishcongress.org/en/main/showNews/id/8854?print=true.

86 Interview with Russian Deputy Foreign Minister Alexei Borodavkin, accessed at
    http://edition.presstv.ir/detail/108016.html.

87 Taheri, Amir. "Whose vision will build the new Egypt?" *New York Post* (March 5,
    2011). Accessed at: http://www.nypost.com.

88 Mahmoud Ahmadinejad, "The World Without Zionism," Tehran (October 26,
    2005). Quoted from the MEMRI translation (October 28, 2005). Accessed at:
    http://www.memri.org.

89 Mahmoud Ahmadinejad, speech to UN United Nations, New York (September
    17, 2005). Text in http://www.globalsecurity.org/wmd/library/news/iran/2005/
    iran-050918-irna02.htm

90 Cleric Mojtaba Zolnour, Supreme Leader Ayatollah Ali Khamenei's represen-
    tative in the Guard: State IRNA news agency. Quoted in an AP story, *Tehran
    Times* (www.tehrantimes.com/politics).

91 General Effie Eitam, in a wide-ranging briefing for journalists, hosted by *One
    Jerusalem* (January 7, 2009).

92 Jeffrey L. Sheerer and Mike Tharp, "Dark Prophesies," *U.S. News and World
    Report*, 15 December 1997.

93 Steven Levy "Playing the ID Card," *Newsweek*, 13 May 2002, 44-6.24.

94 http://en.wikipedia.org/wiki/Doomsday Clock.

95 See Matthew 24:4-5.

96 Malcolm Muggeridge in verbal communication.

97 Erwin Lutzer, *Hitler's Cross* (Chicago, IL: Moody Press, 1995), 16.

98 Joel C. Rosenberg, "Today in Bible Prophecy" Blog, http://www
    .todayinbibleprophecy.org/n/world_leaders_consider_single_global_currency.html.

99 Quoted in Hal Lindsey, *The Late Great Planet Earth* (Grand Rapids, MI: Zonder-
    van, 1970), 130.

100 Mark Hitchcock is Quoting from Charles C. Ryrie, *The Best is Yet to Come*
    (Chicago: Moody Press, 1981), 106.

101 T.S. Eliot, "The Hollow Men."

102 Gallup Poll, http://www.gallup.com.

103 David Jeremiah, *What in the World is Going On* (Thomas Nelson, 2010), 189.

104 Douglas Brinkley, ed., *The Reagan Diaries* (New York, NY: HarperCollins, 2007), 19, 24.

105 David Jeremiah, *What in the World is Going On,* 194.

106 Fareed Zakaria, "China's Century," *Newsweek* (May 9, 2005).

107 Luke 12:43-44, AMP

108 Randy Alcorn, *Heaven,* 88.

109 C. S. Lewis, *Letters to Malcolm,* 93.

110 Julie Jargon, "A Fan Hits a Roadblock on Drive to See Every Starbucks," *Wall Street Journal* (May 23, 2009), accessed at http://online.wsj.com

111 2 Corinthians 5:14, my paraphrase.

Other Books by Greg Laurie

Are We Living in the Last Days?

As I See It

Better Than Happiness

Daily Hope for Hurting Hearts

Dealing with Giants

Deepening Your Faith

Discipleship

For Every Season, volumes 1, 2, and 3

God's Design for Christian Dating

A Handbook on Christian Dating

His Christmas Presence

Hope for Hurting Hearts

How to Know God

"I'm Going on a Diet Tomorrow"

Living Out Your Faith

Making God Known

Marriage Connections

Married. Happily.

Run to Win

Secrets to Spiritual Success

Signs of the Times

Strengthening Your Faith

Strengthening Your Marriage

Ten Things You Should Know About God and Life

The Great Compromise

The Greatest Stories Ever Told, volumes 1, 2, and 3

Upside Down Living

What Every Christian Needs to Know

Why, God?

Worldview

Visit: www.kerygmapublishing.com